The last forty years have seen a massive cha care in the UK. Starting from well outs Bollen negotiated his way through preju and, from a base in one of the most social rose through the ranks to become one of injury surgeons.

Blessed with a few brain cells and educated as a "child of the state", he graduated from a Russell group university. Completely ignoring the then perceived wisdom with regard to career progression, he travelled around the world for a couple of years and then worked in district general hospitals all over the country, at a time when junior doctors were contracted to work for one hundred and twenty hours a week and studied for their higher exams in their "spare time".

Part autobiography, part observation, comment and commentary on the Health Service, health, life, love and death, sprinkled with stardust from his long association with top sportsmen and women, his story shares the laughter, tears, frustrations and triumphs of a long and fulfilling surgical career.

It is arranged so you can dip in and out of the chapters, although the necessarily quite long (there's a lot to tell!) autobiographical parts are in chronological order.

Some stories may be shocking, and certainly not for the squeamish or easily offended, but medicine is involved with the harsh, and some- times unpleasant, intimate realities of life – you have been warned! Some parts will be controversial and may ruffle a few feathers.

Some names, dates and locations might have been subtly, or not so subtly, altered to protect one or two individuals, and there might be some minor embellishments made by a memory that is not quite so sharp as it was when he was in his twenties. All references to politi- cians, public figures and government officials have been gleaned from personal experience and are evidenced by articles posted on Google – the lawyers earn enough money as it is.

All the tales in this book really did happen, no matter how unbe- lievable some of them might seem!

"I had the pleasure of leading sports medicine teams in professional football for over 25 years and was greatly comforted by the fact that with any significant knee or ankle injury, Steve was only a phone call away. He was an outstanding surgeon and in the volatile, uncertain, complex & ambiguous world of football, Steve was a career saver to so many... & not just the players!"

GRANT DOWNIE OBE
HEAD OF SPORTS MEDICINE MAN CITY ACADEMY, MIDDLEBOROUGH
AND RANGERS FOOTBALL CLUBS

"Very early in my career I tore my ACL in my left knee, which was the first major injury I suffered. 5 years later I suffered the same injury to my right knee which Steve also repaired. I went on to win 6 trophies with Rangers, play over 100 times in the Premier League, scoring many goals and representing my country over fifty times. Thanks Steve"

STEVEN NAISMITH
SCOTLAND, RANGERS, EVERTON, NORWICH AND HEARTS FOOTBALL STRIKER

"I was introduced to Steve when I ruptured my ACL before the challenge cup final, as a twenty-three-year-old beginning my SuperLeague career. At that stage I thought it could be over, but Steve fixed me up and gave me belief my knee could still stand up to the stresses of rugby league. I have gone on to have a career of over three hundred games and Steve has played a massive part in that. Thank you and enjoy your retirement!"

DANNY KIRMOND
LONG-TIME CLUB CAPTAIN, WAKEFIELD WILDCATS SUPERLEAGUE RUGBY CLUB

"Steve looked after me for many years both when I was a player and as a manager. For a long time before his retirement he was one of the "go to" surgeons for knee injuries. He's a top man!"

"I've known Steve for over 20 years, both as a player and more recently as Head Physiotherapist of Castleford Tigers and England Rugby League. His interaction with his patients has been first class, always being honest and kind but realistic in communicating bad news. His reputation speaks for itself, both in my personal experience and that of the players who have always had the best outcomes. An outstanding career. Thanks Steve."

"I tore my ACL in 1997. At that time many players went to the States for surgery, but I put my faith in the British system. My choice was vindicated when I returned to playing for Scotland and was "man of the match" in the UEFA cup final with Liverpool. I've never had any problems – Thanks Steve."

I'M
NOT LIKE
EVERYBODY ELSE

The Life and Times of a Top Sports Surgeon

STEVE BOLLEN

ISBN: 978-1-78324-147-7

Published by Wordzworth
www.wordzworth.com

For my four lovely sons.
I have watched you all grow to be kind-hearted,
generous spirited, decent human beings.
My proudest accomplishment.

And for my lovely wife who has supported me,
helped me and loved me through the years –
"You're My Rock", as the song says.

"You're absolutely unique – just like everybody else"

ATTRIBUTED TO MARGARET MEAD

"I started out with nothing, and I've still got most of it left"

SEASICK STEVE

CONTENTS

1

AFTER MIDNIGHT...

The shrill insistence of the cardiac arrest bleep dragged me from the cosy depths of sleep. I glanced at the clock.

"Oh Jesus." It was two minutes past six in the morning and I'd only clambered onto my bed twenty minutes before, having been working since eight a.m. the previous day. I wearily swung round, slipped on my shoes, and was up and running as the message squawked through. I was still fully dressed, including the trademark white coat as, when the opportunity to grab some sleep was so unpredictable and infrequent, seconds spent getting undressed and dressed again were just too precious to waste.

"Cardiac arrest ward twenty, cardiac arrest ward twenty" crackled out the bleep. I loped out of the doctor's mess and along the empty and echoing hospital corridors. Ward twenty, a geriatric (now "care for the elderly") ward, was on the fifth floor and it was always a dilemma – lift or stairs? Discretion overcame valour and I opted for the lift rather than risk a cardiac arrest myself by trying to run up the stairs.

Better to arrive able to function, rather than in a sweaty, breathless, incoherent mess.

Being the youngest, and still keen as mustard, I always seemed to be the first of the arrest team to arrive, which consisted of myself (the medical houseman), the medical registrar and the anaesthetic senior house officer. I jogged onto the ward to see the curtains drawn around a bed at the far end, with a small concerned group of nursing staff gathered around and all the other now wide awake patients, on the old style "nightingale" ward, staring wide eyed and anxiously at them.

The staff nurse started to fill me in on the details of age, medical condition and current treatment plan, as I pushed through the curtains to find a poor old boy receiving basic life support. I stepped up to the patient to feel for the carotid pulse in the neck. There wasn't one, which wasn't really surprising as the patient was stone cold. I tried moving his arm, but it was stiff with rigor mortis.

"I don't think we're going to win with this one, he's been dead for hours". I gently closed the unknown patient's eyes, whispered "RIP", and backed through the curtains to walk down to the ward office and write things up in the hospital notes. As I trudged slowly back down the ward, I could see the other patients looking at each other wondering… "who's next?". I was almost at the office when the other two arrived.

"Been dead for hours." I informed them.

"Bloody hell! Not again." was the response. It was like this on an almost daily basis. The lights of the geriatric ward were turned on at six a.m. and it was only then the nursing staff would notice that one of the patients was unresponsive. Automatically (nobody was allowed to just die anymore, no matter how old, sick or untreatable they might be), they would hit the "crash button", summoning the arrest team. This was bit irksome for the on-call team, who had usually been working through most of the night and would be dragged from their beds to try and resurrect someone who had actually died peacefully in their sleep several hours before. This was known in the hospital as a "Lazarus call".

I sat down in the office, wrote up the notes, and headed back to the doctor's mess to have a shower, change my shirt and grab a bit of breakfast. I was then ready to start work again at eight a.m. with the post-take ward round, having had the grand total of twenty minutes sleep in the previous twenty-four hours. After the ward round with the boss (often a four hour affair), the rest of the day would be spent organising investigations, sorting out treatment plans and writing discharge letters, before finishing about six p.m. with the glorious prospect getting out for a run, a relaxed meal, and then snuggling down under the duvet for a night of undisturbed rest.

Many people, including the "young doctors of today", struggle to get their heads round the working conditions of junior doctors at that time. I was put in mind of the above story when my hairdresser told me of a current book that she had just read, written by a junior doctor, and that she had been astonished to find out "he had been working fourteen-hour shifts without a protected break!"

My brain instantly engaged Monty Python mode and I thought "Luxury... I used to DREAM of working fourteen-hour shifts!" Throughout most of my junior doctor career and "training", I was working the dreaded "one in two", meaning you were on call for emergencies every other night and weekend, as well as working your normal week. This meant the standard contract was a hundred and twenty hours a week and, when you were on call for the weekend, you would start work at eight a.m. on a Friday and finish at about six p.m. on the following Monday, snatching what sleep you could along the way. There was no protected rest or break time and food, if and when you could get it, was generally shovelled in as fast as possible (there was always the possibility of the arrest bleep going off) while writing up notes (my wife and family always chide me about the speed with which I eat, but it's been habit I've never been able to break!).

There was little incentive to change this state of affairs by management or government, as overtime was paid at only thirty percent of the normal rate (not time plus a third), so the more overtime they had everyone working, the cheaper it was. On one occasion as a senior registrar, operating at two in the morning one bank holiday weekend when everyone else was on triple time, I realised I was being paid less than any other person in theatre, including the porter. It only seemed we were well paid, as we were working over three times as many hours as the average person.

Sadly for me, it was the month I became a consultant they outlawed the infamous one in two rotas. There was only a significant change to these working practices when overtime became paid at more than the standard hourly rate. Suddenly there was a dramatic drop in the contracted hours, insisted on by "caring" politicians. Shows where their priorities truly lie. It was much, much later that the "European Working Time Directive", with all its associated problems, became legally enforceable.

At Rotherham hospital, where I was working as a surgical registrar, they had "four-day weekends", meaning you were on call from eight a.m. Friday until eight a.m. Tuesday, and then went straight into a normal working day. During my worst ever weekend, I managed four hours sleep in four days, operating unsupervised through the night and day, on patients who were often desperately ill. On the Tuesday morning we then had the busiest outpatient clinic of the week, and then I had an unsupervised, routine operating list of my own in the afternoon. When I came to sign my letters from the clinic, I could remember absolutely nothing about it. The whole thing was a complete blank.

I can, however, vividly remember standing at the operating table that afternoon with a scalpel in my hand, swaying gently, so tired I was struggling to keep upright, and the anaesthetised patient being wheeled into theatre in front of me. The scrub nurse prepped and draped the patient. I turned to her…

"What operation are we doing?"

"Hernia" she replied, looking slightly concerned.

"OK… hernia", I muttered and stepped up to the table and started to slice into the skin, operating on what must have been complete autopilot. By some miracle, the surgery went smoothly, the patient made an uneventful recovery and was very grateful for their repair. This sorry state of affairs was happening in every NHS hospital, every day, all across the country.

My longest continuous shift was actually two hundred and fifty-two hours, when I was a cardiothoracic (open heart and lung surgery) registrar. One of the other two registrars was off sick, and then the other one had to suddenly fly back to Canada as his father was gravely ill, leaving me as the only middle grade around. The professor called me into his office, looked sternly at me over his pince-nez and declared, "Well Steve, you're it."

Over the next ten days I was averaging less than three hours sleep every twenty-four hours, opening chests and keeping patients alive through the night on the cardiac intensive care unit, as well as ward rounds at seven a.m. and assisting in the operating theatre from eight a.m. until seven p.m. In the middle of the night in cardiac ITU, I would be sat, head slumped on a desk, snatching a few moments rest, when sister would shake me awake, as yet another patient's replumbed heart was not beating to the rhythm it should.

After a week of this, I was so tired I had to put a stick-it note on the wall by my bed in the hospital on call room, saying "You are SteveB, cardiothoracic registrar". I was so disorientated, that when the phone woke me from the brief moments of snatched sleep, I genuinely couldn't remember who I was.

Sleep deprivation is defined as an "enhanced interrogation technique" by the CIA, as it "attacks the deep biological functions at the core of a person's mental and physical health". This apparently produces feelings of fatigue, irritability and difficulty concentrating, ending with disorientation and social withdrawal. No wonder we were such a crabby lot!

Not only were we all working flat out for the health service, but a lot of us were also trying to climb the greasy pole of our profession and were studying in our "spare time" for the very tough, two stage exams of the Royal Colleges. Passing these in turn would enable you to apply for the next level of your chosen speciality and move slowly closer towards the holy grail of becoming a Consultant. By the time you eventually arrived there, you knew you could cope with pretty much anything that came your way, having had a long and arduous baptism of fire.

When I was a senior registrar, a group of us sat down after a "teaching afternoon" and after the usual grumbles and a pint or two of beer, worked out that by the time we became consultants we would have already worked more hours than the average nine-to-five worker would do in their entire working lifetime.

Times have changed enormously. Not long ago I was talking to a trainee who'd come down to theatre to have his log book of operations signed off by another consultant, before taking the final orthopaedic speciality exit exam which, if he passed, would allow him to begin the process of working towards a consultant post.

The temptation was just too great...

"I did that exam, but we didn't have electronic logbooks and on my evenings off I had to drive round to the various hospitals I'd worked at, go through the theatre logs then write it up long hand. How many cases do you think I did in the four years before I took the exam?" You could see him thinking that he should err on the high side.

"Thirteen hundred?" was his guesstimate. This would be a large number of cases for today's trainees and deemed, by those now in charge of training, as an appropriate amount of experience to allow career progression and eventual appointment as a consultant in independent practice.

"No... it was actually something over five and a half thousand. How many do you think I was supervised in?" You could see him thinking this time he needed to aim very low.

"Twenty-five percent?" he tentatively replied (this would be unacceptably low in today's training environment).

"No, four."

"What, four percent?!"

"No... four."

You may be wondering as to why we put up with it and, looking back, I find it hard to believe myself. As mentioned above, the government and hospital management had no interest in changing things. Junior doctors did a huge amount of the routine work and almost all of the emergency work in the health service. At that time there was no European Working Time Directive and there were no touchy-feely post-graduate deans looking out for you and making sure your training was up to scratch.

Mostly, it was because those of us who had ambitions to reach the top just couldn't afford to make waves. Contracts (until you reached senior registrar level) were generally short term (six months, a year or at most two years) and fixed. This meant you were often applying for your next job within a couple of weeks of starting a new post. You were changing posts every six months, even within a two-year contract. The next job pretty much depended on a good reference from the current one, and a label as a "troublemaker" or "shop steward" was the kiss of death to your career progression.

I moved eleven times during my training, sometimes from one end of the country to the other. August the first and February the first were bad times to get sick for patients, as frequently the entire junior team of a consultant changed en mass. When I was driving down the motorway to the next hospital with all my worldly possessions in the back of the car, I would often see people heading in the opposite direction, similarly burdened, and wonder if they were another doctor heading off to do the job I had just left behind.

You would arrive at your new hospital, head for switchboard to pick up your bleep, grab a white coat from the laundry, and then you were straight to work. No protected induction period, no explanation of how to order a blood test or an x-ray etc., and no familiarisation with hospital policy. You were learning how the systems worked as you went along, sometimes in at the deep end being on call for emergencies as you walked through the door. If you survived, it was because you were mentally tough, adaptable, competent and learned quickly.

This was the all-consuming life of a junior doctor. It was accepted as a "normal" working pattern at the time, and did produce a great camaraderie amongst us, as we were all in the same boat, in what felt like an almost wartime footing. You felt you belonged as part of a team, you were given substantial responsibility, and knew that what you were doing was worthwhile. I knew every one of the patients under my care, not only their medical details but also about their families and all their hopes and fears. Your patients effectively became part of an enormous, extended family.

We worked very, very hard but also played very hard. It was also fun, and I loved my job, looking forward to going to work almost every day. This is something that now seems to have been sadly lost with the current generation of trainees who, while working far less hours, are all on shift work and seem to have a (documented) diminished job satisfaction.

In my last year as a consultant in the NHS, I was complaining to the postgraduate supervisor in the hospital that I hadn't seen the doctor who was nominally my SHO (senior house officer), in the previous four months. He'd never been on a ward round, or to outpatients, or theatre (he always seemed to be on some weird shift pattern, working nights, or on "compensatory days off"), so quite how I was supposed to be responsible for training him was difficult to work out. The supervisor told me he thought it would be well worth my while seeking out my trainee and introduce myself to him. I looked at him quizzically.

"So, you think that I, as the boss, should spend my time seeking out the most junior member of the team who is working for me, and introduce myself to him? Don't you feel that's the tail wagging the dog?" He told me he didn't think so, and I was left pondering what my bosses would have done if I had neglected to go looking for them to introduce myself when I'd been at that stage of my career. Probably removed my testicles with a blunt knife. They would have certainly made sure I never made it up the next rung of the career ladder.

I've had an unusual and atypical career. In one part of my practice I have been privileged to have treated many extraordinary figures from the sporting world, from dancers to cage fighters, and everything in between. I have been part of a generation who were responsible for dragging the treatment of professional sportsmen and women into the modern era, from a time when it was almost inevitable a top soccer or rugby player would head across the Atlantic to seek surgery in the States. I think we have done all right, and our television screens are now full of players, of many different disciplines, who have been returned to their pre-injury best after being treated in the UK. I have lived out my sporting ambitions vicariously through the sportsmen and women I have treated, from the elite level down to weekend warriors, and it has been enormously rewarding to return so many to the sporting arena.

During my forty-year career as a medical student, junior doctor and consultant orthopaedic surgeon in the NHS, I have seen the health service evolve with many improvements in the technical side of treatment, but mostly a steady deterioration of standards and personalised care, hand in hand with an explosion of bureaucracy. As far as I've experienced, most of the positive change has been instigated and driven by clinical staff, not by politicians and managers. The health service has changed beyond recognition, and I wanted to document some of how things used to be, before they are lost in the mists of time.

The NHS has become almost soulless, with managers obsessed with hitting politician's targets, and patients becoming numbers on a production line, or profits on a private hospital's balance sheet. After years of a relentless battering by governments, managers, lawyers, private healthcare companies and the media, a large proportion of the once proud, independent and caring medical profession (who incidentally, were the only advocates for patients), seems to have been reduced to a disillusioned bunch of browbeaten yes-men, just turning up to work in the morning, doing what they're told, and what the system allows them to, and then going home again.

The characters, the humour (some of it very black!) and the patients with their bravery and often blind faith, who have touched my life and who I have been very privileged to have known, are all part of a rich mosaic of story and legend, with many, many tales to tell! This book documents some of the memories of a rich and fulfilling career and the long, long journey from school to retirement from the health service.

It tells of the highs and lows, the frustrations and fulfillments, and the resilience of our health service, often in the face of overwhelming odds.

The National Health Service is a precious thing and when I travel abroad, it is always the focus of admiration from colleagues from around the world. We need to look after it, nurture the staff and care for the patients. There is little in life that is more important than the health of your family, friends and yourself.

2

FOLLOW YOUR HEART

How I ever became a surgeon is difficult to understand. Nobody in my family had ever been at school beyond the age of sixteen, let alone been to university, let alone entered the medical profession.

My grandmother was of Irish decent, and one of eleven children, brought up in the East End of London. As a young child she had slept six to a bed, using discarded newspapers for blankets, and often spent days scavenging for scraps of food on the streets. At the age of eleven she had been "put into service", having to get up at five-thirty every day to set the fires in the house, and then spend all day tidying and cleaning. At least she had three meals a day and only shared a bed with one other girl. She was allowed to see her parents one afternoon a week.

Whilst having little education, she was a wise soul and clearly where the brains of the family came from. She had taught herself to read, write and play the piano, and we would often spend comfortable hours discussing current events. The night of the first Apollo landing we stood on the front porch of the house gazing up at the moon, on what was a very clear night, while she told me tales of her childhood, when the whole street would turn out if an automobile passed by, and how things had changed during her lifetime. We looked on in awe, picturing the two human beings so very far away. I was very close to her. It was she that gave me the advice I have lived by – "follow your heart".

My grandfather had lied about his age to join the army at fifteen, rising to the rank of a sergeant in the cavalry, at a time when they still actually rode horses. He was a very good footballer, and apparently on Arsenal's books, until a horrendous tackle left him with a compound fracture of his tibia (where the broken shin bone comes through the skin). The doctors wanted to amputate his leg (in the era before anti-biotics, a compound fracture often led to gangrene and death), but he refused, and spent nearly six months in hospital before his wounds and fracture healed and he was discharged. He then worked for the railway police for many years, living with my grandmother in a small bungalow in a village outside Cambridge. My sister and I spent many happy childhood Summers there, helping my grandmother pick fruit from the local orchards for making jam and pickles, and playing in the surrounding fields.

When we first stayed with them, they had an outside toilet and bath time was in an old tin bath in front of a roaring, open fire in the living room. The outside toilet of one of their neighbours was an old style "earth closet", with a wooden plank with a hole in it over a small pit. There was a bucket of earth, and a trowel next to it, to sprinkle over whatever you might have deposited. Toilet paper was a bunch of torn squares of newspaper threaded through with a loop of string.

Having lived through two world wars my grandparents were of that generation who never threw anything away. Every cupboard and shelf were crammed with stuff that "might come in useful one day", which led down many interesting conversational avenues. They also grew, and preserved, a huge amount of their own food on a patch of land next to their property.

My father was tall and raven haired and had left school at sixteen to join the Merchant Navy (he had wanted to join the Royal Navy but his severe colour blindness prevented him) at the tail end of the second world war. By his eighteenth birthday he had been twice round the world, been shot at by Japanese fighter planes and fought off the amorous advances of older, inebriated shipmates.

My father and mother married at a young age by current standards. My mother came from a Catholic family who did all they could to persuade my father to convert from his protestant faith, but he just couldn't buy into it, and so my mother made the reluctant decision to leave behind her Catholicism. Her local priest addressed her in his broad, Irish brogue.

"Well my dear it's your decision… but you'll burn in hell forever."

After leaving the Merchant Navy my father joined a finance company and went back to "Night School" (the then equivalent of The Open University), to obtain his accountancy qualifications. He must have been bright and driven, as in the meritocracy of the sixties he had a meteoric rise in the business world. During my early childhood we moved to successively larger and grander houses, ending up in a huge detached house with one of the most exclusive addresses in South Manchester.

Then things went pear shaped and he lost everything. A boardroom coup and a blade in the back (seems not uncommon in the world of high finance), left him with a mountain of shares, now worth bugger all, securing an enormous business loan in his name. The saving grace however, was that he owed so much money to the bank they were reluctant to make him bankrupt (the Aristotle Onassis principle) and, as long as he continued to pay off the interest (at that time running between ten and fifteen percent per annum), they allowed him to continue to work – he finally went into the financial black at the age of sixty-three.

I had got it into my head at quite a young age that I wanted to be either a doctor or an astronaut, even though in reality I had little idea of what either involved. My mother of course, also knowing nothing about what either would mean, thought these were great ideas and did nothing to discourage my ambition. One of my dreams was shattered when at the age of eleven it was discovered I was very short-sighted in one eye. In those days, to be an astronaut you had to have twenty-twenty vision, and so my whole future became chanelled in a single direction.

I was lucky enough to be a true child of the state. My education has been entirely state funded and it breaks my heart that it was a Labour government that introduced changes to the university system that meant if I was thinking about applying for medical school now, and was in the same circumstances I was in back then, it is very doubtful as to whether it would be financially viable for me to do so. I think I have made a reasonable fist of things and have certainly repaid the state many times over.

At the end of my primary school years we all took the "eleven plus" exam, which at that time started the massive social divide by consigning a chunk of the eleven-year-old population into the "failed already" bin. I was lucky enough to do well. The only question I struggled with in the whole day of tests was "A place to store food – P_ _ t _ _". Having answered everything else with about fifteen minutes to spare, I sat and wracked my brains trying to come up with the answer. My parents, originating from down south, had never used the word "pantry".

I was fortunate enough to obtain a state scholarship to a decent grammar school in Manchester (sadly, now a private school). It was whilst I was at that school my parents separated, leaving myself and my sister being supported by my mother, who went back to work as a secretary at the Gas Board (how things have changed – I was the only person in my school year of one hundred and twenty whose parents were not together!). My father actually left us twice, returning a couple of years after the initial separation, then going again, on both occasions leaving us on Christmas Eve, meaning the festive period is always tinged with a few sad memories.

My father later went on to remarry. He met a high-class call girl who had been drafted in to entertain at a "business meeting" and fell in love.

To be fair, their relationship stood the test of time and she looked after him the rest of his life, even through his last, debilitating, terminal illness.

Maintenance payments to my mother became infrequent and unreliable (my father used to send cheques either unsigned, with the words and numbers not matching, or with the wrong year on the date, meaning it usually took three or four goes to get each cheque cashed), and we were forced out of our house by the bank as my father had failed to maintain the mortgage payments. Barclay's Bank, bless them, sent us a letter explaining that if we hadn't sold the house within three months, they would auction it, in the week before Christmas. Listening to my mother sob herself to sleep every night added to the previous trauma of my father's departures and is a memory I can never erase. Having moved to successively larger houses during the good times, we then moved to successively smaller ones on the way down, ending up in a small, two-up, two-down terraced house on a cobbled street in Stockport. I can tell you it is much, much psychologically harder moving down the ladder than climbing up it.

I don't think my Mother ever recovered from the blow of my father leaving. In addition, her family (all Catholics) disowned her when the marriage split up. In the end I think it was the bitterness slowly eating away inside her that eventually killed her.

My formative early teenage years were during the "Hippie" era with the famous "Summer of Love" having an enduring impression on me. We really did believe it was "The Dawning of the Age of Aquarius" and that love was going to change the world and make it a better place. This stuck with me through the years, right into the "aging hippie/ wannabe rockstar" phase in later life!

I'm happy to admit I was pretty lazy at school. I hated rote learning, and as natural ability became less important than being able to regurgitate reams of irrelevant facts, I slowly slid down the rankings, becoming less and less of a "golden boy". I was jolted to my senses when, seven months before my A levels, my mother was summoned to the school to be told "We have no idea why Steven has applied for medical school, he'll never get good enough grades to get there."

I took stock, realised that my notes for each subject seemed to be a fraction of the size of those of everyone else in my classes, and also that there was no way I could start from scratch and learn everything by the following June. I gave the matter some thought and obtained the exam papers from the previous twelve years in the subjects I was taking – Physics, Chemistry and Biology.

I then plotted the subject and type of question against the year it had been set. I was astonished to find that the questions seemed to be entirely predictable i.e. "Describe the Industrial Production of Sulphuric Acid." came up every third year without fail, some questions came up every other year etc. etc. I found the same in all three subjects. I made my predictions, revised constantly, and learned the answers off by heart having also obtained the marking schemes from the previous years. I knew it was a calculated risk but didn't think I had much choice.

I can vividly remember sitting in the first exam, chemistry, and being told to turn over the question paper and begin. I did so and burst out laughing, much to the consternation of the invigilator. Every one of my predictions had turned out to be correct and I set to with a vengeance to get it all down in the answer books. I knew I couldn't get less than a hundred percent, as I knew the questions and their marking schemes, so could get every point they were looking for into the answer.

Not surprisingly, I achieved and exceeded the grades I needed for my entry to medical school. My grammar school had a "celebratory dinner" in the school canteen for those of us who had succeeded in getting to university, and I could see my teachers looking at me curiously, obviously puzzled and suspicious as to how I had obtained top grades. Their congratulations were somewhat muted as they had all predicted I would fail. Personally, I found it difficult to understand as to why if I, as a mere schoolboy, could make such accurate predictions, they had been unable to do so.

I was actually offered a place at three medical schools, after going through the usual interview process. I would churn out the stock answers to the stock questions and try to sound sincere when I said

I read the Guardian "because although some people say it is more comments on the news rather than the news itself, I think it presents a balanced and thoughtful analysis of current events", and a load of other bullshit that I didn't really believe but was what I thought the interview panel wanted to hear.

I put Birmingham as my number one choice (ahead of Kings and Manchester), as a result of one of those odd twists of fate. The train broke down on the way to the interview, meaning I arrived an hour after the scheduled tour round of the medical school for the day's interviewees. I was standing there feeling a bit lost and awkward in my ill-fitting suit, not quite sure what to do with myself, when a passing medical student took pity on me and asked what the problem was. I explained what had happened. He told me he had no commitments for the next couple of hours and would be happy to give me a personalised tour. This random act of kindness (together with a delicious fish mornay for lunch in the student refectory) swayed my decision. I've never regretted it.

I had never been a rugby playing type at school, and hadn't really done anything to distinguish myself, done any voluntary work or obtained piano grade eight, seemingly requirements for a place in medical school these days, as apparently these give a better indication you are going to be a good doctor. Indeed, although I had been in the "top set", I was the only member of my class not to have been made a school prefect (I was actually rather glad about that, as at that time one of their duties was to cane miscreants, something some of my year took a sadistic delight in, but wasn't for me).

This was largely because the headmaster had absolutely no idea who I was. I had fairly long hair and wanted to keep it that way (I really, really wanted to be a Hippie), so spent much of my school time keeping a low profile and checking around corners to make sure the Head wasn't there. If he clapped eyes on you, you were suspended until you had a haircut that he felt was acceptable which, as he had come from the military, was pretty much prison regulation.

Having successfully negotiated the interview process and achieved the required grades at A level (I thought my mother would burst with pride when the big, fat, brown envelope plopped through the letter box), I arrived at Birmingham University for "Fresher's Week", full of excitement and optimism for the future.

I hit problems almost straight away. The grant application procedure had been complicated by the fact that my parents were still separated, rather than officially divorced, and the paperwork had gone to my father who assured me he would sort it out. I turned up to the Great Hall to collect my grant cheque only to find nothing there. It turned out my father had not actually done anything at all, so I was left penniless. Fortunately, my hall of residence agreed to allow me to pay at the end of the first term, so at least I had two meals a day and a roof over my head. My mother got on quickly with trying to sort things out, but I had no money at all for the first six weeks. I learned the valuable lessons that you can survive happily on two meals a day, walk to most places you want to get to, and that you don't need to buy a lot of expensive textbooks as you can access them in the library.

During my second week at university, I saw a notice pinned up in the Students Union asking for volunteers for "Nightline", a student telephone helpline a bit like the Samaritans. They were having a selection weekend and, being a bit of an altruistic hippie, I thought I'd give it a go. Perhaps equally important was that it was free, and they were providing lunch!

About sixty of us turned up on the Saturday morning and underwent a day of talks, and several sessions of role playing. Gradually, people were getting weeded out, and half had gone before we resumed on Sunday morning. By the end of that day only six of us were left. I'm still not sure quite how I made the cut.

I manned the phones regularly for the next couple of years. Sometimes nothing would happen at all, sometimes it was frantically busy with everything from "what bus number do I need to get from Y to Z", students who wanted legal advice having been picked up by the police and been told they were in possession of prohibited substances (not all our policemen are knights in shining armour), and the lonely and depressed. I think I was able to help some of them.

You always worked in pairs with one male and one female. You would answer the phone alternately, so if someone rang and I answered and the phone immediately cut off and then immediately rang again, you knew they wanted to speak to a woman. My lifelong disaffection with my own gender (summed up in the Never2Late track "Sometimes I'm Ashamed To Be A Man"), started by having to listen to my opposite number talking to one of a number of sad men who would ring up, as they could only get off listening to a female voice talking about sex while having a wank.

There was some debate within "Nightline" about whether this was a morally justifiable approach, but the consensus was it was probably preferable (in the days before the open access to pornography) to them having to go out and find their jollies elsewhere. I had nothing but admiration for my female colleagues who could talk about a made-up sexual encounter to a complete stranger on the other end of the line, whilst at the same time reading a textbook for their next essay assignment.

I had arrived at university with very little. I had one pair of jeans, a cheap pair of felt "fellboots" from the "Army and Navy Store", a few T-shirts, pants and socks and a paint stained, quilted jacket I had found in an old garage. I remember telling a girlfriend that I only had one pair of jeans and her puzzled look as she asked me when did I wash them? Her puzzled look turned to horror when I told her I had never washed them, except on the infrequent occasions I went home to visit my mother!

Before arriving at Uni, I had the vague idea that I would be mixing with a collection of likeminded people from diverse backgrounds but found out that eighty-seven percent of my year at medical school had been to public school and, out of the one hundred and seventy students in my year, there were only two of us whose parents had a sufficiently low income to qualify us for a full grant.

Things actually haven't changed a lot. In November 2019 the British Medical Journal published a piece "Shut Out: the medical profession's intractable class problem.", bemoaning the lack of medical students from poorer backgrounds and pointing out the proportion of students coming from lower socioeconomic backgrounds was half that among university students overall.

Most of the friends I made were studying subjects other than medicine. Like most groups of students, we drank too much, experimented with drugs (one afternoon someone excitedly rushed into the medical school common room shouting that there were magic mushrooms growing on the front lawn, which was followed by a mass stampede – they make interesting omlettes!), and argued and debated into the small hours, confidently thinking we had worked out the answers to all the world's ills. This was great until the end of the third university year when they all disappeared off around the country to pursue their chosen careers, leaving me at Birmingham with two more clinical years to go and most of my year at medical school in established cliques.

On a more positive note, it was a great time to be at University if you were a live music fan (you might have worked out the names of the chapters in this book are all song titles). In those heady days, bands and individual artists toured to promote their new albums, rather than nowadays where it seems the other way round. Universities were seen as great, and financially lucrative, places to play and we had numerous high profile and upcoming bands entertain us in the Students Union. We weren't overburdened with security, and bands would often pop into the bar either before or after playing. One night I had a long conversation with Al Stewart (about the time of the "Roads To Moscow" album), earnestly discussing our views on what might happen in the forthcoming decade. (He felt there was "change in the air", I was a little more skeptical)

It was a time of great lyricists and singer songwriters – ("in no particular order") Joni Mitchell, Al Stewart, Roy Harper, Bob Dylan, Paul Simon, Leonard Cohen and Jackson Brown, to name but a few (I'd developed a fondness for wordsmiths after being introduced to Dylan Thomas during English Literature at GCSE and this never left me). Their songs are forever associated with segments of my life.

One afternoon, the entertainments secretary was sat in his office in the Students Union when there was a knock on the door. When he opened it, he was surprised to find Paul McCartney standing there, who asked him if he could play (for nothing) that night. There was a van outside with the band (Wings) and all their gear and they were looking for some gigs to try out their new material. Word spread like wildfire (pre mobile phone and social media days!) and they played a great set in front of a packed house.

Even the halls of residence had great, live music events. One of the best concerts I have ever been to, was when "Thin Lizzy" played in front of about two hundred of us at the Christmas party in the hall of residence next to mine. I was standing about ten feet away from Phil Lynott when they played "Still In Love With You", which remains one of my all-time favourite tracks to this day. A year later they had become famous and were filling concert halls around the world.

I was voracious reader in those days before social media, computer and console games, and You Tube. My children are aghast when I tell them I had no TV, no computer, no mobile phone, and my entertainment consisted of reading, a radio and an old-style vinyl record player (now back in vogue!). When I arrived at Uni, I had been an avid science fiction fan, but by midway through my second year I'd worked my way through most of the genre's titles in the University book shop.

Stuck for something to read, I remembered a previous girlfriend, who'd been studying English Literature, telling me how she thought the writing of Herman Hesse was brilliant. I scanned the shelves and came upon "The Prodigy", a slim volume that was relatively cheap and wouldn't take me long to work my way through.

Back at my hall of residence I made myself a cup of tea, sat down and started to read. It was an epiphany. The prose just blew me away, and a door opened into a marvelous, magical new world. I was unused to the sheer quality of the writing and it spawned a life-long love of literature. I worked my way through the entire collection of Hesse's works, then moved on to Thomas Hardy, D.H Lawrence, Raymond

Chandler, Evelyn Waugh, Gabriel Garcia Marquez and then one by one, pretty much all of Penguin's "Modern Classics" from A to Z.

There are occasional episodes that change and shape your entire approach to life. At the end of the first year we had the usual lengthy, university summer holidays and, to supplement my grant, I managed to get a job in a factory local to home. "Wylex" was the firm, making three pin plugs and circuit breakers. I was employed as a "general labourer" – the absolute lowest of the low. I swept floors, cleaned toilets and fetched and carried, in an environment that was constantly deafening (no ear protectors) and, as shafts of sunlight came through the grubby windows lighting the gloomy interior of the shop floor, you could see the air was thick with metal dust.

It was physically punishing work and not surprisingly the three other general labourers, who'd been there for years, didn't bust a gut to get anything done. I have always preferred to be busy, and it didn't take long before they would leave me to it and go and read "The Sun" in the toilets for hours at a time. When the women who were working there, placing small metal blocks in slots in a rotating table all day long, found out I was a medical student, they would come and ask me questions about what the best sort of tablets were to take for depression. It dawned on me that I had been blessed and that this was not going to be my future. I had the chance for a career in a profession which was varied, challenging and rewarding, rather than something mind-numbingly bleak, just to put food on the table and a roof over my head. I felt an obligation to make the most of the chance I had been given and would never forget what it felt like to be bottom of the heap.

The first couple of years at medical school are fairly standard university fare, with lots of lectures, tutorials, study time and exams. I didn't enjoy this stage very much, as it didn't seem to have a lot of direct relevance to treating patients and I spent much time learning things by rote (my pet hate!) that I have never, ever used again.

I was more interested in chasing girls, playing my guitar, going to gigs and having fun, so I did the bare minimum I could get away with, scraping through all the exams in the first year with a "just pass" in every subject. I was subsequently told the medical school wanted to make me take re-sits, as they knew I'd done bugger all and hadn't attended a single tutorial but couldn't actually justify it as I'd actually passed everything.

In the second year, I really enjoyed the hours spent dissecting a cadaver, and this possibly pointed at the future direction of my career. Beneath the skin, the human frame is a truly fantastic, soft machine, and I loved chasing and defining the structures responsible for moving us around and keeping us alive. I actually did quite well in the anatomy exams, I think because I could understand the relevance of what I was learning (a thorough knowledge of anatomy, however, no longer seems to be required for the modern breed of medical student. I was appalled when, not too long ago, one came to join me in a fracture clinic and was unable to name the two bones in the forearm!!).

I found the clinical years much more interesting, experiencing a taste of the whole host of different specialties that deal with all the things that go wrong with the human body. At various times I decided I wanted to be a cardiologist, a dermatologist, a psychiatrist and a surgeon. The only things I decided I definitely didn't want to be were a paediatrician (just too scary, and the parents were often nuts), or an obstetrician (largely because midwives were horrible cows to medical students which made the experience very unpleasant and... you just can't joke with pregnant women). Weirdly though, on the day of my twenty first birthday, I was actually delivering babies (in the days when medical students actually did this), in the very same delivery room I had been borne in, and at the same time, twenty-one years before!

Hospital medicine was all very exciting and new, and I loved talking to and examining patients and trying to work out what was wrong with them. I enjoyed the immediacy of surgery and watching the technically skillful was awesome and inspiring.

The clinical years did mean moving out of university accommodation and living in the real world, renting a house, doing laundry, paying bills etc. Five of us ended up in a house in Sparkbrook, at that time not one of the most select areas of Birmingham, but pretty good if you liked curry. Unlike my children's university accommodation, we had no central heating or ensuite facilities. It was cold, draughty, we had mould on the walls and, like the song says, "rats in the kitchen" (really!).

One winter it was so cold I was going to bed fully dressed, in a sleeping bag, under a duvet. During the night, I must have kicked my hot water bottle out of bed and when I got up in the morning it had frozen solid. It was generally a relief to get to the warmth of whichever hospital you were attached to and get a hot shower in the student's mess.

Finances for me were difficult, as although being on a "full grant", you received the normal grant for thirty weeks, but only a third of this weekly amount for the additional eighteen weeks. As you only had a couple of two-week holidays during the year, there was no opportunity to sub your income with a holiday job.

I was faced with the prospect of going steadily into the red, as I worked out my basic living expenses of rent, food, bus pass, electricity and a weekly visit to the launderette, came to three pounds a week (a lot in those days) more than my grant. My father's various financial problems had left me with a morbid fear of going into debt (Phillip Larkin you were so right!), so I went out and found a job answering the phones at a doctor's deputising service, from seven p.m. to seven a.m., two nights a week.

This put my finances on an even keel and also opened my eyes to the amazing things that patients will ring their doctor about in the early hours of the morning. I will never forget having a bizarre conversation with a patient, just after midnight on a Saturday, about the fact he had found he only had one "Sterident" tablet left to sterilise his false teeth, and the chemist was closed the following day, so should he use half now and half tomorrow, not use it tonight and use it tomorrow night, or use it all tonight and not tomorrow night?

One lady rang up late at night to say she had been cooking tripe a few days before but it had burnt, so she had put the frying pan outside the back door where it had been festering, and her son had just gone outside in bare feet and trodden in it. Should the doctor come out to inoculate him or did he need to go to hospital?

Back in the medical school there was still a great deal of snobbery around, with one of the first questions you were asked by a consultant you were attached to generally being "and what school did you go to." There was usually a disdainful look when you said you had been to a state grammar school. An older, spinster paediatrician told me that the problems of the health service began when "they started letting the wrong sort of people into medical school". For her, this meant grammar school educated, rather than public school. It didn't take me long to realise that I had far more in common with the patients than I ever did with the vast majority of my colleagues, and this feeling stayed with me until retirement.

There were a fair number of students in my year whose parents were either consultants or GPs, and it seemed to be pretty common for children to follow their parents into the medical profession. This is perhaps another of the more noticeable changes I have seen over the last thirty years. Medicine is still usually seen by those outside the profession as a highly desirable and prestigious career but there seem to be few doctors who would recommend it in its current form.

I did a survey of consultant colleagues at the Bradford Royal Infirmary (BRI) a few years back, asking if they would encourage their children to follow them into medicine. The vast majority of replies (eighty-two percent), indicated they would actively discourage their children from doing so (none of my four children have followed me into medicine).

One of the "joys" of moving into the clinical years at medical school was the daily session in the post-mortem room, always scheduled just before lunch. In those days, many people died without the cause of their demise being known, something that modern diagnostic techniques such as MRI and CT scanning have almost abolished.

At the end of every morning on the wards, we all trouped down to the post-mortem room for a session with the ridiculously cheerful pathologist who enjoyed singing opera as he eviscerated people. He would have half a dozen bodies opened up for us on the shiny metal tables. Anyone who has watched a modern crime series, such as "Silent Witness", on the TV will know what this involves, but what you don't get on the TV is the smell, which can be truly awful.

The human sense of smell is an odd thing, in that it quickly becomes overloaded and then ceases to recognise a particular scent. The pathologist's advice was to take a few deep sniffs and the smell would go away. He was right, but it was often a close-run thing before the urge to vomit won the battle.

The pathologist would gleefully hold up a particular organ or a handful of gangrenous bowel for our closer inspection, and then talk us through the particular disease process that had caused the patient to die. We would then walk down to the hospital canteen for lunch, still trying to get the smell of death out of our nostrils. It does wonders at suppressing your appetite.

You often felt that many of the clinicians who turned up to teach you were doing so out of sufferance. Not infrequently you would turn up for a teaching session, only to sit around for an hour or so before someone would deliver a message saying it had been cancelled. Our attachment to Ear, Nose and Throat surgery was a prime example. We turned up to six consecutive "teaching sessions" only to have all of them cancelled after an hour or so of sitting around twiddling our thumbs.

At the end of our six-week attachment there was an exam, and as a protest I didn't attend, hoping I would be able to put my point that having had no teaching, there seemed little validity in taking an exam. I was surprised to find that when the results came out, I had been awarded a "B". I can only surmise they thought they had lost my paper and so gave me a grade in the middle (this was still a time when less than ten percent of grades were an A), that they felt most people would be happy with.

Things got tougher and tougher as we entered the fifth and final year. As a final year medical student at Birmingham you had an attach-ment to General Surgery, General Medicine, Psychiatry, Obstetrics and

Gynaecology and a bit of Paediatrics, then to finish off, Anaesthetics and General Practice (this was my last attachment and unlike every other attachment there was no exam, so I knew I'd passed everything about six weeks before the end of the course).

In those days, if the houseman on the firm you were attached to was away on holiday, you were expected to do his/her locum, and I ended up working as the locum houseman in General Medicine and General Surgery (and the year before as a locum *Senior* House Officer in Infectious Diseases). At least you were paid a pittance for these jobs, which provided a welcome addition to your finances.

These jobs gave you great experience and insight of what was to come, even though it was pretty terrifying. In General Medicine I was attached to the professorial unit at the Queen Elizabeth hospital, with the Professor at that time being the President of the Royal College of Physicians. Fortunately for me, his ward was run by a fabulous, old-school sister, married to the job, who looked kindly on me and made sure I didn't do anything desperately dangerous.

I remember being left to explain to a patient that he had inoperable lung cancer. In those days we had no lectures or training in "communication skills", or "delivering bad news", you were just left to get on with it, even as a medical student.

Sister sat in with me while I carefully explained to the patient and his wife, as kindly as I could, that he had an inoperable cancer of the lung and that there wasn't a chance of a cure, but we might be able to slow down the progress of the disease with some non-surgical treatments. I didn't use euphemisms such as "tumour", or "shadow on the lung", as I've always felt it is better to be honest and upfront so people can plan their lives accordingly. Even though I had used the word "cancer" several times during the conversation, patients can often hear what they want to hear and can blank out the bad stuff.

After I had delivered the bad news, I paused to let the information sink in. I then asked if he or his wife had any questions about what they had just heard. The patient looked up,

"What was it you said I had again?"

The best bit of that job was the evening ward round at ten p.m. The Queen Elizabeth hospital was in one of the posher areas of Birmingham and the patients were generally better off financially than most people. At that time, on admission, patients were automatically prescribed tablets for night sedation to enable them to get a decent night's sleep on the old-style Nightingale wards. Instead of sleeping pills it was then acceptable to have a shot of alcohol, which could be prescribed from the pharmacy, although the hospital supplied whisky and brandy wasn't exactly top quality.

Patients were, however, allowed to bring in their own alcohol which would be labelled with their name and kept on the drugs trolley. So, the trick was to arrive on the ward as the last drug round was going on and there would be the inevitable "won't you join me doctor?" On the professorial unit this meant malt whiskey or Courvoisier brandy – a nice way to finish up the day before heading off for bed.

Psychiatry is an odd profession and seemed to be populated by some very strange consultants. My first attachment was at a huge, oppressive, old psychiatric hospital on the outskirts of Birmingham. I'll never forget one particular patient I met there, who was a cheerful, old Polish lady with twinkling eyes and a beaming smile. She had been an inpatient at the hospital since the end of the second world war, when she had been admitted for the sole reason she spoke no English. She was, by the time I met her, so institutionalised there was no hope of returning her to any sort of independent life in the community, and so she was going to be there until she died.

Although I was meant to be working with a particular consultant, he didn't turn up for the first week and I spent my time with a very nice Indian lady registrar, being taught about the different psychoses and neuroses and their management. When you spend your whole time in the company of patients whose thought patterns and processes are so far outside the norm, you do find yourself questioning your own version of reality!

At the end of the week the registrar asked to have a private word with me. She then explained that the consultant who I was supposed to be with had a severe drink problem and would periodically go off on a bender whilst his colleagues covered for his absence. She assured me that he should be back the following week.

He was a very odd character and to me seemed unnecessarily aggressive and outrageously rude to the patients. After a long clinic one afternoon he turned to me.

"I suppose you think I'm rude to the patients". I told him I did.

"The problem is you see, I am responsible for these patients out in the community. I provoke them in here and if they react violently, I section them and admit them into the hospital. Can't have them attacking someone they take a dislike to at a bus stop." He then gleefully said, "Look at this." and flicked up the top edge of the desk in front of him, which then rotated up ninety degrees forming a barrier between himself and a patient sitting on the opposite side, and at the same time activated the emergency alarm. He'd had it specially made so that if, after the inevitable provocation, the patient went for him, it would protect him while other staff came to his aid.

The second half of my psychiatry attachment was with the Midland's "premier sexologist", back at the Queen Elizabeth hospital. I learned a lot about the weird and wonderful human imagination when applied to sex. As part of this I was obliged to attend a "sexual therapist" course he had organised, being run for nurses, midwives, health visitors and social workers.

It was with some trepidation I turned up to find I was not only the sole male but was also the youngest attendee by at least twenty years. We were split up into discussion groups, and I found myself with a group of middle-aged women who all seemed to think that sex should only take place within a loving relationship and preferably not until married.

Every time a question came up, I'd have to listen to their various discussions until inevitably they would look at me and ask, "And what do you think?". The concept that you could actually have sex just for the enjoyment of it, and that as long as something wasn't physically or psychologically damaging it was ok, seemed a complete anathema to them. At least, after four days of skin crawling embarrassment, I was handed a certificate saying I was a qualified sexual counsellor. It is, however, not something I generally put on my CV.

My final year at medical school was the first year they had scrapped the "matching scheme" for house officer posts, where a huge list of available medical and surgical posts around the region was put up. You then put your name against the ones you wanted to apply for and eventually everyone was fixed up.

My year was a free for all. After doing quite well on the medical professorial unit, their house officer post had been tentatively offered to me, but when it came to the crunch, they gave it to someone else. I was pretty disillusioned but reckoned there would be some people who would fail the course and the consultants they had been scheduled to work for some six weeks later would be desperate to find a replacement.

This did indeed turn out to be the case and, as our results came out, a job became available at the Worcester Royal Infirmary. I rang them up and was given an invitation to attend for interview the following day. The consultant was a Mr. Williams, a rather dry Welshman with an interest in urology (waterworks), as well as his general surgical commitment.

I turned up in my ill-fitting suit and was ushered in to meet him in his outpatient clinic. In five minutes, he quickly ran through what the job involved and then asked me if I wanted to take the post. I tentatively asked if I could have a look round the hospital first. He picked up the phone.

"John, get in here." His senior house officer who had been in the room next door, popped his head around the door.

"John, this is Steve. He might me coming here to work as my house officer. Show him round and make sure he's impressed." I think John was quite pleased to be able to escape the clinic for an hour or so, and we set off to have a look at where I might be working.

Situated near the centre of the town, the Worcester Royal Infirmary was an old, smallish hospital with a large green space in the middle containing a magnificent walnut tree, which gave the name to the doctor's residence – "Walnut Tree House". Everyone seemed very friendly, and John and I hit it off straight away. At the end of the tour I turned to John.

"Are you going to be working here for the next six months?" He said he was, which made my mind up straight away. A truism that was passed on to me early on in my career, is that it doesn't matter what you are doing or where you are working, it is the people you are working with that makes a job viable or not, and I have always found this to be correct.

I didn't live to regret my decision and had a great time over my first six months working as a pre-registration surgical houseman. Mr. William's "team" consisted of myself, John and a registrar who was also a bachelor. We had a riot, and even though working one hundred and twenty hours a week, we laughed a lot and had great fun. Working through the nights, we would pass the time by reenacting Monty Python or Derek and Clive sketches over the operating table and laugh until, behind our operating masks, tears rolled down our cheeks.

The boss could see I was keen and anxious to learn and taught me how to operate on varicose veins and hernias. At night I was able to take on a fair amount of the emergency work myself. In my six months as a pre-registration house officer I performed thirty-two appendicectomies, the last sixteen unsupervised, something completely unheard of today.

At that time, every patient who came into the hospital, whether it was for a minor or major procedure, received a full examination (literally top to bottom with the old saying "if you haven't put your finger in, you've put your foot in it" still holding sway), ECG, chest X-ray and routine blood tests. I listened to hundreds of hearts and lungs, palpated hundreds of abdomens, stuck my index finger up hundreds of bottoms and by examining so many people became competent at picking up the difference between normal and abnormal. Over the subsequent years I identified several melanomas (a malignant skin cancer), countless cardiac arrhythmias (irregular heartbeat), and a whole host of other, previously undiagnosed pathologies, including other cancers and neurological conditions. This was happening to all patients, in all hospitals, all across the country, every day, an aspect of "health screening" that now sadly seems to have disappeared.

Things were a lot more laid back at that time. If we were on-call and during the evening things were quiet, the team would relocate to the pub about a hundred yards from the front door of the hospital. The front desk by the entrance of the hospital was manned by a lovely chap called Ron, who had been working in that role for as long as anyone could remember. As we walked by him, we would say.

"Just off to church Ron." And he would reply.

"Right, ho doctors", and with a wink and a smile, "Bring me back a bottle." He would then reroute any calls for the team, from GPs wanting to refer emergencies to the hospital, to the phone behind the bar in the pub. Over the many on-call nights during the six months I worked there I took numerous calls trying desperately to not make it too obvious we were in a busy public house.

On nights off we would party hard, often in the nurse's home situated not fifty yards from the doctor's residence. Several times I crawled into bed in the early evening, having had a heavy night on call the night before, only to be woken by a phone call from a nurse inviting me to join a party. The speciality of the nursing home was dope cakes, as several of the nurses grew marijuana on their windowsills.

Those were the days when AIDS didn't exist, herpes was a vague rumour, nobody had heard of chlamydia, and almost every girl you met was on the contraceptive pill. It seemed everyone slept with everyone else. This reached an unfortunate and inevitable conclusion when a consultant psychiatrist (female!), that I had a passionate few nights with, popped her head around the door of my room in the doctors mess and informed me she had just been diagnosed as having a trichomonas infection in the STD clinic. She worked out it must have been me that gave it to her, even though I was completely asymptomatic.

This was serious. The bachelors sat down and tried to work out who had slept with whom, and how many people might be infected.

After a few phone calls and difficult conversations, we totted up the numbers and realised… there were fourteen.

The treatment at that time was six tablets of Flagyl (a type of antibiotic), and then another six tablets twelve hours later. We decided to have a Flagyl party and invited all those affected. The only trouble with Flagyl is that it is a bit like "Antabuse" in that it makes you vomit if you drink alcohol while taking it.

The designated evening arrived. A raiding party was formed, and we silently sneaked down to the porter's desk in the front hall and waited for them to be called away. All the keys for the hospital (including those to the pharmacy) were kept in a tin under the desk, so once the desk was vacated the keys to the pharmacy were borrowed (no CCTV or alarms in those days!), and we quietly let ourselves in. It wasn't difficult to locate the Flagyl and one hundred and sixty-eight tablets were carefully counted out. The keys were clandestinely returned and, once we were back in the doctor's mess, the tablets ceremoniously taken. The pharmacy never did quite work out how or why their stock of Flagyl went down so quickly.

I had started at Worcester without the second six months of my pre-registration year being organised, but sure something would turn up. Sure enough, several jobs became vacant as graduates from my year cracked under the strain of the first six months. Half the housemen at one teaching hospital in the centre of Birmingham ended up having in-patient psychiatric treatment.

I fell into a job as a medical houseman at the Walsgrave hospital in Coventry, a massive hospital complex on the outskirts of the city, which had a main hospital, a psychiatric hospital, a maternity hospital, a geriatric hospital and a multi-story nurses home, all on the same site. The only thing it didn't have was an A&E unit, which was located in the centre of town. The ambulance service would triage the emergency calls, taking everything but physical trauma to our hospital.

I thought my time at Worcester had been busy but was in for a rude awakening. We averaged twenty-seven emergency admissions every twenty-four hours, and you generally had less than three hours sleep when on-call. In fact, three hours was regarded as a bit of a luxury.

My fairly young consultant took the team out for a beer one night and, as is the way, told us how lucky we were to be on the rota we were on. It was a bit like the Monty Python "Four Yorkshiremen" sketch, as he told us that "when he was a houseman" they were on call six nights a week and only had one afternoon and evening off a week.

Further questioning revealed it wasn't as bad as it sounded. They were only on-call for their own patients, there were no bleeps and no cardiac arrest calls. If a patient came in during the night, the night sister would assess them and would only call the doctor if she felt it was really necessary. There were no lab tests available and no monitoring systems so, as an example, heart attacks were treated by some morphine (prescribed by sister) and an oxygen tent.

Most evenings, a sit-down dinner would be served in the doctor's mess, following which everyone would do a ward round of their own patients. Then they would all go out to one of the numerous pubs that used to be dotted around most hospitals. If Sister wanted you she would ring the porters, and one of them would be delegated to tour the local hostelries until they found you and politely request you returned to the hospital, "when you had finished your drink."

How times had changed. When you were on-call at the Walsgrave, your bleep would go off about eight-thirty a.m. and the cheery sister on the admissions unit would gleefully inform you "There's two waiting". It then generally didn't stop for the next twenty-four hours. You would be trying to cover the day-to-day ward work, as well seeing the constant stream of emergency admissions, and intermittently running off to attend a cardiac arrest in another part of the hospital. It was frantic, but you genuinely saved some patients lives as they were brought in in extremis and you pulled them back from the brink.

Some of it was horrible. One Sunday morning the ambulance service brought in a tramp who they had found collapsed by the side of the road. He stunk to high heaven and was dressed in layer upon layer of clothes. As we peeled them off him the body lice jumped and scurried for cover, but between each layer of clothes were hundreds and hundreds of pounds in bank notes. When we counted it up, he had over five thousand pounds in cash on him. He was complaining he'd had a lot of diarrhoea (which was pretty obvious from the state of his trousers).

After we'd managed to prise him out of his clothes and clean him up a bit, I eventually got to examine him. Any feelings disgust were quickly replaced by pity when I found he had a huge, inoperable cancer of the rectum. He was referred to the surgeons who told me there was no hope for him and he hadn't long left as it had already spread all over his body.

We used to have some fantastic mess parties at the hospital and one Friday night (having had pretty much no sleep the night before as I'd been on call), I was having a good time at one of them, drinking plenty of beer and convincing myself I was well on the way to seducing a particularly good looking student nurse, when the phone went off behind the bar. I was surprised when my name was called out and I was asked if I could speak to the on-call houseman.

"You know that Irish navvy you looked after last night, the one who'd taken a massive overdose of aspirin? He's gone bananas and barricaded himself in a room and says he will only talk to "that there doctor what saved his life".

Aspirin overdoses, which were potentially lethal, were a real pain (as opposed to the take three Valium and call an ambulance brigade, who were generally treated with a stomach washout and a night in hospital), as the treatment of "forced alkaline diuresis" meant you had to take and check their blood samples every hour through the night, and then adjust the treatment accordingly. This basically meant you didn't get to bed at all and would only be able to snatch a few minutes rest at a time, while slumped over the desk in the ward office. In this particular case as the aspirin was cleared from his system, what we hadn't known was that he was also an alcoholic and, as the alcohol also disappeared, he developed the "DT's" (delirium tremens), a type of acute paranoid psychosis.

I made my way up to the ward to find a whole host of clinical and security staff gathered outside a side room, where all the furniture from inside had been piled up in the doorway. The on-call psychiatrist was there but was a tiny Sri Lankan lady who insisted we didn't inject him with any "Largactyl" (a major tranquilliser and the standard way of subduing this type of patient), as this would "mask" the symptoms of his psychosis!

I'm five-foot-nine in my socks, the patient was huge. About six-feet-five tall, with years of hard manual labour having honed his physique into that resembling a professional wrestler. He was obviously very paranoid, and still shouting he would only talk to "that there doctor what saved me life", so in my slightly inebriated state I was ushered forward whilst everyone else took two steps backwards.

"Jesus" I thought, "I'm going to get killed." In accordance with the psychiatrist's wishes I didn't take any Largactyl with me but a syringe containing thirty milligrams of injectable Diazepam (Valium). This is a huge dose, and if given all at once into a vein in a standard patient, would normally stop them breathing. I spoke to him calmly, reassuring him that I was there, and telling him I was going to help him sort out his problems.

One thing you do learn when dealing with difficult or confused patients, is that there is a "voice of command", and when using it the patient will often respond automatically, without thinking. I pushed through the piled up furniture and noticed he had pulled his IV line out of the cannula in the back of his hand and was dripping blood from it onto the floor.

"Sit down! Let's sort out this bleeding." He looked down noticed the blood running down his hand and meekly sat down in a chair.

"Now then, let's just put some of this in to stop the bleeding." I connected the syringe and gave him the whole dose in one go, half expecting him to stop breathing (this is a temporary effect, and the "crash trolley" was ready and waiting outside). It hardly touched him.

"Hmmm... that didn't work, I think we need some more." Somebody from outside passed me another syringe with another thirty milligrams of Diazepam and, fearful I was going to get punched at any second, I again gave him the whole lot in one go. He started to look sleepy.

"You look very tired. Now lie down on the bed and have a rest!" He lay down, closed his eyes and was very quickly in a drug induced slumber. That dose would have stunned an ox, but it had barely touched him. He never did stop breathing and, with a gargantuan effort, the team transferred him onto a trolley and wheeled him off to the secure unit in the psychiatric hospital. It turned out his wife had run off with another bloke and he was homeless and penniless, spending any cash he did earn on alcohol. Some people's lives are complicated.

And so it went on, the days blurring into weeks and the weeks into months. A haze of hundreds of patients, lives saved and lost, with plenty of parties, booze and sex, much of it whilst half asleep. I learned much, gained enormous experience, and my confidence in treating the acutely ill grew steadily.

Then, suddenly it was over. I had survived! Twelve months of extreme, battle front pressure, and I hadn't killed anyone or cracked up mentally. I could now call myself a proper doctor and place my name on the medical register. It was an almost hysterical feeling of relief that it was finished. If only I'd realised that it had actually only just started…

3

NO MORE HEROES, ANY MORE

They Don't Make Them Like They Used To

During my medical school and junior doctor years, consultants were "gods", and there were many who seemed to have modelled themselves on Sir Lancelot Spratt of the "Carry On Doctor" films. Their generation were almost exclusively upper middle class, and many had little in common, or empathy, with their patients.

When I was starting as a medical houseman in Coventry, the registrar in my team (who was only three years ahead of me) told me he had been a houseman in a big London teaching hospital. When the consultant came for his weekly ward round, the whole team would be assembled on the front steps of the hospital. The consultant would arrive in a chauffeur driven Rolls Royce and the houseman's job was to run down the steps, open the car door and take "Sir's" briefcase. The team would then fall in behind him as he swept imperiously through the hospital to do the weekly ward round.

His ward would be in total silence, with the nurses stood at attention around the walls and the patients tucked neatly in their beds. On one occasion a priest was giving the last rights to a dying patient at the end of the ward and his quiet mumbling disturbed the sepulchral quiet. A scowl of anger crossed "Sir's" face as he pointed a quivering finger at the offending individual.

"What the hell is he doing here?! Get him out!" And the priest was ushered from the ward.

At the beginning of my journey, clinical investigations were fairly primitive and, as a surgeon, there were many times you opened up a patient having little idea what you might find and would then have to make things up as you went along. You had to be technically skilful, able to think on your feet, and have a thorough knowledge of anatomy and your field. A degree of self-confidence and raw courage were also useful attributes!

The "intellectuals" of medicine were the physicians, particularly the neurologists and cardiologists, who were brilliant at eliciting and interpreting the symptoms and then performing the esoteric art of examination, with few tools except a stethoscope and their eyes and hands. They then weighed up the accumulated evidence, arriving at a final diagnosis.

Neurologists and neurosurgeons were definitely a breed apart. At the Queen Elizabeth hospital in Birmingham, an attachment to the neurologist was regarded with trepidation by the medical students. You would be allocated patients to take a history from and examine, with a view to presenting your findings on the weekly ward round.

The neurology ward was in the basement and on the designated day the team would be assembled in the office with the notes trolley. The consultant would stride down the corridor, turn left past the office without casting so much as a glance in their direction. The team would then wheel out behind him with military precision and follow him down onto the ward. He would walk up to the first patient and stick out his hand, expecting the appropriate set of notes would be placed in it, all this without any acknowledgement of the presence of any of the staff. He would peruse the file and if he didn't like what he saw, fling it dismissively across the ward, still in complete silence.

The neurosurgeon in the same hospital had a similarly fearsome reputation. He liked to operate in complete silence and, when wanting a different instrument, would just put out his hand. If sister put the wrong instrument into his palm, he would look down at it and then hurl it across the operating theatre, on one occasion shattering a notice board attached to wall, then put out his hand again, still without saying a word.

During one list, progressing in tomb-like silence, he suddenly let out a groan.

"Are you all right sir?", asked sister anxiously. He nodded he was OK, stuck out his hand for another instrument and, after about another thirty minutes, finished the delicate operation on the patient's brain. As he cut the last stitch he sighed, "Pass the diamorphine sister, I've had a coronary." He was put onto a trolley and rushed down to the coronary care unit where it was confirmed he had indeed had a heart attack midway through the surgery.

As a consultant back then, it seemed you could be as rude as you liked to staff and patients (it almost felt like this was expected), as long as you were good at what you did. Whilst the ideal is obviously a combination of politeness and great treatment, if push came to shove and my life was on the line, I'd take the technically brilliant every time, irrespective of whether they were nice to me.

I think to some extent it was because the NHS had only been formed in 1948, so in the early seventies the ability to access free treatment was still regarded as a privilege by many patients. They could still remember the bad old days when an inability to pay might mean a denial of healthcare, except via charity.

Certainly, through my training and early consultant career many consultants not only expected respect, they demanded it. More than once I witnessed the cancellation of an operating list because the consultant surgeon couldn't find his operating theatre clogs and, on one occasion at the Leeds General Infirmary, a list was cancelled by a consultant anaesthetist because his lunch had been sent to theatre on a paper plate rather than a china one, and he'd "never been so insulted in all his life". He clearly grew up in a very different neck of the woods to me.

Some of what follows may be shocking by today's standards (and rightly so), but you must remember this was a time when it was deemed acceptable to have "comedies" on mainstream TV in which a white family referred to their black neighbours as "sambo" and "nig-nog", and Alf Garnett was verbally abusing and bullying his wife on a regular basis. Homosexuality was actually still illegal in parts of the UK.

Sexual harassment and misogyny were part of everyday life. One only has to look at the early "Carry On" films, when a sexually suggestive remark or a friendly pat on the bottom, were dismissed with a laugh, and an exclamation of "Saucy!". Political correctness had yet to appear over the horizon.

I don't think you can judge behaviour in the past by what is not acceptable in today's world. I'm not sure that many of the consultants were actually aware they were indulging in a ritual humiliation of their patients, or were being upsetting in their remarks, and it never seemed to be done maliciously.

My first surgical attachment as a medical student In Birmingham, was with a fearsome general surgeon, Mr. G, who had the nickname "slasher". One of his favourite sayings was "I don't believe in keyhole surgery", as he made another huge incision. He had beetling eyebrows and a large hook nose but his eyes, despite the fact they were capable of a glare that could melt a hole through metal, had a mischievous twinkle in them. He was a technically proficient and brave surgeon and would often take on patients that other surgeons were reluctant to operate on because of the high risks involved. His patients loved him for it.

His outpatient clinic was at the General Hospital in Birmingham, where the new referrals would be made ready by the super-efficient sister in charge. All the patients would be put in curtained off cubicles and told to strip off. Everybody would be stark naked, irrespective of whether the problem was an ingrowing toenail or an abdominal mass. The senior registrar would then see the patients, take a history and examine them, then present the case to the boss, who generally had an entourage of several medical students, houseman and visiting surgeons, trailing in his wake.

The senior registrar emerged from one of the cubicles and explained to the boss that the GP had referred this patient with what the GP thought was a femoral hernia, but that he couldn't find it on examination.

"Let me have a look." sighed the boss with exasperation, as he pushed through the curtains with the team behind him. We were confronted by a thin, pale, middle-aged gentleman who looked terrified of the assembled throng all gawping at his groin. He was, like all the other patients, stark naked.

"Up on the couch!" snapped the boss. The poor patient looked confused.

"Stand up on the couch!" The patient reluctantly climbed up onto the couch, so his tackle was now at eye level, as the boss prodded around in his groin trying to find the elusive hernia. The patient was clearly (and understandably) very embarrassed and was shifting his weight from foot to foot. The boss was getting increasingly frustrated by the patient's inability to keep still. He looked up at him.

"What's the matter with you man? Are you embarrassed?"

"I am a bit Mr. G." was the timid reply. Mr. G. turned and barked an order to sister to go and fetch a towel. She scurried off and quickly returned with a small white towel. The boss took it and spoke to the patient.

"Lean forward." The perplexed patient slowly leaned forward from the waist and the boss put the towel over his head! At the time, it seemed that patients expected this sort of behaviour and that some of them were almost disappointed if they hadn't had fun poked at them.

A few weeks later I was second assistant to Mr. G. when he was doing a difficult abdominal operation. His first assistant was a career registrar who had already obtained his Fellowship of the Royal College of Surgeons, but in those days this was no guarantee of career progression. The difficult jump was from registrar to senior registrar, and there were many, who having failed to surmount this hurdle over several years, then had to give up their dream of ever gaining consultant status and either move sideways into an associate specialist post or become a GP.

The registrar was a very desperate man with a very brown nose and was desperate to please the boss. Even I could see he was trying too hard, with his hands constantly in the wound and frequently getting in the way. I could also see that Mr. G was getting more and more irritated. This was always a bad thing to do. After about an hour of this, he turned to sister.

"Scalpel please sister." She handed him a clean blade. He lent forward and quite deliberately, gently stabbed the registrar in the hand.

"Oh, sorry. You'd better get down to Casualty and have that looked at." The registrar was profuse in his thanks for the boss's considerate attitude, unscrubbed and hurried off to get his wound checked out and dressed. Theatre went a bit quiet and the operation then calmly continued. Mr. G turned to me.

"I can't stand that bastard." I made a mental note that I would never upset him. I guess in this day and age the incident would probably be treated as assault, whereas in those days it was regarded as all part of the long learning curve, which not only included vast volumes of facts, basic science and experience but the political and interpersonal skills that would enable you to eventually navigate your way to a consultant post and put your knowledge and experience into practice.

I actually ended up on the wrong side of the scalpel with Mr. G when, quite by accident, I discovered I had a breast lump (an unusual thing in a male). I was wheeled out in front of him after a ward round. He examined me.

"Ummm… it's probably benign, but it could be malignant. We'll do you tomorrow." He then turned to the house officer asking her to make sure I was consented for a "radical mastectomy", a procedure where half the chest wall is removed (a devastating and mutilating procedure), in case the frozen-section examination of the lump under the microscope turned out to be cancer.

As you can imagine, I was absolutely terrified, but the following morning found myself on a trolley in the anaesthetic room. The anaesthetist put in an intravenous line and drew up the various drugs into his syringes. I lay there sweating and hyperventilating with my heart beating nineteen to the dozen. Suddenly Mr. G's gargoyle like face appeared above me.

"Fear nothing!" I can remember muttering "Oh Jesus" and trying to climb off the trolley, before the anaesthetist pumped me full of drugs and the world mercifully dissolved into oblivion.

I woke up back on the ward, a little sore, but relieved to find my chest wall was still present. The house officer came down to tell me the lump was a "benign fibroadenoma" and I would be able to go home the next morning. I had some tea, watched Top of the Pops in the sitting room at the end of the ward, climbed into bed between the crisp white sheets and went to sleep.

I was gently shaken awake with the ward in pitch darkness. My head was still a little thick from the anaesthetic, and it took a moment or two to regain my bearings.

"Sorry to wake you." whispered the staff nurse. "It's three o'clock in the morning. The rest of the team are stuck in theatre with a leaking aneurysm (when the main blood vessel taking blood from the heart to the lower half of the body bursts) and will be for a couple of hours yet. Mr. X has been in urinary retention (when you can't pee, usually because of prostate problems) for the last twelve hours and is in agony – you couldn't catheterise him could you?"

I swung myself out of bed and, in my pyjamas and slippers, shuffled down the ward pushing the trolley loaded with the necessary equipment. I washed my hands, donned some gloves and catheterised the poor bloke. His relief was instantaneous, and he was extremely grateful. I then pottered back down the ward, got back into bed and went back to sleep.

As a surgical senior house officer, I worked with a consultant in Bedford, a portly gentleman with a nasal, high pitched voice, whose outside interests seemed to mainly consist of hunting, shooting and fishing, accompanied by imbibing large quantities of good quality wine. He was another who hailed from an upper middle-class background and was legendary in his ability to unintentionally upset patients. He always attracted a houseman to work for him who was interested in psychiatry, as they spent a lot of time counselling patients after his ward rounds. His saving grace was he was a brilliant technical surgeon and was phenomenal to assist in the operating theatre.

He was also very loyal to his junior staff. One SHO who worked for him was very popular with the nursing staff. He was good look-ing, tall and a "person of colour" (to use the current politically correct description). Late one night he was in the home of one of the ward sisters when her husband unexpectedly returned. He hurriedly climbed out the window in his pants and, clutching his car keys, started to drive back to the hospital. About five minutes into his journey some blue flashing lights appeared in his rear-view mirror and he was pulled over.

There he was, a coloured guy in his underpants, with no ID, driv-ing a car at two in the morning. Surprise, surprise (this is the early eighties) he was handcuffed, taken down to the main police station in Bedford and put in a cell. In desperation he asked the police to contact his consultant to come down and identify him.

Despite it being in the early hours of the morning, much to his credit, he duly turned up, but in his nasal twang told the SHO, "I'll only tell them I know who you are, if you tell me who it was you were shagging!"

One ward round we were seeing patients before theatre, with the team gathered around the bed of a poor lady with breast cancer, who was listed to have a mastectomy. He examined the breast and spoke to her.

"Well my dear…, it's cancer. We're going to have to cut it off." She dissolved into tears. Seemingly moved, he sat down next to her on the bed and, in a bid to provide some comfort, put his arm around her shoulders.

"There, there my dear. I was at my tailors the other day and there was a sign in the window which said, 'It's Smart to be Single-Breasted'."

He seemed genuinely puzzled as to why her sobs rose to a howling crescendo and quickly moved off up the ward.

Another day and another ward round, we had a poor old boy in his eighties who had unfortunately developed a rare cancer of the penis. The boss looked down at his exposed organ.

"Oh dear…, it's cancer. We're going to have to cut it off."

"Oh, dear Mr. *… Well, I was a bit of a reckless cock as a young man."

"Well, now you're going to be a cockless wreck!" came the instant reply from the boss. He then turned on his heel and strode off down the ward to the next patient.

General surgeons were a mucky lot. During my junior career, surgical gowns had yet to become impervious and used to soak up bodily fluids like a sponge. This often meant at the end of a case you would be soaked to the skin with the patient's blood. Because of this, many surgeons didn't wear underclothes. When I was a senior registrar, I would enter the surgeon's changing room at the end of a list to find one of my general surgical colleagues washing his tackle in the sink. His consultant would have a shower then open the door and bawl down the corridor, "Sister… a fluffy towel for my genitals, please."

My chosen speciality of orthopaedics has had its fair share of similar stories. Orthopaedics is a particularly macho discipline, as a lot of it involves sheer brute strength. "An orthopaedic surgeon is as strong as an Ox and half as intelligent." was the usual jibe aimed at us, although I preferred "What's the difference between an orthopaedic surgeon and a rhinoceros – one's thick-skinned, horny and charges a lot, and the other is a rare breed of wild animal".

At a nearby hospital they had a poor, low-grade manager whose main job seemed to consist of dealing with the complaints against one near-retirement orthopaedic surgeon. Every Wednesday morning, at the end of an outpatient clinic, she would come down to visit the consultant with a large box file. He would fix her with a steely glare and ask her what they had this week?

"Well… this patient says you called him a malodorous cretin" she would answer, sliding the complaints letter across the desk. He would scan it briefly before pushing it back at her.

"Well, he was." would be his only answer. And so the meeting would continue for half an hour or so before she slunk back to the management offices to try and work out just how she was going to placate the patients.

This would never happen today and in fact, things have swung entirely the opposite way, in that patients can be as rude to you as they like, without any fear of comeback, but any complaint about your attitude or behaviour can result in suspension, with a "guilty until proven innocent" approach.

My favourite story about this particular consultant relates to an incident one evening when he was on his way home after a long day's operating. His most prized possession was a beautiful, vintage Porsche, which he loved heart and soul. His habit was to stop off at his favourite pub for a quick whiskey before heading home for dinner. Whilst he was standing at the bar, looking out of the window at his beloved car, a woman in a Range Rover drove into the pub car park and, with a massive bang, drove straight into his gleaming Porsche.

He was apoplectic. He strode out of the pub, gave the woman a torrent of abuse, then returned to the bar and proceeded to drown his sorrows. About half an hour later, the agitated husband of the woman turned up at the pub and stalked up to him.

"I'm absolutely appalled that a man of your education should use language like that to my wife!" Mr. * blearily looked up from his whiskey tumbler.

"What the hell do you want me to do, swear in fucking Latin?!"

I have seen some terrible technical surgeons as well as some gifted ones. When I was a senior registrar in Leeds and Bradford some of the surgeons were truly awful, and I was witness to some dreadful surgery.

One of the legendary incidents, never forgotten by those of us who were trainees at the time, involved not one but two consultant orthopaedic surgeons at the Leeds General Infirmary. One was nearing

48

retirement and his approach to elderly patients with a fracture of the hip was actually no treatment at all, but to send them to a nursing home where the fracture either joined up, failed to join up but they could walk on it, or they died. But then... the elderly father of one of the consultant gynaecologists at the hospital was admitted under his care with this type of fracture. He therefore felt he should try one of "those new-fangled Austin-Moore jobs" (a type of metal, half hip replacement, designed to replace the broken off "ball" of the normal ball and socket hip joint, which had actually been in regular use for many years).

When getting close to retiring, most consultants if having to try something new, would ask their senior registrar to do the operation, while they held the retractors. Despite having one of the most talented surgeons I've ever seen as his senior registrar, he couldn't countenance asking a junior for a favour, so approached an equally technically awful colleague to help him.

The retinue of junior staff couldn't pass up the opportunity to watch what would happen, so were dotted round the theatre walls quietly observing, when the anaesthetised patient was wheeled into theatre and transferred onto the operating table. The operation began...

"I say *, what sort of approach should we use?"

"Oh, I don't know **. What about one of those Smith-Petersen jobs." (this is a particular sort of surgical incision and approach which is from the front of the hip joint rather than from the more usual side or back, and it is quite easy to get disorientated if you don't use it regularly).

"Jolly good." he said, making a huge incision from groin to halfway down the thigh. They carried on guddling around and managed to get the fractured part of the hip (the "ball" of the ball and socket) out from the wound. The fun started when they tried to insert the metal, half hip joint down into the thigh bone. To those of us stood watching at the back of theatre, two things were immediately obvious. The first was that at the angle they were trying to insert it, there was no possible way it would go straight down the inside of the shaft of the thighbone, and the second and perhaps more alarming, it was a hundred and eighty degrees out of true i.e. the wrong way round.

"I say *, it doesn't seem to be going down:"

"Oh… just hit it a bit harder with the hammer **." Three mighty blows later, the prosthesis sunk into place. They then tried to reduce it back into the socket but found the only way they could do this (as a consequence of putting it in the wrong way round) was by pointing the foot backwards.

"I say *, that doesn't look right."

"Oh, it'll be alright **. Just sow it up." This they did and the patient was sent round to the recovery room with his feet pointing in opposite directions. Of course, as soon as he woke up and his muscles resumed their normal tension, the new hip dislocated and there is a famous X-ray, copies of which are in the possession of most of the junior staff of the time, which shows a pelvis with half a hip replacement pointing the wrong way, with its tip out through the side of the thighbone. The operation was later successfully redone by the senior registrar.

Misogyny was rife amongst the orthopaedic fraternity, and female orthopaedic surgeons are still in a substantial minority. At the Leeds General Infirmary one of the consultants, who had been a surgeon in the Royal Navy before joining the Health Service, particularly enjoyed teasing female medical students. We were on a teaching ward round, when a feisty, female medical student reached the end of her tether.

"But Mr. A…, do you not feel that women have a role in medicine?" He slid his glasses halfway down his nose, peered over them, and fixed her with a steely glare.

"Of course I do my dear… dishing it out to their children."

Medical students were generally regarded as fair game in those days and were expected to take whatever was thrown at them without complaint. As a surgical registrar I was tagging on to a teaching round with the boss, when we approached an elderly lady who had undergone surgery to remove part of her bowel a few days before.

The consultant turned to the group of six students and asked them how we would know when her bowel had started working again. One of them correctly answered that the patient would start to pass flatus (wind) per rectum (out their backside). The consultant suggested he might ask the lady. The student stepped up to the old dear, and in his best medical jargon loudly asked, "Have you passed flatus?" The old lady obviously hadn't a clue what he was talking about, and in addition I'm not sure she had her hearing aid in. The student tried again and in an even louder voice asked, "Have you passed wind?" This was again met with blank incomprehension.

The consultant had become increasingly impatient during this exchange, muttered "Jesus Christ" under his breath, stepped up to the patient and in a very loud voice shouted, "Look dear... have you farted?"

She looked suspiciously at the group gathered around her and in a shrill voice came back with, "It wasn't me... it must have been one of you!"

At Bradford we had a consultant who revelled in his reputation as being an eccentric. His main love in life seemed to be his farm where he kept Jacob's sheep, and he would often turn up to work with bits of straw sticking out of his rather wild hair. He would sometimes address patients in Latin, leaving them somewhat puzzled.

He really cared for his livestock and one day turned up at the hospital with an injured sheep in the back of his Landrover Defender, insisting on taking it down to the X-ray department to X-ray its leg as he thought it might be fractured.

Working in his clinics as a Senior Registrar was a nightmare. He would insist on seeing all the new referrals, and then you would see all the follow ups. His notes from the initial consult were often difficult to interpret, and would consist of almost cryptic puzzles such as "Dear Doctor, thank you for referring Mr. X. I have injected him with this and that and will review him in eight weeks", leaving you to have to work out what he had thought the diagnosis had been (not always accurate!), what he had injected them with, and then sort out further management.

One day a blind lady turned up in the follow up clinic. The letter from her first consultation consisted almost entirely of a description of her two guide-dogs, with no reference to anything she might have been complaining of, or what the treatment plan might be. I chatted to her.

"I can't quite make out what Mr. * thought was wrong or why he has brought you back to the clinic?"

"I think it was mainly because he wanted to see my guide-dogs again, which is why I haven't brought them." I then started from scratch, to sort out what turned out to be her "Tennis Elbow".

Mr. * was a very good hand surgeon but took referrals for all sorts of orthopaedic problems, and anything that required something other than an operation on the hand was left to his registrars, who would be of variable experience. One day a patient came back to clinic having had a hip replacement that he wasn't satisfied with. The pain had gone, but as he pointed out to Mr. *, his left foot now pointed out at a ninety-degree angle to his right. Mr. * stroked his chin, looked up and cheerfully exclaimed, "Well, look on the bright side, you'll make a great left back!"

Occasionally something said in the heat of the moment, or when extremely stressed, can land you in real trouble. On the intensive care unit of my hospital, a patient was inexorably declining towards death, despite every intervention aimed at trying to reverse this having been tried.

A consultant anaesthetic colleague sat down to have a difficult conversation with the relatives, explained the situation and suggested that it might be time to turn the ventilator off and allow them to die peacefully. The relatives failed to take the information on board and were adamant that everything should continue until the bitter end. After failing to convince them and their continuing protestations, he exasperatedly exclaimed, "Look, we're just flogging a dead horse here!", and shortly afterwards found himself having to explain his remarks in front of the coroner.

These are just a few stories of one or two consultants I have come across in my long career. This type of consultant was not uncommon in the past, but they have now pretty much died out. Most consultants, even the oddballs, seemed to care deeply about their patients and got on with treating as many as possible, to the best of their abilities, within the constraints the health service put upon them.

Some were truly inspiring. I was lucky enough to work with a Mr. E in Sheffield. His special interest was in complex revision hip replacement and pelvic reconstruction surgery and we would receive referrals from around the county and beyond. Operations would often take upwards of four hours, in a clean-air tent, wearing heavy gowns and air supplies, and were technically very difficult, putting a huge strain on everyone involved.

Mr. E had decided to pursue his interest in this field after becoming a consultant and had gone on to learn his craft by working as a house-man for a year in a world renowned, specialist unit in Germany. This had required him to learn to write and speak German before he set off. Being a houseman nearly killed me when I was in my early twenties, so it must have been particularly tough for him. He then returned to become a pioneer in his field in the UK.

He became great friends with a French surgeon, Emile Letournel, who had a world-wide reputation in surgery for complex fractures of the pelvis and so he also added French to his repertoire of languages. When we had a difficult pelvic reconstruction case, if Mr. E asked him, Emile would fly his own plane from France to Sheffield, join us in the operating theatre for the day, have dinner and stay overnight at Mr. E's house, and then fly back to France. This just couldn't happen today. There would be so much red tape to negotiate, so many hoops to jump through, that it would be impossible to organise, even if it would be of benefit to the patient.

Mr. E had a massive intellect, and to while away the hours during difficult surgery, we would have long discussions on almost any subject, but usually about philosophical concepts to do with life, death and religion.

It was he who shaped my career. He told me that to be a good orthopaedic surgeon you had to be a bit obsessional, and that you should aim to make every operation perfect. A few degrees or milli-metres out is just not good enough (Mr. Good'nuff' is a nickname sometimes bestowed on surgeons who do not follow such lofty principles), as this can mean a difference of years of lasting success to a patient. While this may not be achievable every time, it doesn't negate the principle.

Mr. E was very sociable, a great raconteur, and could play the organ to concert standard – a true renaissance man. Once every six months or so, all the junior staff would be invited to have dinner at his lovely house in the Peak District, and he would entertain with humorous tales and music. When I was at Sheffield, we all turned up for what promised to be a great evening, to find that Mr. E's son (who was in his twenties) was at home. Mr. E and his son had a difficult relationship, and as the evening wore on his son became increasingly inebriated and aggressive.

It didn't end well, and he ended up picking a fight with one of the other, rugby playing, registrars who proceeded to lay him out with a single punch, bringing the evening to an abrupt end. The registrar was then hurriedly shepherded out and taken back to the hospital.

The following morning the registrar turned up at the hospital with his resignation letter in hand, and went to find Mr. E. He mumbled his apologies and proffered his letter. Mr. E took it, quickly scanned the contents and handed it back to him.

"Don't be stupid, I think he's an arsehole as well."

4

I'M NOT LIKE EVERYBODY ELSE

My career path was very atypical. After surviving my house jobs, I spent a couple of years travelling, quite literally right round the world, including a few months working as a General Practitioner in Australia.

This was virtually unheard of at the time in the UK, whereas now it seems almost the entire student body are on their travels during "gap years". In two years of travelling along the standard traveller routes, I met two British doctors in Nepal, a British couple in Malaysia and that was it. Plenty of Germans, Italians, Ozzies and Kiwis, and in South America a lot from the USA, but almost nobody from the dear old home country.

It was tough if unforgettable (and the stories would fill another book!). There were no mobile phones or internet, and each day's journey was made not knowing where you were going to lay your head that night. I slept in a lot of rough accommodation, ate a lot of bad food and became a connoisseur of gastrointestinal disturbances. I wouldn't have missed it for the world!

Many people told me I was committing career suicide by stepping outside of the system, but I reasoned that as I was at the bottom of the ladder, I couldn't get any lower, so it seemed the ideal time to go. My travels never failed to get me a job interview as I had something different on my CV, and in most of the interviews I attended we spent a lot of the time talking about my experiences in other parts of the world. I have never regretted what was an eye opening and life enhancing journey.

I had no patron pulling strings and smoothing my way up the ladder and on my return, I wasn't too sure what to do next, so applied for a casualty officer post in Stoke. These posts in the accident and emergency department can be the beginning of a career path in going many directions and are a good place to start getting back into the system.

The job I fixed up at Stoke was very busy (one snowy morning, by ten o'clock, there were over two-hundred and fifty people waiting to be seen). As a "Cas Officer" in that particular unit we were dealing almost exclusively with trauma which had been triaged by the nursing staff. A peculiarity of the job was that you also followed the patients onto the ward and then helped in the operating theatre. I manipulated and plastered hundreds of fractures, stitched up countless wounds, as well as dealing with more major trauma arriving in extremis.

I also had my first experience of having to tell distraught relatives that following an accident or injury, their loved one had not made it. Patients were sometimes rushed in by the ambulance service "in kit form", and no amount of effort, or state of the art equipment was going to put them together again. You try and try and try but sometimes nothing works, and despite everything their life just slowly ebbs away under your hands. I have had several patients die while desperately trying to save them. It never gets any easier.

One Monday morning we were trying to contact the medical senior house officer on-call to see a patient with chest pain. He just didn't seem to be answering, and we were getting increasingly frustrated with one or two choice expletives aimed at him. Eventually we had to try the registrar who was also unhappy at being unable to speak to his junior colleague. About eleven o'clock we received a call which answered all our questions about his whereabouts.

A cleaner had gone into his room in the doctor's mess to find him stone cold dead. He'd been feeling unwell and gone to bed on the Friday night, just as the mess emptied with people going home for the weekend. He had actually died from pneumonia, a treatable condition which, in his job, he was curing on a daily basis. It was a sobering time, but no miraculous changes were introduced by the management to ensure it didn't happen again. In fact, death was not infrequent in my peer group. When the medical school organised a twenty-year reunion, over ten percent of us had shuffled off this mortal coil.

One day, I was chatting to retired GP at one of the hospital lunch-time educational meetings. He asked me what I did, and I told him I was working as an SHO in A&E. He told me that he had done the same job many years before and had thoroughly enjoyed it.

As he recalled it, he had spent most of his time playing squash in the hospital squash courts, and if a patient came into A&E, a porter would come across and request his presence. He told me he would generally finish the game, shower, get dressed and then potter across to see and treat the patient. How things had changed!

Throughout my career I lurched from job to job, occasionally being out of work for short spells. You went where the work took you as the concept of "run through training" (where you stay in the same region for your whole training) had yet to be developed.

As previously mentioned, I moved eleven times during my training. This made friendships and relationships, in pre mobile phone and FaceTime days, very difficult to maintain. You'd meet new colleagues, make new friends, and then four months later you'd move to Sheffield and they would take a post in Exeter. You were all working very long hours, and generally only had two consecutive nights sleep once a fortnight on your weekend off. If your every other weekend off didn't coincide, there was actually no chance of ever meeting up.

At Stoke I was very lucky. In the room next to me in the doctor's mess, Rob arrived to take up a spot as an SHO in general medicine.

We hit it off straight away. He was obviously very, very bright (way above me!), and we shared a taste for the same humour and music. Not only was he a phenomenally talented and caring doctor, he had played bass in the national jazz youth orchestra and was an authority on archaeology – another true renaissance man. We managed to keep in touch as we moved around the country, and I was best man at his wedding.

He went on to become a professor at Great Ormond Street children's hospital. He died young and suddenly, with some sort of cardiac event as he slept in the night. His secretary told me she felt the job had killed him. Management had just kept piling more and more work on him. With his caring attitude he felt he couldn't let the patients down and was working all hours God made. I still miss his cheerful smile; he was one of the nicest human beings I've ever met.

The job after Stoke was down in Bedford. When looking for jobs, the back pages of the weekly British Medical Journal were the go-to resource. I saw an advert for a senior house officer post involving six months general surgery followed by six months orthopaedics, and applied. I sweet talked one of the secretaries into typing up my rather limited CV and sent it off. To my surprise the hospital rang back and offered me the job. It turned out they had previously advertised, interviewed and appointed, but one of the two appointed candidates had pulled out just before the job was due to start. The consultant involved in the appointments process was, luckily for me, so disillusioned he instructed his secretary to offer the job to the first UK graduate who had sent in a typed CV. Such was the lottery of the system.

I actually had a brilliant time at Bedford, one the happiest in my junior career. Sam, the other successful candidate (originally from Palestine), and I hit it off straight away and the two of us ended up sharing a hospital house with George, a medical SHO who hailed from Crete. Despite it being a job in a non-teaching hospital, both Sam (now a very successful cardiac surgeon) and I did pretty well for ourselves, both going on to develop national reputations in our respective fields.

The rules of the Health Service at that time meant that if you were on call, either every other night or every third night, the hospital was obliged to provide you with rent free accommodation. Bedford hospital had purchased a row of terraced houses backing on to the hospital car park, so at the end of the day you went through a gate in the wall, across a small yard and through the back door into a normal house. When you opened the front door, you were in a normal street. This did help stave off cabin fever and give you some sense of living in the real world.

The doctor's mess was very sociable and lively, as almost all the junior doctors lived in the hospital. Bedford has no medical school and is about an hour's drive from both Oxford and Cambridge, making it just a bit too far to commute. Most evenings, all those not on-call dropped round at our house after dinner and, when we had a sufficient number, we would set off for one of the excellent pubs scattered around in the picturesque villages not too far from the town centre.

Mess life was where everyone let off steam, and where you could share the traumas and grumbles of the day. Alcohol was always available. There would always be a mix of those working and those on evenings off and, at the end of almost every working day, the "team", including the consultant, would retire to the mess for a pint or two and a bit of socialising. It was even not uncommon for juniors to have a pint or two at lunchtime and then return to the operating theatre!

Alcohol was a huge part of hospital culture. Big drinkers were common and budding alcoholics were everywhere. While at Bedford I saw a senior registrar sink six pints in an hour and a half, then get into his car to drive home, seemingly perfectly sober. It has been estimated that about one in ten doctors become alcohol dependent and a few more become addicted to drugs of one sort or another. As long as you didn't literally fall down while doing the job, the whole system tended to just adapt round you.

In the hospital house in which I was living, we developed some notoriety as hosts of a regular party every eight weeks or so. To reduce the likelihood of gatecrashers we always made these some form of costume party, generally involving everybody being in an advance state of undress at the beginning of the evening, such as a "swimwear party" or "toga party". The parties could get pretty wild.

We would get together a fund for the hospital cleaners who would come in the morning after and tidy everything up for some welcome extra cash. It was not uncommon to come downstairs in the morning to find two or three people crashed out on our lounge floor with the cleaners carefully hoovering around them.

One true story that reached almost legendary status was the "night of the pre-fab hut". In the hospital car park was an orange, wooden, prefabricated hut, held together by wooden dowels, in which the hospital car park attendant would stand, telling patients and visitors, "You can't park your car there, it's more than my job's worth."

In the early hours of the morning, after a mess party, and with everyone being somewhat inebriated, a group descended on the car park and, as quietly as they could, disassembled the orange hut. A second group had purloined the keys to the chief executive's office from underneath the porter's desk and the hut, in kit form, was carried, with much muffled laughter, through the hospital (still no CCTV). We silently let ourselves in and reassembled the hut around the chief executive's desk. After shutting and locking the door the keys were discretely returned, and a group of giggling junior doctors made their way off to their beds.

The chief executive really didn't see the funny side. In fact, he was apoplectic. He demanded that every junior doctor in the hospital attend a meeting in the doctor's mess that lunchtime. He was a small, rotund, balding man, and was purple with rage as he ranted at us, saliva spraying everywhere, that "this sort of behaviour was totally unacceptable".

He then demanded that those responsible, step forward and own up. We all looked at each other and thought "not a chance". The puce colour of his face became almost luminescent as he realised his entreaties were not going to get a result. Just before I thought his head was about to explode, he turned on his heel and stormed out, leaving a group of chastened juniors sighing with relief.

It wasn't all partying, and we worked bloody hard as well. In my time as a surgical SHO I performed over one-hundred and twenty emergency appendicectomies, as well as a shed load of other minor procedures. Not long ago, I was talking to a surgical trainee in the theatre coffee room and discovered she had done less appendicectomies in her training to registrar level, than I'd done as a pre-registration houseman.

One of the more memorable patients I operated on was the owner of the best Indian restaurant in Bedford. Whenever a group of us went out for a curry he would welcome me enthusiastically and then, with his arm round my shoulder, in a loud voice would announce to the whole restaurant, "This is the man who fixed my haemorrhoids!", without a trace of embarrassment, and we would be then be royally looked after.

In fact, problems with bottoms are a staple of general surgical life. I have removed countless objects from people's rectums, including a light bulb (apparently, he had been having trouble with his piles and had been lubricating them with anusol cream. Walking naked across the bedroom, he slipped and accidentally sat down on a lamp which was on the floor without its lampshade on... and the bulb came off), and an altar candle from the colon of a vicar. There might have been an innocent explanation for this latter but when it was removed (and it wasn't a small thin one), it had a condom on it.

General surgery is mostly involved in the very basics of life. An old general surgeon once said to me "To be a general surgeon, you have to love faeces". Oh well, each to their own. To be fair, many of the rest of the population seem to be obsessed with the function of their bowels. There is certainly a lot of shit involved in general surgery. Not many jobs involve regularly staring up people's bottoms at what they had for breakfast the day before.

A standard outpatient examination of the time was a "sigmoidoscopy", when a shiny metal (and usually very cold!) tube was inserted through the anus and up into the rectum and the lower bowel inflated with air so it could be visually inspected. This was known in the trade as "a ride on the silver rocket".

In one of my last outpatient clinics at Bedford, a rather nervous lady was complaining of problems with her bowels that suggested a sigmoidoscopy was indicated. She lay on her left side on the examination couch and the staff nurse bent her knees up to her chest to allow better access. It's about as undignified as it gets.

After lubricating the silver rocket, I inserted it up her bottom into the lower bowel. I got the impression she wasn't enjoying the experience. I leaned over the couch and withdrew the trocar to allow me to look up the tube.

As I did so, a trickle of diarrhoea poured out of its end and across the examination couch. I looked down and realised my tie was draped across the couch, and now had an extra, broad brown stripe across it. I turned to the staff nurse.

"Scissors please." I felt the woman clench, presumably anticipating something painful was about to happen. Keeping nice and still, I reached down and cut off my tie just below the knot, leaving it to be cleaned away with the soiled drapes.

In addition to the busy daily workload, we were also studying for the first part of the Fellow of the Royal College of Surgeons (FRCS) exam, required to take the next step up the career ladder. This was a particularly tough exam, being in pathology, anatomy and physiology, almost a repeat of the first two years of medical school, but unlike back at medical school, you had to know absolutely everything. The examiners didn't see their job as "helping the candidate pass" (as I was told when I became examiner myself many years later) and almost seemed to take a malignant pleasure in failing you.

For the London College, the exam hall was in Queen's Square in the centre of the city. You first had to pass a large multiple-choice paper (with negative marking i.e. if you guessed and got it wrong a mark was deducted), and then a written paper with several hour-long essays (with no choice). If you were successful in these, you were invited back for the "vivas", three, separate, half-hour sessions face to face across the table with two examiners. You can cover a huge amount of the syllabus in these sessions. There was no hiding place, and no room at all for getting anything wrong.

Humiliation can be a great driver in life, and this was certainly true in my case. The first time I took the exam I had surmounted the first hurdle of the multiple choice and the written questions, and a couple of weeks later attended for the long day of the vivas.

Things were going reasonably well, and I was feeling reasonably confident as I walked into the last viva of the day – anatomy. I sat down opposite the two examiners who tried to put me at ease with some standard chat.

"Which medical school did you go to?"

"Birmingham." I replied.

The examiner beamed at me.

"Our new president is from Birmingham!"

To this day I don't know what possessed me, but like a complete prat, I cheerfully replied, "Oh, is he?" The examiner's smile disappeared. He clearly wasn't impressed by a candidate not knowing who the president of the college was. He slid his glasses halfway down his nose and peered over them at me. He murmured, "Yes... he is actually."

In front of him, on top of the table, lay a virtually complete, dismembered bony skeleton. The last chapter in the anatomy textbook is always "The Foot", and consequently is always the last bit to revise. He slowly reached out and without fail picked up the bony foot and pushed it across the table at me.

"When does the talus ossify?" (when you are born your bones are largely made of cartilage which becomes calcified into bone – the human foot is made up of twenty-six small bones, one of which is "the talus").

I knew absolutely nothing about the ossification of bones in the foot, so I gulped and replied, "I'm sorry, I don't know." He looked at me pityingly.

"O.K... well when does the navicular ossify?" And one by one we slowly went through every bone in the foot, to which my repetitive reply was, "I'm sorry, I don't know." By the time he finished I was a gibbering wreck, and I think if he'd asked me my name I would still have replied "I don't know." It was an almost orgasmic relief when the bell rang, and my torment was brought to an end. I had never felt so humiliated in my entire life and vowed to myself it would never, ever happen again.

I revised like I'd never revised before. Everything else (apart from normal one hundred and twenty hours a week!) went onto the back burner. Every waking moment was spent with my nose in the books. I went up for the next sitting of the exam a few months later, went into the multiple-choice exam (three hundred true/false questions with a mark deducted if you answered wrong), and answered two hundred and eighty-seven in twenty-five minutes. I sat there debating whether to take an educated guess at the remaining thirteen, but decided it probably wasn't worth guessing as I was pretty sure I was correct in the one's I'd completed.

I had to sit there for a further five minutes, as you weren't allowed to leave the exam hall until after half an hour had passed. My desk was right at the back of the exam hall and I had to make a long, lonely walk to the front to hand my paper in, feeling the eyes of the other couple of hundred candidates boring into my back.

On the day of the subsequent vivas, the basement of Queen's Hall was a sea of nervous surgical clones. Dark grey or dark blue suits, white shirts, anonymous ties, shiny black shoes and freshly cut hair... except one.

There was an Asian doctor, who clearly hadn't read the script. He had longish hair and stubble, a blue and white striped boating blazer, white trousers, trainers and a hideous floral tie. He stood out like a sore thumb. I thought "he either knows everything or he's an idiot". You can't beat the system by being a rebel on the outside.

We all filed off to the first viva in Physiology. Half an hour of stressful mental gymnastics later, I left the hall thinking I'd done all right. The Asian doctor was standing outside, trembling and looking pale, with sweat beading on his forehead.

"Are you Ok?" I asked. "How did it go?"

He then told me that he'd sat down, and when the bell went for the start of the viva, the first examiner had asked him to speak about "inherited disorders of metabolism that might be important to a surgeon". This is a very difficult and complex question. Examiners back then often had "stopper" questions that they would pull out if a candidate was perceived as too cocky or annoyed them.

The examiner then sat in complete silence, waiting for an answer, periodically asking "have you thought of one yet?", whilst the candidate sat pouring in sweat on the other side of the table. The bell went after fifteen minutes, indicating for the examiners to change over, and the second examiner asked him "well, have you thought of one yet?" and then continued to sit in silence, whilst the first examiner picked up his newspaper and started reading it. Eventually the final bell rang, and he was told he could leave the hall. This type of experience was not uncommon.

After you had finished your three half-hour vivas, you were told that the results would be available at five o'clock, and most people retired to the Ship Inn on the other side of the square for a few well deserved beers, swapping tales of how awful the experience had been. At five o'clock everyone trooped back to the basement and waited in nervous anticipation.

A hush descended as the sound of a lift heading down towards us could be heard. The doors opened and an officious looking college porter, clutching a clipboard, stepped out.

"Pay attention gentleman (There was not a single female in the hundred or so of us waiting there). The following numbers have passed. Will they step forward, identify themselves, and go into the lift." He then paused dramatically before announcing, "Number fifty-six." A groan went up from all those whose numbers were less than the one read out. The day I passed, my number was two hundred and something, so I was one of the last to be called and staggered forward hardly believing it was true. Only eleven of us passed that day. We were then taken upstairs to be congratulated by the examiners, given a thimbleful of sherry, and ushered out.

I had passed! This then meant I could apply for the next level up in my career, of "pre-fellowship registrar". At this stage I knew I would have to move back to a teaching hospital, as to spend too long in district general hospitals in the "periphery", brought a certain end to any progression up the ladder.

A job came up in Sheffield, rotating out to Rotherham and back, involving two six-month posts in Orthopaedics and Cardiothoracics, and a year in two different posts in General Surgery. As was usual, the job advert in the BMJ stated that if you "haven't heard after three weeks from the closing date for applications, assume you haven't been shortlisted".

The three-week deadline passed and disappointingly I hadn't heard anything. To compensate, my girlfriend of the time and I went down to the local travel agents in town and booked a last-minute deal for a holiday in Greece, to use up some leave I was owed.

To my surprise, a week later, an invitation arrived to attend for interview in a further three weeks, the date of which was smack bang in the middle of my holiday. I rang the contact consultant from the ad and left a message with his secretary explaining my situation, as a last-minute cancellation of my holiday to attend the interview was going to mean I'd lose all my money.

Fortunately for me, the consultants in Sheffield had a very low opinion of the medical personnel department and blamed them for the problem. It was agreed that I would be able to drive up and see all the various consultants involved in the rotation, and that this would be counted as an "Interview". For me, this meant instead of the standard half hour interview, in a very much more demanding process, I saw four separate groups of consultants for half an hour at a time, driving from hospital to hospital between each appointment.

I went away on holiday unaware of the outcome. I came back to find a thick brown envelope waiting for me, informing me I'd been successful and would be starting with orthopaedics three months later. I was on my way!

I arrived in Sheffield not knowing anybody. On my first evening in the hospital I walked down to the doctor's mess, expecting it to be full of colleagues looking to go out for some fun. In complete contrast to Bedford, I sat there for two hours and not a single other person came to join me.

Because Sheffield was a teaching centre, with its own medical school, most of the people working there had come through their own system, making their own friendship groups, and mostly living outside the hospital. This made making new friends even more difficult.

For a young, straight, reasonable looking male however, hospitals did have their compensations. You were working in an environment where half the doctors were female, ninety-nine percent of the nurses were female (apart from a few male nurses and, I know it's a cliché, at that time most of them were actually gay), almost all of the physios and radiographers were female, and in fact the only other group that were predominately male were the porters. The normal social dynamics of men chasing women were completely reversed in the unreal bubble that was hospital life.

I've never been a "lad's lad", full of beer and bravado and have always been genuinely fond of the company of women, although this might perhaps have been tinged with commitment issues after my parent's bitter break up. My relationships were, for the most part, fairly short in length, but we almost always finished on good terms.

I was almost sexually incontinent, with a steady stream of female visitors to my hospital flat. I'm not proud of it, but I was working very, very hard in a very stressful environment and, for me, it was a way of leaving behind the cares of the day and spending a couple of hours in pleasant, pleasurable company.

Nurses in particular had a terrible reputation for being "easy". I think this was very unfair. When you spend all day, every day dealing with the dying, the diseased, and the very worst that nature can inflict on an individual, I think you tend to grab on to anything that is life affirming. The pleasures and intimacies of sex, providing they are shared and not taken, are just one of the ways of doing this.

In the early hours the morning, between emergency cases in the operating theatre, I was chatting to an older (early forties), married radiographer and, as was often the case, confidences started to be shared. She was very upset as she and her husband had held a party the weekend before and, at some stage, she'd walked into their bedroom to find her next-door neighbour kneeling on the bed, knickers round one ankle, with her husband enjoying himself from behind.

I murmured my sympathies and half-jokingly offered to help her out if there was anything I could do. A few nights later, on my evening off, I was in my flat, immersed in a textbook, when the doorbell rang. I wasn't expecting anybody and was surprised when I opened the door to find the radiographer, in a very pretty, if very short, dress, heavily perfumed and holding a bottle of wine.

"Surprise!" she whispered as she pressed her mouth to mine and manoeuvred me back into the hall, shutting the door behind her. In all honesty I didn't put up a lot of resistance and things proceeded along the inevitable path. This actually suited me down to the ground. The intensity and stress of the work and the hours involved didn't leave me with a lot of spare emotional capacity, and a no strings, purely sexual, relationship was just what the doctor ordered (as it were).

Somehow word must have gone out, despite the fact that I was utterly discrete, and at one time I was having affairs with several married women at the same time. I never went looking for them, they came hunting for me. They would turn up, spend two or three hours having fun, and then go home again leaving me to catch up with my precious sleep.

One very dangerous relationship (which added extra frisson but in retrospect was completely crazy), was with the wife of one of the hospital consultants. She was lovely but very unhappy in her relationship. She felt her husband had only married her in order to get a hospital consultant post (an absolute necessity in those days) and was probably gay. We spent many happy and passionate hours together in the six months before I moved on to the next job.

Back then, being married was pretty much a requirement to gain a consultant post, as it apparently demonstrated you were a stable individual and not likely to cause scandal or go off the rails. While I was at Sheffield, one of the unmarried, general surgical senior registrars had gone for an interview for a consultant post at a hospital in the Midlands.

His interview went well, and the questions came to an end. The consultant who was the chairman of the appointments panel nervously cleared his throat and there was then an awkward silence. He then addressed the senior registrar.

"Ummm… it's a bit awkward this, but we've noticed you're not married"

"No, I'm not." he replied.

"Well, have any plans to get married?"

"No… not at the present time." The complexion of the chairman was slowly getting redder and redder.

"Uhhh… We feel we have to ask you this… are you a homosexual?"

Quick as a flash the senior registrar, who'd half been expecting a question along these lines, came back with, "Oh, I'm sorry, I didn't realise that was a requirement for the job." At which point the whole panel broke up in relieved laughter. Of course, he got the job.

As far as my "training" went, I had the great stroke of fortune to be following another trainee, H, around the various posts involved in the rotation. He was the only trainee I came across over the years, who was completely hopeless at operating. Every time I started a new job I was greeted with a sigh of relief, as H had left a trail of disasters making me look fantastic by comparison.

He was already a year ahead of me and was looking to take the second part of his FRCS exam, although you'd never have guessed it. I met H again a couple of years later, when I was taking the London version of the FRCS, and he told me he was struggling to find further posts but felt the problem might be that he only had the Edinburgh exam. No trainer had plucked up the courage to tell him that he was never going to make it and help him into a more suitable career path, something we're still very bad at doing in the Health Service.

I had a great time during my orthopaedic attachment at the Northern General Hospital, working with two consultants who were both technically excellent and nice people. I was given a large amount of responsibility and a large amount of unsupervised operating, at which I became steadily more confident. There was certainly not the level of control over the department that management have today.

In those days, hospital management were treated with contempt, and regarded as something lower than pond life. One of the senior registrars in the orthopaedic unit, who has since gone on to become a professor of orthopaedics in Scotland, had a particularly robust approach in his dealings with them. After one particular spat with the management, he famously sent a letter –

"Dear Sir,

Fuck off.

Yours Faithfully…" and then a few lines below "P.S. Strong letter to follow".

On only my second day in post I was scheduled to do the emergency surgery list in the afternoon, on which there was a lady with an ankle fracture that needed operating on and fixing. My boss asked me if I'd done one before, which I hadn't. He invited me to come down to his office where he would talk me through the procedure.

We made our way to his rather chaotic office, cleared some space and sat down. He rummaged around in a drawer and produced a small, stainless steel screw. He held it up.

"Put two of these in," and that was that. My entire tutorial on ankle fracture fixation. Certainly, during my time, the old adage "see one, do one, teach one" held largely true, although frequently the first stage of this was missed out.

If you ever want to see the worst aspects of humanity, try popping down to your local A&E department late on a Saturday night. New Year's Eve is like a Saturday night on steroids. During my attachment to the orthopaedic department, I found myself on-call on a Saturday night that was also New Year's Eve!

It started quietly until my bleep went off at about ten o'clock, and then there was a steady stream of the wounded and head injured. I would do a couple of cases in the operating theatre and then nip down to the A&E department to see the next batch of customers, and alternate between the two.

About two in the morning, I was called down to see a lad who'd cut his hand on a piece of broken glass. A&E was like something out of an end of the world movie. They had cleared away some of the seating and placed a load of plastic covered mattresses in the corner. By that time there were several people lying asleep on them, occasionally waking up to vomit over one another. The whole place smelt of sick, stale alcohol and blood. Outside was a big black police van and, when the intermittent and inevitable fighting broke out amongst the drunk and disorderly, several burly policemen would pile out, break up the fighting and arrest the perpetrators, who would then be shipped off to the police station in town.

The lad I had been called down to see had cut one of the tendons to his finger on some broken glass and needed surgery to stitch this together. I was explaining this to him, when his obviously very drunk girlfriend appeared through the curtains of the cubicle. I explained what was happening, and his mate who wasn't tall but was almost square with a pair of powerful looking shoulders, also joined the discussion.

The injured lad's girlfriend wasn't happy and kicked off with, "I've cut my fucking finger, and they're not bringing me into fucking hospital." His mate then chimed in.

"Don't fucking speak to the fucking doctor like that." but then made the fatal error of putting his hand on the girlfriend's shoulder to try and shepherd her away.

The injured lad took great exception to this and exploded, "Don't you fucking touch my fucking girlfriend", and a fight erupted.

I took a couple of steps back out of arms reach, and a large policeman appeared and grabbed the short, stocky one by the shoulder.

"All right son, break it up." I've never seen anything like what happened next. The injured lad's friend turned, grabbed the policeman and heaved him through the air, clean over a row of chairs. At that point, he disappeared under a pile of policemen and a hail of truncheon blows, meaning we ended up having to admit him for head injury observations, as he had been knocked out!

71

The relationship between an orthopaedic department and A&E is often a sticky one. While A&E departments receive injuries, the doctors working there frequently have very little orthopaedic experience. At the present time, in their five years of training, medical students in Leeds have two weeks attached to an orthopaedic department. The next time they use this miniscule amount of knowledge will be in A&E or as a GP (where twenty-five to thirty percent of all attendances are to do with an orthopaedic problem!).

I was with a fellow registrar who was on-call, when his bleep went off. One of the A&E senior house officers had just seen a patient with a splinter stuck under their fingernail and wondered if he wanted to come and see them. He wasn't best pleased and, to summarise, tactfully suggested they remove it after giving the patient some local anaesthetic.

This is generally straightforward and relatively painless, injecting some local anaesthetic around the base of the finger, which then numbs the whole digit (called a "ring block"). About half an hour later we were taking a shortcut through the A&E department, when the calm was disrupted by a blood-curdling scream coming from one of the cubicles.

We popped our heads through the curtains to find the casualty officer trying to inject the local anaesthetic by sliding a needle underneath the patient's fingernail. We pointed out that this had been used as a form of torture in the war, and politely suggested (!) she go away and read up how to properly anaesthetise a finger.

Sometimes you see some pretty horrific cases. One lady arrived with ninety percent burns, having set herself on fire to try and commit suicide. She was just about alive but was not going to survive, and the thing I'll never forget was the horrible smell of her charred flesh.

Another day, a workman from a building site arrived alive and conscious but looking like something from the first "The Omen" film. They had been prestressing concrete on a building site when one of the steel rods under tension snapped and flew through the air. It had completely transfixed him from his right collar bone, through his chest and abdomen, and exiting from his left thigh. Part of the rod had to be cut off by the emergency services so they could actually get him into the ambulance.

The assembled expertise in theatre was something to behold. Cardiothoracic, Vascular, General and Orthopaedic surgical teams were all scrubbed and ready to go. The patient was anaesthetised, placed on the operating table, and prepped from top to toe. A hush descended, and the rod was grasped where it exited his thigh and, with bated breath, slowly pulled out. Absolutely nothing happened. No change in respiration, pulse or blood pressure, no torrential haemorrage out of either wound. The General Surgeons made a small incision to check out his abdominal contents, where there was only some bruising and very minor bleeding, and then closed him up again. X-rays of his chest showed no collapse of his lungs or collections of fluid. By some miracle the rod had missed every major organ and blood vessel in his body. Sometimes, people are just insanely lucky.

Sometimes some people are insanely unlucky. One of the most mentally traumatic procedures I've ever been a part of, involved a poor lady who'd had a heart-valve replacement and not recovered well. Essentially her heart was worn out and functioned very badly post-operatively. In order to keep her going she was given a number of drugs to help her heart beat properly, the last being an infusion of adrenaline.

This did indeed help her cardiac function, but one of the side effects of adrenaline is that it constricts the blood vessels in your limbs and, in her case, both arms and legs died and went black. She was given the choice to have her cardiac support withdrawn (which would have led to her demise) or to have a quadruple, simultaneous amputation and opted for the latter. Four teams of orthopaedic surgeons were assembled, she was anaesthetised, and wheeled into theatre. Twenty minutes later she'd had all four limbs removed.

As I watched her being wheeled out to recovery, I stood there thinking "Jesus, what the hell have we done?" While you are operating you can concentrate on the technical aspects of what you are doing, and it's only afterwards the awfulness of the situation hits home.

It was while I was working on the orthopaedic unit in Sheffield that an incident occurred that helped shape my whole future. I had injured my knee playing squash and was limping around for a week or two before one of the consultants eventually noticed.

"Steve, you seem to be limping. What have you done?" I explained what had happened, and that I thought I had torn my cartilage.

"Well… we better get that sorted out." I was allowed to go down to the radiology department between the morning and afternoon lists, to have what was then the state-of-the-art investigation – an "air arthrogram". This involved injecting a mixture of air and dye into the knee and wasn't without discomfort! I limped back up to the operating theatre for the afternoon with an audible crackling coming from my knee.

The X-ray confirmed I had a cartilage tear, which then presented the consultants in the department with a dilemma. The standard treatment at the time was to remove the whole cartilage through a large slash in the front of the joint, a very painful procedure and usually requiring six weeks off work, something that they weren't willing to contemplate.

Instead, it was arranged for me to go down to Cambridge to see David Dandy, at that time the only orthopaedic surgeon in the country doing keyhole surgery of the knee. I travelled down on the Wednesday and saw him in outpatients, had my surgery on the Thursday, was discharged on the Friday, and the following Monday was on call back in the hospital.

After the surgery, I remember waking up back in my room, with my first thought being "does it hurt" (doctors are notorious for being terrible patients with low pain thresholds), and realising it didn't. I tried gently bending my knee and no, it still didn't hurt. Having seen patients in agony after an operation done through a large incision, I thought "this has got to be the way of the future." Nearly forty years later I'm still very active and have had no real problems.

In fact, my only concern about the whole procedure was when a nurse from the recovery area of the theatres popped her head round the door of my room and said, "You were the life and soul of recovery!

Some of those jokes were brilliant!", leaving me worrying about how indiscreet I might have been.

From the Northern General, I moved to Rotherham to do general surgery with a surgeon whose additional interest was vascular surgery. I had committed to taking the second part of the Fellow of the Royal College of Surgeons exam some six months later, as I had been told that I would only be on-call only every fourth night and weekend, which would have given me the absolute luxury of having plenty of time to hit the books.

When I arrived however, I was informed that things had been changed, and I would now be on-call every other night and weekend, making revising virtually impossible. I was not best pleased, but there was no right of appeal and nothing I could do about it.

The rota was organised in such a way that you worked consecutive four-day weekends (on call eight a.m. Friday until eight a.m. Tuesday), with a Wednesday on call in between, meaning that in twelve days and nights, you had two periods of twelve hours off. Not only that, but the second weekend you were the only member of one consultant's team in the hospital, and he insisted that nobody except one of his team touched his patients. This meant the jobs generally done by the houseman or senior house officer, such as clerking routine admissions, prescribing painkillers and answering any queries from his ward, no matter how trivial, were done by me, whilst also trying to deal with, and operate on, all the emergency admissions.

This came to a climax when at three o'clock one Sunday morning, having crawled into bed half an hour before, my phone went off. It was one of the nurses from the ward telling me there was a problem with a patient's heparin infusion (a way of thinning the blood). It took my befuddled brain a minute or two to work out what she was telling me. The needle of the line carrying the heparin infusion was stuck into a rubber bung on their normal IV line and had fallen out. The discussion was fairly brief.

"Let me get this straight. You want me to get out of bed at three o'clock in the morning and walk over to the ward to reinsert a needle into a rubber bung." The nurse told me that was exactly what she wanted me to do.

"Don't be so fucking stupid!" And I put the phone down. I received a reprimand and had to write a formal letter of apology as apparently, it's perfectly acceptable for a nurse to wake a registrar at three o'clock in the morning, when he's had four hours sleep in the previous three days, and ask him to do something a monkey could do, but not for him to lose his cool.

To add insult to injury, I really disliked the surgeon I had been allocated to work for. Partly because he was obnoxious, and partly because he left me to operate almost entirely alone.

On my very first night on call, a patient came in with what I thought was a burst appendix. When I opened them up however, it turned out they had a perforated cancer of the first part of the large bowel (the bit the appendix is attached to). This requires a "right hemi-colectomy", a large operation where half the large bowel is removed, and not without potential significant complications. It was now just after midnight and I rang the boss. I apologised for waking him, explained the situation, and that the patient needed an operation I hadn't done before.

"Well, you've seen one, haven't you?" I told him I had, but about eighteen months before.

"Well, you've read it up, haven't you?" I told him I had.

"Well get on with it then." and he put the phone down. So, there I was, at one o'clock in the morning, doing my first major bowel surgery. There was a life saver, in the form of a book called "Kirk's General Surgical Operations", which was a step by step manual of how to do operations. Pretty much all the junior staff took it to theatre for every list so, if needed, somebody could read aloud the steps you had to take to successfully carry out the surgery. The operation went by the book, if painfully slowly, and the patient went on to make an uncomplicated recovery.

Another day, the boss was going to be away at some sort of regional meeting, and he had told me he had arranged for the associate specialist to come and take me through my first gall bladder removal operation. The patient was brought down to theatre, anaesthetised and transferred onto the operating table.

I waited patiently for the associate specialist to arrive, and someone hurried off to find out where he was. The consultant anaesthetist was becoming increasingly impatient and tetchy.

"You know how to start the operation, just get on with it." I made the initial incision and carefully exposed the diseased gall bladder. The associate specialist never did turn up and so I very slowly performed my first cholecystectomy (removal of the gall bladder), completely unsupervised and on my own. To my great relief, and perhaps a tinge of pride, the patient had no problems, and was discharged ten days later.

Another couple of weeks went by and the boss yet again did the same thing to me, telling me to start an operation (an exploration of the common bile duct for gall stones), with a high risk of complications, saying he would come up to do the difficult bit after doing some paperwork in the office. After doing the incision and approach, which turned out to be very tricky with everything stuck to everything else, I rang the office only to be told by his secretary that he'd become fed up of waiting and had left the hospital. Once again, I was left to finish some complex surgery unsupervised. Fortunately, the outcome was fine.

Things came to a head the following week when, on a Tuesday afternoon, he came into the theatre I was operating in and told me he wanted me to assist him in the local private hospital the following morning. I was ordered to bring a set of instruments from theatre, and some blood from the blood bank.

I explained I didn't think I could do that as I was on call for emergencies at the hospital that day, so couldn't really be off site.

"You're my registrar, you'll do what I tell you." he snapped. I pointed out that my contract was actually with the health service so he didn't actually employ me personally, and my NHS contract did not oblige me to help him with private practice. The discussion quickly escalated into a free and frank exchange of views, during which I told him my opinion of him as a "trainer". It ended with him telling me to get out, that he never wanted to see me again, and that if he could block my career in any way in the future, he would go out of his way to do so.

Somewhat worried about my future by this, I rang one of the orthopaedic consultants I'd worked for, and who was on the regional postgraduate education committee. I explained what had happened.

"Oh, don't worry Steve. There's a saying in surgery, that for every enemy you make, you make two friends." It turned out that this was very true. Sheffield had been trying to move the Rotherham attachment back into the teaching hospital and now had the perfect excuse, so it didn't really do me any harm. When I was eventually appointed as a consultant, I sent the Rotherham surgeon a postcard, letting him know I had made it.

After Rotherham, it was back to Sheffield for another six months of General Surgery. This time it was with a surgeon who was a great political animal and spent most of his time away on various national committees and attending as a member of the board of the Royal College of Surgeons of Edinburgh. His practice was therefore run by the very experienced Senior Registrar, although occasionally the boss would turn up and create utter chaos by insisting on doing a ward round.

He would stride up to a patient, turn to us and say, "So, this is the chap with prostate cancer." in a loud voice, and in front of completely the wrong patient. After he left, we would have to do another ward round, calm all the patients down and clarify the various treatment plans.

It was during this job I had my mind finally and irrevocably made up about my career choice. It was three o'clock in the morning, and we were in the emergency operating theatre, operating on an old lady whose large bowel had become obstructed by a malignant tumour at its lower end. This type of tumour gradually constricts the colon, and over the space of a few weeks, the bowel becomes totally occluded.

At that time there were several approaches to managing this problem. The simplest was to perform a "defunctioning colostomy" (where the bowel is opened onto the abdominal surface), let the patient recover and then come back a few weeks later and resect the tumour.

The technique in vogue at the time however, was to do what was called an "on table colonic lavage", resect the tumour, join the ends of the bowel together and then perform a colostomy proximal to this, which could then be simply reversed when the stitched up bowel had healed a few months later.

The "on table colonic lavage" was a way of washing out the bowel so the ends of the resection were clean when they were sewn together, and therefore less likely to get infected and more likely to heal. Essentially, a catheter was inserted into the first part of the large bowel to allow fluid to be poured in, the lower bowel was then clamped and cut above the tumour and then held out over the side of the operating table, the clamp released and the washing out of three or four weeks of accumulated faeces begun.

My job, as a surgical registrar, was to hold the bucket as several litres of stagnant shit splashed out into it. The smell was truly appalling, and it was touch and go as to whether I was going to add my own vomit to the contents of her bowel. I stood there thinking, "And they say being a surgeon is a glamorous job! I've spent years of training to get to this point, where at three in the morning I'm stood here, holding a bucket, collecting shit." It was at that point I made my mind up that I would be an orthopaedic surgeon, and not spend my life dabbling around in the contents of other people's guts.

Orthopaedics or "bone and joint surgery", is a huge discipline, and its scope has exploded over the past thirty years. There are some major differences from some other branches of surgery. It is involved predominately with improving the quality of people's existence rather than merely extending life, there is very little cancer and indeed, there is no shit. This last sentence I used at several interviews as a junior, when asked the inevitable question "Why do you want to be an orthopaedic surgeon."

From general surgery it was on to a final six months on the cardiothoracic surgery unit. If ever you want to look for a bunch of psychopaths, look no further than any cardiothoracic unit. They were all nuts.

Theatre started at eight a.m., following the seven a.m. ward round, and the two cardiac theatres would get going at the same time. Not infrequently, there would only be one bed on the cardiac-surgery intensive care unit, and so there would then be a race to see who could get their patient down, insert all the intravenous and intra-arterial lines, get the monitoring on, and be first into theatre. The first one into theatre then claimed the ITU bed and the other patient would be told "unfortunately all the ITU beds are now occupied so we can't do your surgery now", all the lines would be taken back out and the patient sent back to the ward.

I did get slightly worried when the fearsome professor of the unit asked to see me in his office. This usually meant you were going to get a bollocking for some perceived failure, and I'd seen the walls shaking as he'd ranted at some poor SHO. I was surprised when he told me the consultants of the unit had been discussing me and thought I would be wasted in going into orthopaedics, and that I "had the makings of a cardiothoracic surgeon". He obviously felt that this was a massive compliment, whereas I stood there thinking "Jesus… am I that much of a bastard?"

It was during this attachment, I passed both the Fellow of the Royal College of Surgeons Edinburgh, and the Royal College of Surgeons of London exams. Snobbery was such, that to have a chance of working south of Birmingham, you pretty much had to have the London exam.

I had thought the first part exams were tough, but little did I know! I went through a ten week spell, consisting of the Edinburgh written exams with multiple choice papers and essays, then the following week a whole day of vivas, and finally a day of clinicals (when you have to take a history and examine patients and are then quizzed about them). After a ten-day gap I had the London written exams, vivas and clinicals spread out over a further three weeks. It was one of the toughest periods in my entire life, especially after passing the Edinburgh College exams, when I had to keep myself motivated for the next set of hurdles.

The London written exam consisted of four, one-hour essays with no choice. We all assembled in the hall, took a table and waited for instruction. After the usual health and safety spiel we were told we could turn over the exam paper and begin.

A groan went up from many of the candidates. The very first question was "Discuss the aetiology and management of scoliosis in adolescents." (scoliosis is a developmental curvature of the spine). This is an esoteric subject even for an orthopaedic surgeon, and clearly many candidates knew nothing about it.

I was extremely fortunate. The weekend prior to the exam, I was getting very bored with reading the same articles over and over again. Purely by chance there had been an article on scoliosis opposite a piece on one of the more common surgical problems, and I had read it for something else to do. I could remember just about enough to fashion some sort of answer.

To badly fail any single question in the exam, was to fail the whole thing. In that moment of turning over the paper and reading the very first question, probably half of the hall realised they had fallen at the very first hurdle.

I passed the writtens and went on to the vivas and then the clinicals. This time, the results were to be given in the imposing front hall of the Royal College of Surgeons in Lincolns Inn Fields. Once again, about seventy of us nervously waited for the porter with the clipboard to appear. Out he strode.

"The following numbers have passed. Will they step forward, identify themselves, and wait in the corridor behind me. Number twenty-eight." Everyone whose number was before that, turned and trooped off out of the building, failure weighing heavily on their shoulders. My number came closer and closer, and my pulse progressively beat faster. Suddenly there it was, my number! The porter then finished with "and that is all the successful candidates from today", turned on his heel and walked off.

I could hardly believe it and staggered round the corner to join the other successful candidates. There were five of us. We were then ushered into a college boardroom, where the assembled examiners congratulated us, and we were supplied with the inevitable thimbleful of sherry. The examiners then quickly disappeared, and an official from the college gave us all standing order forms for our annual subscription to the college which we were asked to sign before we left.

The following day, back at the hospital I was back down to earth on the early morning ward round in the cardiac surgery unit. As we finished, the professor asked for quiet as he had an announcement to make.

"Ladies and Gentlemen, I am pleased to inform you that Steve passed the Fellow of the Royal College of Surgery exams yesterday. You will now refer to him as *Mr. Bollen.*"

People often ask why surgeons are referred to as "mister" rather than "doctor", and it's often a cause of confusion when talking to colleagues from abroad. It is because originally, in the 1700's, qualifying as a surgeon was with a diploma rather than a degree in medicine, and therefore they could not call themselves doctor.

Anyway, my euphoria was short-lived as no suitable jobs were being advertised and, after obtaining fellowships from both colleges, I spent several months unemployed. I did a few locums around the country, for a week here and a week there, to keep myself financially solvent and my skill set intact. Just as I was reaching desperation point and thinking my career was over, a job in orthopaedics came up for a year in Bradford followed by a year in Leeds (designed ostensibly, to bring the departments closer together), as a "post-fellowship registrar". I applied, and after a successful interview, was appointed.

I spent two years getting experience in my chosen craft, and then once again was facing the spectre of unemployment. The difficult hurdle was coming, which was the move to senior registrar. In those days to stand a chance of being shortlisted for a post, you had to have the higher degree of an MD, or at least have spent time doing a year's research working towards one, in addition to having several peer reviewed research publications in the orthopaedic journals.

Fortune smiled on me, and I was once again in the right place at the right time. The Rheumatism Research Unit in Leeds was looking to forge closer ties with the orthopaedic surgery unit and had suggested a year's research post for an orthopaedic registrar. I was it.

At this stage I had an interest in shoulder surgery and was keen to follow this path but the only project available at the research unit was to do with the measurement of knee laxity (looseness) after knee ligament injury and surgery. It's strange the way things turn out sometimes, and I was unwittingly chanelled in the direction my future career would take.

Although appointed, there was no funding for the post, and I had to then apply for a research grant. I was fortunate to be successful in obtaining a grant from the Arthritis and Rheumatism Council which, while not generous, would keep the wolf from the door for twelve months. On the first day of my year's research, I turned up at seven thirty a.m., as I would have done for my regular orthopaedic job. I then sat there, intermittently making cups of coffee, until about ten to nine when one other person turned up. The world of academia was a very different place.

The unit was run by professor Verna Wright, a fundamentalist Christian, who would walk down to the town centre at lunchtime and, bible in hand, preach to any members of the public willing to listen. He truly lived by his Christian principles and I admired him greatly for it. He also had a superb intellect and was fundamental in pointing me in the right direction with my research, helping me produce a number of scientific papers.

It was very different to my previous frantic post. The whole unit would stop for coffee in the morning and tea in the afternoon, which the professor insisted we all took together in the unit's large sitting room. This was actually a great idea, as we were all from completely different disciplines and much exchanging of ideas went on during this protected time. It's often a good idea to get someone who is not intimately involved in your work to look at it from what was a completely different viewpoint and provide valuable, independent input.

The most amazing thing for me was not being on-call, so every evening and every weekend was free (allowing a few locum weekends to supplement my income), something that I hadn't experienced for many years. My two major interests outside work at that time were rock climbing and playing in a band, formed with three other junior doctors, rejoicing in the name of "Brain Dead". We were awful but gained enormous pleasure from thrashing out a load of rock covers, having some great nights playing in front of bemused audiences.

Whilst I was at the unit, the British Mountaineering Council wrote an article in one of the popular climbing magazines, saying they were becoming increasingly concerned about the number of top rock-climbers who were getting injured, and were wanting to set up a study looking at the problem. I wrote to them saying I was happy to help out, and they almost bit my hand off.

Like any aspiring trainee of the time, I went to the published literature to see what was already out there and found that there was exactly nothing. I had to start completely from scratch, but it did mean I had the field to myself and, within a couple of years, because of the scientific papers I was able to produce, I became the "world authority" on rock climbing injuries (only because there wasn't anyone else!), being invited to lecture around the globe. I later went on to become the medical adviser to the British Mountaineering Council, and the British representative in the "Union Internationale des Associations d'Alpinisme".

By the end of my year's research I'd done the work for my MD, had two published book chapters, and sixteen scientific papers published in peer reviewed journals. This stood me in good stead when applying for the next step of senior registrar.

I kept applying and kept getting shortlisted. You would then make the expected visit to consultants on the training program, ask the right questions (generally getting exactly the same answers), and then attend for the interview. There must have a small group of us who were roughly the same standard, as you kept meeting the same half dozen people at each interview.

Too long spent at post-fellowship registrar level was another way of bringing your career to an early finish. There were a couple of candidates at the first interview I went to, who were also at the last interview when I was appointed and became stuck at that level never gaining a senior registrar post. After years of filling in doing locums, they were sometimes lucky enough to obtain a consultant post at what was perceived to be a less desirable hospital, when nobody else had applied.

Almost inevitably, the "local guy" ended up being appointed at the first few interviews I attended, and this continued until it was my turn and I was the "local guy", shortlisted for a post on the Leeds/Bradford training programme. I think it was the worst interview I've ever given. The pressure from being the local candidate weighed heavily, and I really didn't want to let my referees down. I stumbled and mumbled through the questions, hoping for the best.

I have never been so relieved as when I was asked to go back into the interview room and offered the post. I had made it. Short of doing something catastrophic, I would now go on to become a consultant in another six years or so. It was time to celebrate!

5

RAISED ON ROBBERY

Every time I pick up a paper or watch a TV program with adverts, there seems to be yet another legal firm specialising in suing doctors and hospitals. I cannot actually think of another profession where there is a huge chunk of another profession, amounting to an industry, whose sole aim in life is to try and prove you've been crap at your job. I don't see adverts asking if your lawyer or accountant have done a bad job, and that this or that company are experts in getting you suitable compensation.

This is perhaps one of the most notable changes I have seen as the years have gone by. When I first started, patients generally had faith that you were trying to do your best (and that was almost always the case), and that if something went wrong, "shit happens".

When I was a senior registrar in Bradford, I would be summoned into the boss's outpatient room to find a patient sitting there with X-rays displayed on all the screens around. The boss would introduce the patient and tell the story of their initial presentation. He would then describe the unfolding of events.

He would explain that when the patient presented with this problem, he felt the best approach was to try this particular procedure and display the X-rays of before and after the initial surgery. He would then turn to me.

"Of course, that turned out to be completely the wrong thing to do." He would then talk through the various problems and solutions he had to devise to get the patient to a satisfactory conclusion in the end. The patient would sit there, listening with interest to the discussion, and would always express their thanks for the eventual outcome. I can't imagine a consultant doing this in today's litigious atmosphere.

We have gone from that position of trust, to a point where it almost seems that if a patient gets out of hospital in one piece, it is more by luck than judgement. Lawyers seem to encourage patients to sue, however trivial the problem has been, and there has been a massive surge in litigation over the last thirty years.

A massive amount of NHS funding is spent practicing defensive medicine. It seems doctors are not allowed to work off probabilities anymore but have to exclude any remote possibility, and so investigations are ordered "just in case", not because you really think they are needed. Perfection in management and treatment now seems to be the only acceptable standard. We also work in situations where a wrong, split-second decision, made in complex and stressful circumstances, can result in disaster.

Doctors don't just laugh this off but carry the burden through the rest of their lives. Not only do we face the prospect of persecution by the media, who seem to sensationalise everything, bandying around words like "murder", and "killing", but also the real possibility of being prosecuted for manslaughter – the "criminalisation of unintentional error", a situation that is treated very differently in other parts of the world such as New Zealand.

In my hospital Trust, a new and grossly overweight chief nurse was appointed. This was roughly the time new legislation meant that chief executives could be held accountable for disasters in their organisations. The new chief nurse barely emerged from her office in the subsequent twelve months, producing page after page of "trust policy". I counted close to twelve hundred pages produced in that year, most of which seemed essentially to be management arse covering.

I don't think anybody actually read it all, it was just so that if anything went wrong, management could say "It clearly says in paragraph thirty-two B on page twenty-six, blah blah blah... and put the responsibility back on the clinician. We were constantly asked to cut corners to save money and hit targets, but if anything went wrong, the blame was laid entirely on the doctor.

I spend a bit of time doing medical negligence work, as an expert witness, and in most of the cases no-one has actually done anything wrong, the poor patient has just had a bad result. Unfortunately, the legal profession the UK have fought tooth and nail against a system of "no fault compensation", such as exists in New Zealand, so the only way to get compensation is to try and prove that the doctor or hospital have been negligent.

There was an article in the Times newspaper in 2018, where the author stated that "The Cost of NHS Litigation Is a Price Worth Paying.", explaining that this was a way of protecting patients, and encouraging better practice. He may have been slightly biased however, as his job was as a solicitor in a medical negligence firm, but it is a good example of the skewed logic the legal profession applies to the problem.

The cost of litigation to NHS is truly staggering, currently running at about two-point-two billion pounds a year. If the claim is for less than one-hundred-thousand pounds, and ninety-eight percent are, the legal costs run at about fifty-three percent of the claim. It doesn't take a genius to realise this means something over a billion pounds a year, of hard-earned taxpayer's money that has been allocated to the NHS, goes straight into the lawyer's pockets. The Medical Defence Union recently reported a case where the patient's compensation was about five thousand pounds, but the legal fees were over a hundred thousand!

Even worse for the NHS, is that in the current climate, if the claim is below twenty thousand pounds, and there is a sniff of a case, the NHS will generally settle out of court, as it cheaper to do it that way, rather than to try and fight on behalf of the staff or hospital. There are possibly some unscrupulous lawyers (!) who are well aware of this and encourage patients to make claims for minor problems. In February 2020 the BBC reported the estimated outstanding litigation claims against the Health Service amounted to a staggering eighty-three billion pounds.

Nobody is saying that if doctors or hospitals are truly negligent, they should not take responsibility, and patients should not be suitably compensated. Despite every effort, sometimes things do go wrong, or a patient will get less than a perfect result. That's just the way life is. Doctors, surgeons and nurses don't deliberately try and inflict a poor outcome. No operation or treatment works a hundred percent of the time, and every treatment or operation has complications.

Part of the problem is that you can tell a patient a complication can occur in one in a thousand cases, but if it happens to them, it has happened to them a hundred percent of the time. They don't see the big picture.

An older surgeon once said to me that when things go wrong in the NHS "It's a bit like trying to pass a knitting needle through a piece of Swiss cheese. Every now and then, all the holes line up." This certainly seems to be the case. It is rarely one single thing that has caused a problem, it is an accumulation of errors that produces the final disaster.

Although doctors are often accused of not fully explaining risks to patients, in current times, with almost universal access to smart phones/tablets and the internet, there can be little excuse for patients not taking some responsibility and reading up on their potential procedure. A few keystrokes will allow access to information to that was previously arcane, and only obtainable through a library.

We still have an historical "consent for treatment" process which implies patients are almost being strong armed into having procedures performed on them, whereas in the current climate of fully involving them in decision making, and always offering the option of not having anything done (providing they understand the implications of this), they are effectively *requesting* intervention. As I understand it, lawyers would hate this, as *requesting* treatment puts the onus on the patient to understand potential complications and outcomes, as opposed to *consent* where the responsibility lies with the treating physician.

It seems to me the whole thing is a chicken and egg type problem. Underfunding of the Health Service leads to inadequate staffing levels, with the staff trying to do their best to cope in poor working environments with inadequate equipment, leading inevitably to more mistakes and undesirable outcomes. We need to stop spending money on lawyers and put more funding into the NHS, hopefully improving outcomes for everyone (apart from the lawyer's bank accounts).

You never forget the first time you get legal action taken against you. A pompous letter arrives, from some legal firm specialising in suing doctors, telling you that you have been guilty of "gross negligence" and have "fallen far below the standards that would normally be expected". You sit there crestfallen and questioning yourself and your abilities. It really hurts.

The first time it happened to me was after performing an osteotomy (where the shin bone is cut and the leg realigned to take pressure off the damaged part in the knee) on a lady, which had failed to improve her symptoms, following which she'd gone on to have her knee replaced by another colleague, which also hadn't helped with her pain. She had initially been referred to me by yet another consultant, and all three of us were in the firing line. This is a common legal tactic, with a scattergun type approach, to serve notice on everyone involved, obtain all the relevant notes and then trawl through them trying to find something they can hang a case on.

I was upset to find they felt I'd given the patient a "completely unrealistic idea of potential outcomes" following her operation. The patient was a little odd, and I'd been very careful about documenting our discussions in the notes. I'd quoted success rates that were published in the orthopaedic literature, and the pre and post-operative X-rays showed the operation had been carried out exactly as planned. I provided my defence organisation (This was before the NHS ran its own insurance scheme) with the relevant literature and a written report (how many NHS hours are wasted going through this process?), and the action was dropped a couple of years later.

Once notice is served, the lawyers have three years to move things forward. One later case where a patient sued (and before you think this seems to be happening a lot to me, the average orthopaedic surgeon is said to be being sued by six patients at any one time!), hung over me for this length of time, as the lawyers touted the case around the country trying to find an "expert" who would support their allegations. Through the grapevine I heard they'd given up, after trying about six different specialists who all said I'd done nothing wrong, but they didn't have the good grace to let me know.

I rang my defence organisation when the three years were up, to ask if I could now consider the case closed, only to be told that the lawyers were entitled to an additional period of three months grace, just in case they hadn't had enough time! I have been fortunate during my career to have been in the firing line only a couple of times and, to date, have never been successfully litigated against. In the ten years before I left the NHS, I was one of only two surgeons in our department who had never had a complaint made against them.

Other than being sued, appearing in court as an orthopaedic surgeon generally occurs in two ways. Either as an "expert" witness, when you are giving your expert opinion about either a personal injury claim or allegation of negligence, or as a "witness to fact" when you have been involved in the immediate care of an accident or assault victim.

There is apparently, "no authority higher than the law". If the NHS is a system in need of repair, our legal system needs to take a long hard look at itself. I have been subpoenaed to appear in court, as a witness to fact, on quite a few occasions. This has often been with less than twenty-four hours notice, necessitating last minute cancellations of NHS operating lists or clinics. Once at court I have rarely been called, meaning I have often sat waiting all day, to eventually be told that I'm not actually needed and can go home.

This also frequently happens in litigation cases, where the lawyers play brinkmanship, and then settle at the last minute "on the court steps". I was once subpoenaed, with three days notice, to appear as an expert witness in a case in Manchester. I was actually due to go on holiday with the family that week and hurriedly had to rearrange my flights, while they all jetted off to the sun.

After turning up at court and sitting around for a couple of hours, together with another expert witness who had flown back from Venice to be there, the solicitor came out and spoke to us.

"Good news! We've settled, so you can both go home now." Both myself and the other expert witness were incensed but were dismissed with the words "Sorry about that, vagaries of court and all that." You can't help but think this is being replicated across the country on a daily basis, at what sort of cost to the nation?

Appearing as an expert witness can be intimidating, as the opposing counsel's job is to try and diminish your evidence, and make you look like a fool, and some of them are very good at doing it! Personally, I have always quite enjoyed the verbal jousting, and as a colleague said to me when I first started, "Keep calm and remember that however knowledgeable they might seem, you know more about your subject than they do."

Some counsels are well prepared and discuss the case with you before putting you in the witness box, some are definitely not. With the legal system we have, it is not uncommon to turn up to court and find a barrister you've never met before who has been handed the case that day (as the previous barrister has gone to do something more important), and read the brief on the train on the way there. Some are quite brilliant and can grasp the essential facts of the case in a flash, some can't!

After a couple of times of standing there while our counsel went round and round the houses, seemingly not sure what evidence I could provide that might be important to the case, I decided to take matters into my own hands.

To get around the problem, I started writing a script of the questions and my answers to them (in large font), that I felt were the most relevant points of the case and would give it to the counsel just before the hearing started. My scripts were generally well received and when standing in the witness box, you could see it on the desk in front of them. The counsel then stands, looks down at the desk, and starts to read from the script as though they are utterly familiar with the complex issues involved. I then give the answers that support our case. Using this system, I have never been on the losing side.

I was involved, as an expert witness, in the landmark case when Gordon Watson sued another player and his club, after he had his leg broken in a tackle, during the traditionally fearsome local derby between Bradford City and Huddersfield Town in February 1997.

Gordon was a talented striker who had been a high profile signing for Bradford City, and had scored in his first two games. I was actually at his third game, watching from the stand (at the time I was actually club surgeon to both teams), when he received the ball in the midfield. He had just laid the ball off when Kevin Gray of Huddersfield Town came flying in with a tackle described by the ex-footballer and pundit Jimmy Hill, as "late, dangerous, violent, and one of the worst tackles I've ever seen".

I hurried down from the stand as Gordon was stretchered off the pitch and into the treatment room. I examined him which confirmed his leg had been broken. Fortunately, he had just taken his weight off the leg at the time of impact, so had been spared a compound injury, where the bones come through the skin. I followed the ambulance to the local hospital and two hours later was operating on him to fix the fracture.

After an emergency meeting, the Bradford City board of directors decided to proceed with legal action. I was called as an expert witness, as I had calculated that at the height and angle that Kevin had contacted Gordon's leg, together with the site of the fracture, he would have gone over the top of the ball, even if it had been there at the time.

As usual, the opposing barrister spent about an hour trying to rubbish my testimony. The discussions became quite heated but after the showing of a video of the tackle in the courtroom, things quietened down, and his attempts to phase me were to no avail.

Gordon set a precedent by winning the case and being awarded nine-hundred and sixty thousand pounds. He returned to playing about a year later, helping Bradford City during the season they achieved promotion to the Premiership.

The most dramatic case I have been involved in as a witness to fact, was a murder trial that took place when I was a senior house officer in Bedford. A poor woman had been rushed into casualty having been stabbed in the chest, with a small, two-centimetre wound, just below her right collar bone.

Her lung hadn't been punctured and she wasn't bleeding profusely, but her blood pressure was a little low. She was reviewed by the registrar and consultant and was about to be admitted to the ward for observation, when she suddenly collapsed and, despite our best efforts, sadly died.

At post-mortem she was found to have had a "cardiac tamponade". The knife used must have been some sort of thin, stiletto blade as it had slid down inside the chest wall, and inflicted a small puncture wound in the front of the heart. The heart is surrounded by a tough fibrous sac, so if there is bleeding into this, it compresses the heart and prevents it from beating.

If Bedford had been a major teaching hospital with a cardiac surgery unit, then she might have been able to be saved, but we had none of these types of facilities. The nearest cardiac unit was a forty-five-minute, blue light ambulance drive away, which she would not have survived.

I was slightly puzzled as to why I had been called as the only witness from the hospital, as I was the most junior member of the team who been involved in her care. The reason quickly became apparent when I was called to the witness box, and the defence counsel waded in.

For nearly an hour he tried every which way he could to get me to say that she would have survived if she had received the correct management. I had no brief from anyone, and this was my first experience of court. The whole thing was incredibly stressful. It felt as though I was on trial and I was being accused of the murder.

Prior to the trial I had a vague inkling that this might have been the case and had read everything I could about stab wounds to the chest. I knew my stuff and quoted the published work on the subject from the time, which said that these types of cases rarely survived, and back and forth we went. I started to get a little irritated when he asked exactly the same question, worded a slightly different way, for about the eighth or ninth time. I fired back.

"Look, let's put it this way. If she hadn't been stabbed in the chest she wouldn't have died." We then had a debate about whether this was the point or not, with him saying he felt this wasn't relevant, and me disagreeing with him. He eventually seemed to run out of steam, and with a sigh snapped.

"No further questions". The judge then turned to the prosecution counsel and asked him if he wanted to put any questions.

He stood and declared, "I don't think so my Lord". The Judge thanked me, and I was then told I could step down and leave. The prosecuting barrister spoke to me later and told me he thought I had handled myself very well.

Lawyers are an interesting bunch and seem to work on a different timescale to most of us. I was involved in a litigation case involving a professional soccer player, where the sum involved was in excess of twenty-eight million pounds. The legal team for the case contacted me late on a Friday afternoon to ask if I could give an expert medical opinion on the problem.

After they had supplied a few more details, I felt it was within my field of expertise and I could supply a report, once I had all the relevant notes etc. They then told me there was a bit of a time constraint and the report had to be in by the following Wednesday! I was staggered that a case involving such huge sums of money seemed to have been left to the very last minute. This is not an unusual state of affairs!

I spend my working life treating professional sportsmen and women, but this has now reached a stage where you have to ask if the potential risks are worth it. Indemnity costs (the insurance that covers you if you are sued) constantly go up and currently the maximum you can get insured for is twenty million pounds.

This might sound a lot, but as the average weekly wage for a premiership footballer is now running at fifty-thousand pounds a week, if something went badly wrong with a twenty-year-old soccer star, and you lost a negligence case, you could be looking at a claim for in excess of fifty million pounds, not taking into account the loss of income from advertising and image rights, and for a Sanchez, Pogba or Neymar, the sum is unthinkable.

When I first became a consultant, the legal profession was our peer group, with a GP earning the equivalent of a solicitor, a consultant earning roughly the same as a barrister and a top consultant, a QC. This is certainly no longer the case.

After years of relentless government downward pressure, wage freezes in the NHS and even most private practice fees not having increased since 1991 (and for many procedures were halved four or five years ago), the most recent BMA figures report that in real terms, doctors are now earning thirty percent less than ten years ago. In the private sector, in real terms, I was being paid seventy percent less for the same procedure than I was when I started twenty-five years ago. One of the peculiarities of the system is that all consultants are paid exactly the same for a given procedure, whether they were appointed last week, or whether they have twenty years experience and an international reputation.

When working in the NHS, there was always the promise of a decent, index linked pension at the end of it. This was seen as compensation for working like a dog, having no social life, and not being paid extravagantly. Over the last twenty years the politicians have kept moving the goalposts, and this is no longer the case.

In 2004, new tax regulations regarding "pension pots" were introduced, hitting a lot of consultants. Encouraged to save hard for their retirement, they were suddenly subject to a new level of taxation. We now have the ridiculous situation that consultants are requesting a reduction in their working hours, as with the new regulations they effectively end up working a day a week for nothing. As they say, there are only two certain things in life – death and taxes!

Interestingly, there is only one group who are not affected by the new pension regulations. An emergency piece of legislation was put through parliament at the time to exempt judges, as there was the threat of mass resignation if the government didn't roll over. Probably nothing to do with the fact Tony Blair was an ex-barrister and his wife a member of the judiciary.

I first started to realise the gulf between our professions when I was a senior registrar. I was attending a course in Edinburgh staying in a tiny B&B on the outskirts of the city. One of the other attendees was another trainee from Leeds who suggested we go for a bite to eat after the day's instruction.

We finished at about five o'clock and he invited me to have a coffee at the place he was staying before heading out. We walked through the picturesque streets of Edinburgh, ending up at a lovely mews house. He was staying in an apartment on the top floor, full of designer furniture, looking directly out at the castle, somewhat of a contrast to my meagre accommodation. I asked him how he had managed to end up in such luxurious surroundings.

"Well...it belongs to a friend of mine from school. She went into law and I went into medicine. She's working in corporate law in London and bought this place last year with her Christmas bonus. She already has a place in Milan and London. This is just part of her property portfolio."

How far the medical profession has fallen behind our peer group in the law, really came home to me when I was having a conversation with a colleague who is a professor of orthopaedics, and one of the most brilliant and unconventional minds I have ever met. His brother was a barrister in London and had recently been involved in a government enquiry for a year. He asked me to guess what his brother's personal fee for the twelve months work had been. I wasn't too surprised when he told me it had been three million pounds. We looked at each other...

"We're in the wrong bloody job!"

6

BRING IT ON HOME

The Senior Registrar Years

I n my day, senior registrars were effectively "junior consultants". We had already trained as general surgeons, and had then gone on to specialise in orthopaedics, so were confidant clinicians and operators with significant experience in our chosen speciality. You had already been through a baptism of fire and, after all the exams and time doing research, had a huge wealth of knowledge.

You were expected to operate unsupervised and often had two or three operating lists of your own each week, sometimes in a different hospital to where your boss was based. The emergency work was done almost entirely by the junior staff. In six years as a senior registrar, I didn't see a single fracture fixed by a consultant.

This might sound poor, but most of the consultants in the hospitals I trained in were within ten years of retirement, and many of them were technically awful. They had been appointed at a time when you went into orthopaedics because you'd failed to make the grade at general surgery and, at one hospital, the consultant I worked for had been appointed two years after gaining his FRCS, with a total of four years surgical experience. When they started, there were no joint replacements, fractures were treated with plaster or traction, and most of them wouldn't have known which way round to hold an arthroscope.

When I was a senior registrar, orthopaedics was undergoing an exponential increase in new techniques, and few of the consultants had moved with the times. As senior registrars we spent a lot of time keeping the patients away from the consultants, as no matter what was wrong with them, they would end up worse off if the boss tried to fix the problem surgically. The senior registrars taught each other new techniques we had picked up by attending conferences, and I was fortunate that my peer group were a great bunch of guys, all of whom were excellent with a knife in their hand.

There were a couple of consultants on the Leeds/Bradford rotation who were undoubtedly the worst technical surgeons I've ever seen. It was always an education if you were helping them do an operation! At that time, surgeons were allowed to operate on private patients on their NHS lists, and this was generally when you were called upon to assist the boss.

One consultant asked me to help him with a private hip replace-ment, and so I duly turned up in theatre at the appointed time. He was never a delicate surgeon and didn't believe in "keyhole surgery". The hospital had actually purchased the entire stock of a particular scalpel blade (that was more like a small carving knife), which the manufacturers were going to be discontinue, so he would never run out of his favourite cutting tool.

He made his usual huge incision and began the procedure. He managed to dislocate the ball out of the ball and socket and removed the damaged, worn end of the femur. At one point during the proce-dure he turned to the scrub sister.

"Large swab please sister". She handed him a large swab. He then pulled down his mask, blew his nose on it, pulled up his mask, threw the swab on the floor and put his hands back in the wound. I was flabbergasted and looked at sister, not really believing what I had just seen. Sister winked at me, confirming that it had really happened.

The operation was truly awful, with the boss seemingly not being au fait with any of the up-to-date techniques of cementing a joint replacement in place. I was left to stitch up the dog's dinner that had been left behind, which was less than easy, and the artificial joint actually looked loose even before the skin had been sewn up.

Amazingly, it became horribly infected (who'd have thought it and a real puzzle to the consultant!), pouring pus out of the wound, and a week later we were back in theatre taking it back out. This was fairly straightforward, as the joint replacement hadn't been cemented in properly in the first place.

One day, the same consultant asked me if I had done a knee replacement. At that time this was still nowhere near as common a procedure as a hip replacement. I was a fourth-year senior registrar and hadn't yet done one. He told me he would sort it out and get a suitable patient in so he could take me through the operation.

On the due day, the poor patient was anaesthetised and wheeled into the operating theatre. I set them up on the operating table, scrubbed up, and started the prepping and draping, getting them ready for the surgery to begin. The boss was still unscrubbed, wandering around the outside of the clean air tent. I finished getting the patient prepared and stood waiting for the boss to join me. He looked at me through the plastic panels of the clean air tent and shouted, "Are you ready?" I told him I was. He then turned around and picked up the instruction manual from a shelf behind him and opened it on page one. He then proceeded to shout the instructions from the book to me, as a I slowly progressed through the operation.

As I said in the introduction to this book, supervision was somewhat limited. Without doubt though, most of the time, the patients were far better off having my generation of surgical trainees operating on them, than they would be if the boss came anywhere near them with a knife.

Unlike the current generation of trainees, we would never turn anything down we were asked to do, no matter how complex or difficult. To do so would have meant a big, black mark against your record. This was never more apparent than when the boss was going on holiday. He would put a chummy arm around your shoulder and tell you he had some "interesting" cases coming in for you to operate on in the next two weeks. This would generally mean the cases he didn't want to be involved in, as the surgery was going to be difficult and the outcomes unlikely to be great. In fact, a sort of game was played, where you brought in cases that you thought were horrendous when you were away, and vice versa.

One day I had joined a ward round for another consultant, as the other senior registrar was away. We came to a side room where a patient had been admitted for a second time, re-do knee replacement scheduled for the following day. The houseman presented the case and put up the X-rays, which showed it was likely to be a technically very difficult operation.

The consultant looked unhappy, as he clearly didn't fancy taking on the case and also, he wanted to get off early that day so he could get to the races. He thought for a moment, took off his glasses and vigorously rubbed his eyes until they were bright red. He put his glasses back on and went into the patient's room. Pointing at his eyes he explained, "I'm terribly sorry about this, but I have terrible conjunctivitis. The last thing we can afford to do is to get this operation infected – that could lead to amputation. I think the safest thing to do is to delay the surgery a couple of weeks, until this is all cleared up." The patient was extremely grateful for this considerate attitude and went home without a murmur.

I think I actually spent more time mentally filing away things I would never do when I became a consultant, rather than learning from my bosses as to how it should be done. Most of them were very old school and certainly one or two regarded their NHS time more as "charity work" than anything else. They often had the attitude that they were really granting the NHS patient a huge favour by devoting some of their precious time to see and treat them.

One consultant at the LGI really loved the sound of his own voice, although, to be fair, he was a pretty good at teaching the students. His special interest was back pain, and his clinic room was like a lecture theatre. He would be sat at a large desk with his secretary, her shorthand pad in hand, perched on a stool at one side. Behind him, on benches, were several medical students, houseman, senior house officer, physiotherapist, and pretty much anyone else who'd expressed an interest. Opposite him were several cubicles with wooden doors, in which the patients would be prepared by sister. They would be stripped off and asked to put on something that had all the appearances of a large, white, linen nappy, with ties on either side.

When the boss was ready, he would nod to sister, who then approached a cubicle, opened the door and encouraged the patient to shuffle out into the room in front of the assembled audience.

The boss would look up and address them, "So… what's the matter?" The patient would usually mumble a reply and be asked to speak up, as the boss was a bit hard of hearing.

"It's me back, Mr. *, I have really bad pain." The boss would turn to the secretary and tell her to record that the patient is complaining of back pain, and then there would be a series of questions and answers.

The boss would then give the poor patient a long, hard, disdainful look and turn to the secretary, "On examination… poor posture, pendulous abdomen, flabby musculature…" And continue in this ilk, then finish with a short examination and then a dismissal, following which he would turn to the students and talk about the problem and its management for fifteen minutes or so. As his senior registrar, you were working flat out in the clinic next door, seeing dozens of follow up patients through the afternoon.

One of the other consultants took a slightly different approach, and never actually spoke to the patients at all. They were sent for an X-ray, which had been based on information in the GP referral letter (not always accurate in the identification of the problem!), before coming up to the clinic. He would look at the letter, look at the X-ray and the patient would then be shown in. He would look up from the desk and tell the patient he would write to their doctor. The patient would then be smartly wheeled round and back out of the door by sister, without actually having sat down. They usually asked what was going to happen, and sister would tell them that Mr. * would be writing to their doctor to advise on treatment and that would be that.

As a senior registrar you worked hard, studied hard and operated around the clock. There were no protected, daytime "trauma lists", and so all the emergency fracture treatment was done through the night. As the other surgical discipline's emergencies were frequently life threatening, they got to go first, and orthopaedics was well down the pecking order.

You were often on call with a junior registrar who was on a surgical rotation, with no aspirations to become an orthopaedic surgeon, or any previous orthopaedic surgery experience. This frequently meant being called in during the early hours of the morning to do fairly routine fracture treatment that could have quite easily waited until the following day.

You would finish, drive home, have a shower, change your clothes, have some breakfast, and then head back into the hospital to do a routine day's operating and clinic work, having had just a couple of hours of sleep. You were still on call every other night and weekend, and if the other senior registrar was away on holiday or study leave, you filled in for them (unpaid!), and were on call every night for a couple of weeks, because you really didn't want to leave the patients to the mercies of the consultants.

Being a surgical trainee was not without its hazards. One of the other senior registrars was replacing a fractured hip and, right at the end of the operation, was struggling to get it back into the socket. The reduction was very tight, and as he strained to get it back there was a loud crack. "Oh, Jesus" he thought. "I've fractured the femur" (thighbone).

He carefully inspected the operative site but could find no sign of anything amiss. As he stood there puzzled, he suddenly noticed his hand was starting to throb. Looking down, he could see his hand starting to swell within his glove, and it was becoming increasingly painful.

He managed to finish the operation and headed down to A&E to get an X-ray, which showed he had fractured a bone in his hand. He went on to have a few investigations, just to make sure he hadn't developed some rare form of osteoporosis, but they were all normal.

When regaling this tale to fellow trainees, he would find that other colleagues had similar tales of injuries sustained while operating, and it started him thinking. He wrote to all the senior registrars around the country asking the question "Have you ever been injured while operating?" and received an astonishing number of replies.

There were loads of self-inflicted needle stick and scalpel wounds, but many instances of injuries caused by faulty equipment (including electrocution), and clumsy consultants. Probably the worst instance, was a trainee who had a lung punctured when a consultant pushed a drain so hard through the abdominal wall (drainage tubes are attached onto a sharp metal spike so they can be pushed through muscle and skin), that it shot through and into his chest, where he was steadying the patient on the other side. He needed a chest drain put in for a week or two and was off work for six weeks. The accumulated data of disaster was turned into a scientific paper, which was published in the Christmas edition of the British Medical Journal.

Occasionally the dangers were more external. A&E could be hazardous during the night, as fights frequently erupted. A couple of the hospitals used to train individual soldiers from elite units, to stitch wounds, put in cannulas and manage trauma. They were sometimes very useful to have around when things kicked off. They had the ability to just look troublemakers in the eye, and somehow through the alcoholic haze, the miscreants would realise it would be best for their health to just sit down and shut up.

Late one night I was down in A&E seeing a patient with an injured leg, when a "hot hatch" screamed to a halt outside the front entrance. A couple of burly blokes jumped out from the front, opened the back door and roughly pulled out a third, who was bleeding profusely. As they dragged him over the ground and into the department, a second "hot hatch" pulled up. The windows went down, and they started shooting at the first group, with bullets whizzing round the inside of A&E. Everyone hit the deck and after a dozen or so shots, the second car zoomed off at high speed. They were terrible marksmen; they didn't hit a single thing except the walls.

This was my first experience of being in the line of fire, as I had grown up in the post second world war era of small skirmishes, but then Iraq went and invaded Kuwait. I was working at the LGI, when it was designated as one of the reception hospitals for wounded flown back from the battlefront of Desert Storm, and we were told to prepare for the worst. Previously starved of funding for state-of-the-art equipment for treating fractures, suddenly money was no object. Anything we wanted magically appeared. New phone lines, message boards and enough external fixators (a frame applied to the outside of the leg to stabilise fractures), nails, plates and screws to treat dozens of patients. It occurred to me that two groups of people make a big profit from conflict – those who supply the tools to kill and maim, and those who supply the kit to put the surviving wounded back together.

Someone high up in the medical side of the Ministry Of Defence came to talk to us. It was a chilling lecture, delivered in a slightly pompous style and a plummy, cut-glass accent.

"In the event of hostilities kicking off, we will expect approximately five thousand casualties a day. Of those, half will be dead, half the survivors will have wounds that are incompatible with survival, and will be triaged to be kept comfortable, the rest will be patched up and sent home as soon as is practicable." He then went on to give details of how they would be dispersed around the country, and warn us, that as a receiving hospital, we would be considered a legitimate target for terrorist attacks. He advised us to look under our cars before driving home. All leave was cancelled, and we waited nervously for the coming storm to break.

As it turned out, he had mercifully and grossly overestimated the toll. Only forty-seven UK troops were killed (nine of them by the Americans) and, according to Wikipedia, out of the six hundred and seventy thousand allied troops from sixty-three nations, there were only seven hundred and seventy-six who were injured.

In my personal life things had settled down. I bought my first house, had a steady girlfriend who was physiotherapist, and we moved in together. Then things took a major turn for the worse. I received one of those phone calls, you really never want to get, from my mother.

She had been feeling poorly, and after several visits to her GP, they had decided yes, things don't seem to be right and done a few blood tests. The hospital rang back the next day and asked my mother to attend the haematology unit at Christies hospital in Manchester that afternoon. She had acute leukaemia.

She was told that without treatment she would survive only two or three weeks, but with treatment she had a ten percent chance of survival. Initially, she thought she would just let go, but when it came to the crunch, she grasped the straw and started chemotherapy.

It was a horrible time. In the next eleven months she spent nearly nine of them in an isolation room, having aggressive chemotherapy and feeling dreadful. Of the other ten patients who were in the unit when she first started her treatment, none survived, with one dying almost every month, not exactly inspiring confidence in my mother.

Back in Leeds I was still on call at the hospital every other weekend. Every weekend I was off, I'd drive over to Manchester to visit my mother in the hospital. I'd clean and tidy her house, buy frozen microwavable meals from Marks and Spencer (the only food you were allowed to take in), visit the hospital twice a day and then head back to Leeds on Sunday evening. My sister would travel up from London on the alternate weekends.

The saddest thing for me was that after many months of this, I started to resent the burden of spending every free weekend I had visiting my mother, and then I would feel horribly guilty for doing so. It really messes with your head. Despite having a horrendous time with the chemotherapy, she bore her illness with great bravery.

On one of my on-call weekends (with just an SHO, the registrar was away), on a Sunday morning, I was just finishing the third fractured hip operation when my bleep went off for an outside call. It was the Manchester Royal Infirmary to tell me my mother had been admitted with a minor stroke, but she was recovering well and would be transferred back to Christies hospital either that evening or the following morning.

I rang the boss to explain the situation. He was unusually kind and told me that of course I should go across to see her, and to tell casualty to ring him at home about any patients they wanted an opinion on.

It took me two hours to drive across. I spent a few hours with my mother, reassured that she seemed reasonably well, and drove back to Bradford arriving at the hospital about seven in the evening. I went down to casualty to find they had been too scared to ring my boss, so had saved all the patients for my return. There were eight of them, who had been waiting up to seven hours for my learned opinion. I finished operating, on those that needed it, at four the following morning.

After a couple of hours sleep, a bit of breakfast and a ward round, I drove to the orthopaedic hospital to do my normal Monday list. Near to lunchtime (not that I ever got any lunch), I was actually in the middle of doing a hip replacement when my bleep went off, and one of the nurses ran off to answer it.

"It's Christies Hospital, can you ring them urgently." As a doctor you know this wasn't likely to be good news, but I had to carry on and finish the operation, and then went to make the call.

They asked me if I could get to the hospital as soon as possible. I asked them if my mother had died. They were reluctant to give this information over the phone but after explaining who I was and where I was, they told me my mother had suffered a catastrophic haemorrhage and had died very quickly about an hour before.

I sat there, sad and crestfallen. My boss came into the room.

"Are you OK Steve?"

"No, not really, my mother has just died." You could see him worriedly thinking that he might have to finish the list himself (he usually buggered off early to go to the private hospital, leaving me to do the last two or three cases). He looked at the floor.

"Well, it was expected, wasn't it?" I came very close to punching him. I vowed there and then I would never, ever be so unsympathetic to my junior staff. I changed out of my theatre greens and drove over to Manchester.

I went up to my Mother's ward and was shown into the side room where she was lying. I sat down next to her, held her cold hand, told her I was sorry I wasn't there for her in her most desperate moments, and sobbed helplessly with tears running down my cheeks and splashing onto the floor.

When I had regained my composure, I went back out to see the nursing staff, who all expressed their sympathies and were genuinely kind. The houseman was waiting for me and, looking embarrassed, asked if they could have permission to do a post-mortem.

"No, I don't think so. You know what she died of, and I think she's suffered enough." He seemed very disappointed. I had one further difficult thing to do. My sister had already been travelling up from London on the train when the hospital rang me and had no idea what had happened. She was also seven months pregnant. I waited on the ward to give her the news.

Perhaps one of the saddest things was that my mother was so looking forward to seeing her first grandchild. In fact, I think it was one of the major drivers in keeping her going. Now, this was never going to happen.

We spent the next week arranging the funeral, visiting banks, building societies and solicitors, and attending to the myriad of things that a death requires you to do. We started to clear the house taking all my mother's clothes to the charity shops in the local village. Driving into the solicitor's office one morning, I turned to see all the mannequins in the front window of the Oxfam shop dressed in my Mother's outfits.

Her funeral was astonishingly well attended, and having been so busy during the previous week, it was only during the service it really started to hit home. After the service we were sat at home, all feeling a bit shell-shocked, when the front doorbell rang. It was the undertaker. He proffered me a small black box, explaining it was my mother's ashes. I was horrified to find it was still warm.

There was no "leave to grieve", so no matter how much pain I carried inside, it was back to Leeds, and straight back to work. It was only another twelve weeks before my partner's mother rang to say she had found a breast lump. It turned out to be malignant and had already spread outside of the breast itself.

Another difficult three months went by, as she underwent surgery and chemotherapy, when one of our best friends was suddenly admitted to hospital with a swollen abdomen. She underwent emergency surgery, only for them to discover she had inoperable ovarian cancer, despite only being in her early thirties.

Over the next year, my partner's mother became increasingly ill, to the point it was getting obvious she didn't have a lot of time left. We made the decision to get married, so her mother would be able to attend the wedding, and our best friend could be a bridesmaid.

Everything was organised over a hectic six weeks and the big day arrived. Sadly, my wife's mother arrived looking yellow with jaundice, legs grossly swollen with excess fluid and mildly confused. It took a bit of the shine off the proceedings, but the day otherwise went well.

We set off on our honeymoon, only to be called back three days later, as my wife's mother had taken a turn for the worse. We sat by her bedside for forty-eight hours as she slowly drifted away and died. Ten days after our wedding we were attending the funeral.

It was a very sad and difficult time and you wonder at the relevance of still having to go into work every day. I guess like many people you find yourself repeatedly asking the age-old questions of why are we here and what's it all about? Life goes on however, and my calling still continued.

Things had been progressing slowly but surely. I had taken and passed the very last FRCSEd Orth exam (a specialist orthopaedic surgery exam exclusive to the Edinburgh College of Surgeons, that afterwards became an exam common to all three colleges), another tough hurdle to overcome. It consisted of several hour long vivas and a long day of clinicals, with again, absolutely no margin for error.

In the very first viva I sat down and the examiner pushed a photograph across the table at me. It was something called a "radial club hand", an incredibly rare genetic condition that, in my entire career, I've never actually seen in the flesh. He then asked me to talk about the surgical management of the condition.

Fortunately for me, in the run up to the exam I had talked to a candidate from a previous sitting, who had been asked exactly the same question. At that point I knew exactly nothing about the condition and had gone away and read it up. There I was in the exam regurgitating the information like I was an expert.

The rest of the day went well, apart from one sticky moment when there was some argument about the anatomy of "the posterior branch of the obturator nerve" (another esoteric bit of information), whilst stood over a dissected cadaver. Both of my examiners were professors and, in the end, one sided with me and the other disagreed. I left thinking I had ploughed it but fortunately the envelope confirming I'd passed arrived a couple of days later.

During this period, I was chatting to one of my fellow senior registrars at the weekly teaching afternoon, congratulating him on just having obtained a consultant post up in Scotland. He was telling me his only regret was he was going to have to back out of a six-month fellowship in "sports surgery", he had organised in Australia, in a unit which had an international reputation.

"Fellowships" were becoming increasingly common at that time, allowing you to gain knowledge and experience in a specialist field, before taking up your consultant post. I asked if he minded if I wrote to the unit in Australia, suggesting that I step into the now vacant post, which he was happy with, and I sent off my letter and CV. They were only too happy to take me at short notice, and eight weeks after my wedding and my wife's mother's funeral, I was heading off "down under" for six months of specialist training.

Before I departed, my consultant (mentioned above in the private hip replacement anecdote) asked to see me. He took me down to his office, sat me down with a cup of coffee and we talked about my impending time abroad. I explained what I would be doing, how this dovetailed with my previous work in the rheumatism research unit and the various publications I had written, and how it was what I wanted to do in the future. He looked at me gravely.

"Well Steve, you're a talented chap, but I think you're wasting your time. There's no future in this keyhole surgery stuff. You can't possibly see as much through a hole this big (holding his index finger and thumb about a centimetre apart), as you can through a hole this big" (holding his hands about eight inches apart). I begged to differ, and I think time has probably proven me to be correct.

I arrived in Australia, jet lagged and alone, checked into a motel and attended the unit the following morning. There were actually three of us starting at that time, with the other two being from Switzerland and the USA. After filling in the inevitable paperwork, we were ushered in to see the great man.

Merv Cross was another inspirational character. An orthopaedic surgeon with a world-wide reputation in knee surgery, he had been raised in a small town, out in the middle of nowhere, in less than ideal circumstances. He had paid his way through medical school by playing professional rugby league. From there he had gone on to study sports surgery in the States, before returning to Sydney to set up his clinic, which rapidly developed into a unit with one of the best reputations in the country. He was also straight as a dye and wasn't shy of telling it like it is. I liked him a lot.

I was a bit surprised and disappointed to be told I would be working with one of the other surgeons in the unit, who had a special interest in ligament reconstruction. At that time nobody outside Australia had heard of him but, because of his technical brilliance, he has since gone on to be one of the world's leading figures in knee ligament reconstruction.

The first two weeks I was there, he was abroad attending a scientific meeting, so I had a bit of time to myself. This was very useful as I had to find somewhere to live. I ended up sharing an apartment with the Swiss surgeon, who had also left his wife back in his home country.

One of the Australian fellows in the unit had just been appointed to a consultant job in Perth and was getting ready to move out. He had done a huge study on patients who had just had a ligament recon-struction but told me he didn't need to actually publish it now he had his post.

This was too good to be true, and I offered to turn the raw data into a scientific publication, with his name as first author, which he was more than happy for me to do. I set to, sorted out the statistics and illustrations, and worked into the nights writing the scientific paper. I had it all ready for when my new boss returned.

There is a tradition in the UK, that when writing a scientific paper, the person who does the most work gets their name as the first on the list of authors (this is the most prestigious). The consultant, who has usually just had an advisory role, puts his name at the end of the list, and anyone else involved goes in between, in order of amount of input. When my new boss returned, I was summoned to his office.

"So... what have you been doing while I've been away?" Rather pleased with myself, I pushed the finished scientific paper across the desk to him. He looked at the title page.

"Well... The first thing that's wrong is, my name goes first." I struggled to take this on board, as he had put very little into the pro-cess. I made my protests and explained how things were usually done in the UK, but he wouldn't budge. I disliked him at that moment and our relationship has been "frosty" ever since. This was reinforced over the next few months by him repeatedly slagging off Merv behind his back, despite the fact it had been Merv who had given him a job when apparently no-one else would employ him.

I was determined the paper would never be published with his name first, so I hung on to the data, and when I left the unit at the end of six months, I downloaded the data onto floppy discs (how old am I!) and, as part of my "housekeeping", wiped it off the hard drive before I headed back to the UK.

About two months after I returned, the phone went off in the early hours of the morning, on a night when I wasn't on call.

"Steve... it's X" I sleepily told him it was two o'clock in the morn-ing, something I'm sure he was fully aware of.

"Oh, I'm sorry about that. What's happened to the data from that study?" I explained that I had "housecleaned" before I left, but still had the data on floppy discs.

"I need that data for my MD." I expressed my surprise at this, given that he hadn't been involved with the data collection or its' interpretation. After some discussion, I offered to return it if he signed a "letter of transmittal" confirming he was happy to submit the scientific paper I had written to a peer reviewed orthopaedic journal and returned it to me. I had him trapped between a rock and a hard place.

He somewhat reluctantly signed the letter and returned it, and I then sent him the data. The paper was accepted and published by a European orthopaedic journal, with the Australian fellow as the first author, myself as second and the boss, third and last. It's the only paper he doesn't mention in his online CV!

I learned a lot in Australia, particularly how far the UK was behind the rest of the world in our treatment of ligament injuries of the knee. In the early nineties, the general standards were rudimentary to say the least, resulting in a steady stream of our top sportsmen and women trekking across the Atlantic to have their surgery abroad. I returned to the UK determined to drag our management of the injured athlete into the twentieth century, just before we moved into the twenty-first, a few years later.

It was a bit of a come down to return to being a senior registrar, managing the plethora of problems coming in through the door, without having a specialist focus. In fact, it was nearly eighteen months later before I performed my first arthroscopic knee ligament reconstruction in the UK. As a senior registrar at that time, you could just keep going round and round the rotation of posts in the training programme until a job you felt suitable became available. There was no time limit, as there currently is today.

Another of the obligatory hoops you had to jump through on the way to a consultant post, was to have attended some form of "management course", so I signed up for the one run by the Regional Health Authority. This was a series of study days at the White Hart hotel in Harrogate, then actually owned and run by the Health Authority as a training facility. I didn't want to do it, but it was a necessity, so I duly turned up on the designated day. Little did I know that a few years down the track, this type of pointless exercise was going to become an integral part of consultant life.

The other attendees were all senior registrars from across the region, and from many different disciplines. To start the whole process, the management consultants running the course sat us all down in a big circle and asked us to say who we were, what was our speciality, state two qualities we thought made a good manager, and then name someone who exhibited those qualities.

As this slowly progressed around the seated circle, it was immediately obvious who were the other surgical trainees, by seeing who was getting increasingly impatient and irritated. There were several answers from trainees working in the more touchy-feely disciplines along the lines…

"I think to be a good manager, you need to be a good timekeeper with a sympathetic ear, and I would nominate my mother", which resulted in a few muttered "what a load of old bollocks" from the surgeons among us. Then it was my turn, so I thought I'd think out of the box, do some blue sky thinking, run my flag up the pole and see who saluted.

"Well… I think to be a good manager you have to be ruthless and be able to take tough decisions, and I would nominate the entire management staff at the Leeds General Infirmary, who balloted the staff as to whether to take the hospital into a Trust or not, and when eighty-five percent of the staff voted against, they did it anyway." The moderators weren't quite sure what to say, muttering a few "well, management can involve difficult decisions" type platitudes.

The people running the course clearly hadn't had a bunch like us before. They would set us one of the standard management problems (similar to the David Brent "fox, chicken and sack of grain") to solve and then disappear off, giving us forty-five minutes to come up with a solution. We were a bright, highly motivated bunch, entirely used to taking in and rapidly processing information. We had normally found the solution within five to ten minutes. We would then sit there for another forty minutes, chatting about how crap the training system was. The only useful things I took on board from the whole course were to always make notes before attending a meeting, and never go to a meeting without an agenda.

A job then came up in Sunderland for a consultant with a special interest in arthroscopic knee surgery, a post that had my name written all over it. At that time Sunderland was the "jewel in the crown" of the training programme in the North East and had an excellent reputation.

I made my enquiries and found there was not a single other surgeon in the entire North East carrying out surgery similar to that I had been trained to do. The unit seemed a happy and cohesive one, so I put in my application. I made the usual visit to the department to meet the other consultants and have a tour round, with everyone seemingly very welcoming. I was duly shortlisted and started practicing my answers to the standard, stock interview questions.

The day before the interview, I was attending yet another of the days of the management course in Harrogate, when I received a message asking me to ring one of the consultants at Sunderland. Puzzled as to what this could be about, I rang him.

"Yes… it's a bit embarrassing this, but we feel none of the candidates shortlisted are really what we want for the job and so, if you were successful, I'm not sure we could support your appointment." I was a bit shocked and asked him if he was trying to get me to withdraw from the interview, because that was actually illegal. He muttered an incoherent reply before ringing off.

I was absolutely furious, having let one or two other advertised posts go by, as I felt this was going to be the one for me. I rang one of my referees, who happened to be the professor of orthopaedics in Leeds. He exploded.

"What!!!! Are they saying a fully qualified Leeds trainee isn't good enough?!" He asked me to head home and wait by the phone. The phone lines went white hot, with messages of support from fellow trainees and previous bosses flying in. The last call I received was actually from the president of the Royal College of Surgeons, who spoke to me at length and insisted I attend the interview the following day.

The next day arrived and I travelled up to Sunderland and found myself sitting in a waiting room with the other two candidates who'd been through an identical experience. The college assessor came out and told us the interview panel were fully aware of what had happened the day before, confirming that they would definitely be appointing that day.

It turned out I was the successful candidate and was asked by the appointments panel if I would be willing to accept the job. I said I would, but on the proviso that I came and spoke to all my future colleagues the week after, making sure there would be no bad blood. If I was going to move to an unfamiliar part of the country and then be ostracised by my colleagues, it really would make life untenable.

I travelled home a bit unsure about it all, but happy I had finally made it all the way. I opened the front door, ready to get the champagne out of the fridge and celebrate, to be met by my wife sobbing uncontrollably. She had also had a job interview that day but had not been appointed to the supervisor role in her physiotherapy department and was inconsolable. It took a little bit of gloss off the occasion.

The following week I went back up to the hospital, chatted to all the consultants who, while a little embarrassed, didn't seem openly hostile. My wife and I then went on holiday with some friends to the Lake District for a week (arranged months before and purely coincidental), to mull things over.

When I returned home, there had been an official looking, brown envelope put through the letterbox, which contained a letter from the North East Area Health Authority saying that because interview protocols had been breached, they didn't feel they could ratify the appointment, but would be re-advertising the post and hoped I would reapply! Someone had been got at!

The powers that be at the colleges were not too impressed with this, and the hospital was banned from re-advertising the post for a period of twelve months. When they did eventually advertise again, no UK trainee applied as they had all heard about what had gone on.

Shortly after the Sunderland debacle, one of the consultants at Bradford announced he would be retiring. The unit was an odd one but had great potential, having a small orthopaedic hospital situated almost exactly halfway between Bradford and Leeds. As I saw things, it was a perfect location to develop a sports injury unit.

Once again, I jumped through the hoops, but this time was successful without any come back. At last, after all the years of hard work, I had finally made it. I wrote and posted a postcard to my previous boss in Rotherham, letting him know I had been appointed, went home and opened a bottle of champagne with my wife. This time we did celebrate together. The next chapter was about to begin.

A day at the seaside with the family.
Woollen swimming trunks knitted by my Nana! As they absorbed more
and more water the crutch ended up around my knees!

A rare happy memory with my father.
Winning the parent's race at school sports day,
in the days when there were winners and losers

Travels round the world, pre mobile phone and internet!
Muktinath in Nepal, Easter Island and Machu Picchu – cool shorts!

Receiving my "Fellow of the Royal College of Surgeons"
diploma at Lincolns In Fields in London.
The first hurdle on the way to becoming a consultant

Climbing demands your full attention.
Tarana in Australia and soloing one of my few new routes,
at Almescliffe Crag – "Envy of Angels"

*The last exam! The FRCSEd Orth specialist diploma in Orthopaedics.
I'd been taking regular exams from my schooldays into my early thirties!
Finally, I was on my way to becoming a consultant*

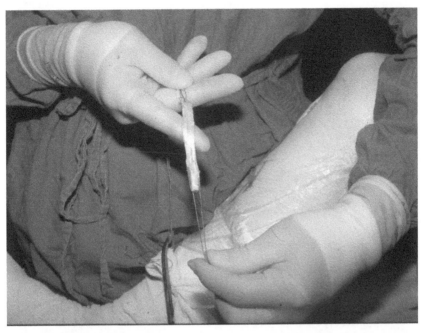

The surgery that made my limited fame and fortune.
A middle third patella tendon graft (the middle bit of the kneecap tendon),
to replace a torn anterior cruciate ligament

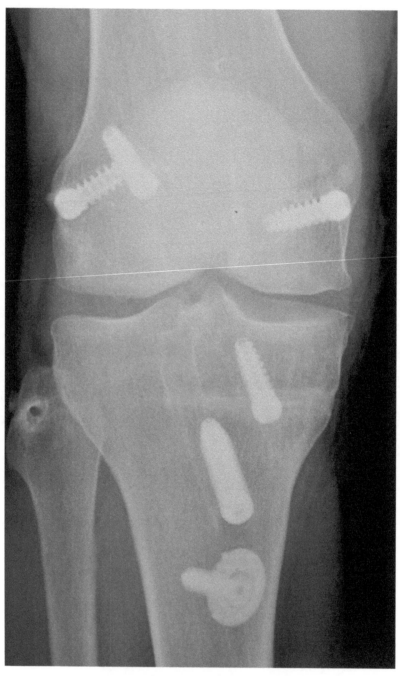

Sometimes, things get complicated!
Post-op X-ray following a reconstruction of a dislocated knee

Official Independent Singles Breakers Chart
Top 20
03 May 2015 - 09 May 2015

http://www.officialcharts.com/charts/in ... ers-chart/

1 6 2 Twayne - Nasty Freestyle (T-Wayne)
2 1 2 Markus Feehily - Love Is A Drug (Harmoney)
3 NEW 1 Bradford City FC & Never2Late - Everywhere We Go (Bradford City FC & Never2Late)
4 NEW 1 Armin Van Buuren & Mr Probz - Another You (Armada)
^another dumb mistake, Van Buuren has had TWO UK top 40/20 hits!! 😩 this is meant to be a chart of "unknowns" yet to break the top 40 singles/albums

5 7 3 Touch Sensitive - Pizza Guy (Future Classic)
6 5 83 Edward Sharpe and The Magnetic Zeros - Home (Rough Trade)
7 15 2 Pvris - St. Patrick (Rise)
8 8 4 Andy Grammer - Honey I'm Good (S-Curve)
9 NEW 1 BigBang - Loser (YG Entertainment)
10 4 6 Purity Ring - Bodyache (4AD)
11 14 8 Stormzy - Know Me From (Stormzy)
12 NEW 1 The Japanese House - Polls To Bathe In (Dirty Hit)
13 10 26 Family Of The Year - Hero (Nettwerk)
14 18 21 Sofia Karlberg - Crazy In Love (X5)
15 19 3 Syn Cole - It's You (Icons)
16 16 5 Tez Cadey - Seve (Roch Music)
17 11 2 Wolf Alice - Bros (Dirty Hit)
18 NEW 1 The Living Tombstone - Die In A Fire

Riding high in the charts with my band and Bradford City. Whatever happened to the guy eight places below us at number eleven?!

Swapping my scalpel for an axe. Playing Blues at The Blues Bar

*I was forty-two when I went on my first snow sports holiday.
For some reason I thought it would be cooler to learn to snowboard,
at a time when it was far from a mainstream activity. It was one of the
hardest and most painful things I've done! There's nothing like mountains,
snow, blue sky and sunshine – champagne for the soul*

7

DO THEY KNOW IT'S CHRISTMAS?

Christmas used to be a time of fun and excitement for those working in the NHS. It has now become almost just another working day, the patients served heated up turkey slices as part of an unappetising Christmas dinner, with the overstressed staff doing their best to jolly up the occasion.

In the days when I was a final year medical student in Birmingham, we were still expected to do a locum for the pre-registration house-man if they took their holiday during your ten-week attachment to either a general surgical or general medical firm. I happened to be scheduled to be with a general surgical firm at Dudley Road, a large teaching hospital in Birmingham, over the Christmas period, when the houseman contacted me to say he was taking two weeks off over Christmas and New Year, which fell on consecutive weekends. In fact, he'd done the dirty on me and swapped some of his weekends round so I was going to be on call on successive weekends, for both holidays.

Although this sounds a bit miserable, I had a great time! In those days every single patient that could be managed at home was discharged to be with their families, and no routine surgery (other than minor day cases) was admitted. This meant the ward I was looking after had the grand total of three patients staying in, who were all patients whose social circumstances didn't allow discharge. My daily ward round was fairly swift, leaving the rest of the day to enjoy what was on offer in the hospital.

For weeks before Christmas the wards would be selling stuffed toys and doing raffles to raise funds to look after the staff over the holiday period. The ward staff room would be festively decked out, and all sorts of goodies brought in for the nurses and doctors to enjoy.

On the ward I was attached to, the storage room for bags of intravenous fluids, dressings and other bits and bobs was emptied out, and the shelves filled with bottles of alcohol. Two bottles of whiskey, two bottles of brandy, two bottles of vodka, two bottles of sherry and in fact, pretty much every tipple you can think of. When you went to visit a patient on any ward in the hospital the first question was always "Can I get you a drink doctor?"

Every lunchtime of the week before Christmas, there was party in a different department in the hospital – radiology, switchboard, path lab, physio etc. This was a great way to get to meet and socialise with members of the backroom staff you would normally never come face to face with, and things always ran smoother afterwards when you could actually put a face to a name. By two o'clock in the afternoon a substantial proportion of the junior hospital doctors (except those with on call commitments) would be hammered but ready to carry on partying through the rest of the day and evening in the doctor's mess.

I had a great week, obtaining a degree of notoriety. The Sister on my ward was of Caribbean origin and very attractive. Although she was ten years older than me there seemed to be some mutual attraction, which may have been because she had an acrimonious split from her husband just a few months before.

After one of the lunchtime parties, and being a little worse for wear, I was sat in the ward office with her having a long heart to heart conversation. One thing led to another and before long we were in the drink's cupboard, carried away by passion. Things were getting close to the inevitable climax when suddenly the door opened behind me.

"Oops... sorry." said a soft female voice. The door was quietly closed, and we carried on. We never did find out the identity of our mysterious visitor, although the following day the incident seemed to be common knowledge around the hospital.

There was a certain Christmas tradition, which has now sadly died out, when every ward would cook their own turkey for Christmas dinner. It would then be wheeled, with great ceremony, into the centre of the ward and either the consultant, or the on-call senior registrar would do the honours and carve the bird for the patients.

One Christmas that I was working, the cooked turkey was wheeled onto the ward and the registrar was asked to do the honours. He had been somewhat over imbibing in the doctor's mess and was very, very drunk. He staggered forward, grasped the carving knife, closed one eye, took careful aim and plunged it into the top of the carcass. He then took a step back to admire his handiwork as the blade quivered in its vertical orientation. Then with a beatific smile on his face he slowly slid onto the floor and passed out, to a loud cheer and round of applause from the patients. He was put to bed in an unoccupied side-room and left to sleep it off.

This tradition still continued into my early consultant career. On Christmas Day at our little orthopaedic hospital, the Salvation Army would come in to play Christmas carols, the Mayor would visit, and the consultants and their families would go in to distribute presents to the patients.

Every year a local farmer would donate a huge turkey, and Sister would come in at two o'clock in the morning to put it in the oven in the hospital kitchen. This would then be brought onto the ward and one of the consultants would then proceed to carve. This all seems to have disappeared now, which I can't think is for the better.

Almost every department, ward and speciality would have a "Christmas Do" usually organised about six months before the festive season. As a senior registrar, one two-week spell before Christmas I went to eight different events, five of which were at the same venue, with the same menu, Christmas crackers, DJ and disco! Again, it was a great way of mixing with staff that you might not meet on a day to day basis and worked well as a team bonding exercise. These "Do's" have now all but disappeared.

One of the other great Christmas hospital traditions that has gone a similar way is the "Christmas Show". Every hospital had them and was a great way for the junior staff to let off steam and bring some of the more pompous senior members of staff down to earth.

About eight weeks before Christmas, a notice would go up in the doctor's mess announcing a meeting to discuss a show. Generally, about thirty or forty people would turn up to the first meeting which would quickly whittle down to a hard core of about twelve by about the third week. Scripts for comedy sketches and songs would be written, discarded, rewritten and honed to "perfection", then read throughs and rehearsals started.

In fact, there is a long tradition of medics in comedy. Graham Chapman (Monty Python), Graeme Garden (The Goodies), Harry Hill, Phil Hammond, Simon Brodkin (aka Lee nelson) and Adam Kay have all trod the wards before the boards.

My first participation in a Christmas show was at Stoke. I hadn't been one of the "In Crowd" as a student in Birmingham, so most of the stuff at medical school passed me by. At Stoke however, I had a fellow Cas officer who seemed to be on the same wavelength, and we wrote and rehearsed many of the sketches. Over a post rehearsal beer, he confessed to me that he had seriously thought about a career in the performing arts before entering medicine. He has since gone on to become a national authority on the management of bone tumours.

The night of the first performance arrived. The lights dimmed, the audience hushed, and the show started. I suddenly understood how people get hooked on show business. The feeling you get when the whole audience are roaring with laughter at material you've written, and then being applauded off stage, is like no other. After the final curtain call, I thought to myself, "I could do this for a living."

It was at Sheffield my performing career peaked. The Northern General hospital in Sheffield had a large social club which actually had a proper stage, with curtains and backdrops, giving the potential for putting on an almost professional show. In addition, we had a houseman who had an interest in dance and offered to choreograph any dance numbers. Also, amongst our ranks there were a couple of junior doctors who had previously been involved in amateur dramatics.

We had a number of booze-filled script writing meetings. Most of the stuff we wrote went into the bin the following morning, but some of what was left seemed of acceptable quality. These scripts were not only performed in Sheffield, but later went with various cast members as they moved with their jobs around the country, to be reprised into future years. We rehearsed regularly, becoming tighter and tighter knit as a group as we neared our run of three nights just before Christmas.

The shows were done to raise money for charity, so the audience didn't have high expectations, but they were a great way of pricking the pompous while having a laugh. The show ran for three consecutive nights and went down a storm. As word quickly spread that the show was actually quite good, more and more and more people turned up. On the third night, we were breaking the fire regulation capacity of two hundred and fifty by a considerable number.

Much of the material was pretty corny and obviously medically orientated. We had a sketch about the birth of twins, a song about haemorrhoids (where three of us wore white gowns and carried large red balloons which contained some fake blood – at the end of the barber's shop style piece "We're Your Piles", these were popped, spraying the front rows).

It may seem strange that haemorrhoids can be a source of humour, but the audience loved it!

"Though you don't know we're about,
We're there ready to pop out,
Don't forget we three...
For when we're out and swinging free,
That's when we itch like buggery,
Not only irritation then but heaven knows,
We'll show what pain's really like...
When...we...thrombose!"

At one part of the show we needed a front of curtain piece while the scenery was shifted, and stupidly I volunteered to do a monologue (I must have been very, very drunk at the time). It was a piece I had worked up based on a patient I'd been presented with as a casualty officer in Stoke, where at two o'clock in the morning a gentleman snuggled in a purple, nylon, Woolworths sleeping bag, and wearing a Stoke City bobble cap was brought in to the A&E department by ambulance.

When I asked him what the problem was, he proceeded to tell me.

"I've had a heart attack... I've had three before... so I know what's going on... the wife insisted I went to the hospital, but I've ten pounds hidden in the bottom of the sleeping bag to take a taxi home". He talked at me solidly for about fifteen minutes while I tried desperately not to laugh.

"I'm not coming in here to the coronary care unit. It's beep, beep, beep... beep, beep, beep all bloody night long, except sometimes it goes beeeeeeeep, the curtains get drawn round, a load of half dressed, half asleep doctors come charging in, jump up and down on someone, then ten minutes later it's "well we didn't win that one, fancy a pint in the mess?" Then the porters bring in the big grey metal box, draped in a cloth, pretending it's the tea trolley, and 'thump' he goes in it. Then they wheel him down to the morgue. Then... they draw back the curtains and you all stare at each other wondering... who's next!" He went on in similar vein to describe the various shortcoming of the hospital, and its different departments.

136

The first night I went out, the piece went down a storm. Everyone was laughing and cheering, and I came off buzzing to rapturous applause. The second night I went out and there was not a titter. I suddenly understood what it meant to "die" on stage and sweat poured down my back. It's a very, very lonely experience. Then suddenly, someone at back of the hall started laughing, and in a wave, it swept forward through the audience. I have never been so relieved.

One of the sketches involved a couple of ladies sat with a large shopping bag between them. Behind the middle of the curtains Richard, one of the SHOs, had his arm pushed between them and onto the bag, so it looked like the bag contained a dismembered limb. The ladies started talking, discussing that he didn't look well, and that he'd only gone in for an ingrowing toenail but there had been "complications".

Each night we identified a particular consultant that we wanted to have a go at, who was sitting somewhere near the front of the audience. Suddenly the arm would come to life, vigorously pointing at the audience.

"What's the matter George? Oh, it's that nice Mr. X... The one who did your operation!" The audience loved this. The hand would then start making obscene gestures.

"There's no need to be like that George, I'm sure he was doing his best" etc. etc.

On the last night we had secretly prepared a huge white arrow with "Dr Richard T..." on it. Richard's boss was in the audience and was the night's chosen victim. As Richard started to make some obscene gestures, one of the other SHOs sneaked out in front of the stage and held up the arrow. The audience erupted. Richard couldn't see what was going on, and thinking they were laughing at him, the gestures became even more vigorous and obscene!

I think we would have gotten away with it, except somebody had taken a video of the performance, and then put it on in the bar for the after-show party. As it got closer and closer to the "One Arm Sketch" the bar started to empty out.

As I tiptoed out, I heard Richard saying, "Oh, this is my bit, the audience loved it… hang on a moment what the hell is that? YOU BASTARDS!" By which time he was in splendid isolation.

The show had finished with a sketch based on "This is Your Life" but changed to "This Was Your Life", which gave us an opportunity to poke fun at consultants across the hospital. It started with two of the cast wheeling a big, grey mortuary trolley in from the back of the hall. Then the Eamon Andrews character jumped out from behind the curtains with the big red book, stopping them, flinging open the top and a zombie like character suddenly sitting bolt upright, shocking the audience. The story started…

"Mr. Higgins, you thought you were on the way to the mortuary for your postmortem. But tonight Mr. Higgins… This Was Your life." The story started with him attending A&E with a boil on the bum. After four hours of extensive tests and X-rays the casualty consultant Mrs. X (who had an awful reputation for being painfully slow) made the diagnosis and ordered the boil to be pricked. The third-year student nurse delegated to do the treatment, misheard the instructions, and he was admitted with third degree burns to his private parts. Everything sequentially went wrong, leading inevitably to his demise. It finished with a song and dance number based on Frankie Goes To Hollywood's number "Relax" but reworked into "Relapse (don't do it)".

I was working for the same boss as Richard, and we had unmercifully taken the piss out of him all the way through the show. I went into work the following morning, a little nervous as to how he would have taken it. He came into the office. I needn't have worried –

"That was brilliant! Best show I've ever seen. Well done!"

While Christmas can be a time of fun and laughter, it can also be a time of tears and dismay. Injury can be bad at any time but to happen on Christmas Eve or Christmas Day means the memories will recur every year. Working over the holiday can also sometimes be sad and difficult. When I was working in A&E, Boxing Day was also known as "Granny dumping day".

A family would turn up to visit Grandma on the annual visit, to find her living in squalor. Not infrequently they would then bundle her in the car, drive to A&E and try to get her admitted to the hospital. I thought one family were going to lynch me when, after finding nothing physically wrong with the very pleasant, but mildly confused grandmother, I suggested they should take her home and care for her. Their attitude was that it was the NHS that should take over the responsibility of care for their mother, as they had other commitments and were too busy to look after her.

I'll never forget working on Christmas Eve at St James hospital in Leeds, when I was called down to A&E to see a young man who had been injured in the train yards in town. Somehow or other he had managed to get his feet on the rails as a shunting wagon went past, crushing both his feet.

He'd had plenty of morphine by the time I got down to see him and seemed quite cheerful. His feet were screened off by a large green towel. I raised it to inspect the damage. His feet resembled something from a Tom and Jerry cartoon, being about two centimetres thick and both about the size of dinner plates, a mangled mess of blood, bone and work boot. I spoke to him as kindly as I could.

"I'm sorry mate, these can't be saved. We're going to have to amputate them." He protested and asked if there was nothing else that could be done. I asked him if he'd actually seen the injury, which he hadn't. I explained it was probably a good idea for him to see the damage, and then he could get his head round the necessity of the surgery.

I told him to take a deep breath and lifted up the green towel. He looked down at his mangled feet with a puzzled expression, I don't think quite believing what he was seeing, then sighed and passed out. I was able to save his heel and ankle making the amount of amputated tissue less dramatic, and so some eight week later, he was walking on his new prosthetic feet. Not quite what he had probably asked Father Christmas for.

8

THE PRETENDER

The Early Consultant Years

I n the early 1990's consultant status was actually worth something. You were effectively an independent practitioner with professional autonomy, working within a massive organisation and were allowed to organise your working life in the way you wanted it. You automatically received enormous respect and could treat patients with whatever you thought was best for them. I didn't have to obtain a GP's permission to refer a patient to a colleague who I thought was better suited to treat them, and if I wanted a state of the art piece of kit to treat a specific condition, I just asked sister to get it for a particular operating list and it would appear, without having to fill in endless bits of paperwork.

I would drive up to our little orthopaedic hospital to do a ward round and there was a parking space with my name on it by the front entrance. I would walk through the door to be welcomed by the receptionist, sat at a large wooden desk, who would greet me by name and tell me he would let the ward know I was there. As I set off for the ward, I would hear him on the phone telling them I was on my way.

When I arrived at the ward, there would be a notice board outside saying "No Admittance. Ward Round in Progress". On the ward the whole team was assembled – Sister, Staff Nurse, physiotherapist, occupational therapist, radiographer, senior registrar, senior house officer and secretary. All the patients would be tucked up in bed, and all the notes and X-rays would be ready for inspection.

We would then slowly go round the patients, taking time to talk to them all, showing them their X-rays, listening to any cares and concerns, discussing their treatment and making whatever decisions needed to be made. The secretary would take all this down in shorthand, ready to type it up in the notes.

After the round we would all sit down in Sister's office and be joined by a Sister from theatre (who was my own, designated scrub Sister, responsible for making sure everything I needed would be there), and over tea and biscuits discuss any problems, who was going to be discharged and when, who was coming in for surgery the following week, and any specific equipment I might need.

Fast forward twenty odd years. I would walk on to the ward and a harassed looking nurse would look up from a computer screen and tell me "Your patients are in bay five". My SHO would be on "compensatory days off", so I would go to see them on my own, have a futile and frustrating hunt for the appropriate notes and X-rays, see the patients and then walk back down to the nurse's station. The same harassed nurse would look up and ask me if there was anything they needed to know about. I know which system I preferred!

Starting as a consultant held no fears for myself or my peers. All that happened was the name on the end of the patient's bed changed. We had all been practicing pretty much independently for years. The consultant I took over from was technically excellent and a great decision maker, so I wasn't left with a trail of disasters to sort out. In fact, he'd stopped seeing new patients some twelve months before, as he had a year long waiting list for surgery and didn't want to see patients, agree a treatment plan, and then not be able to carry it out. He gave me only two pieces of advice – "Always offer a patient a second opinion before they demand it." and "Beware of knee replacements that require you to replace the patella (kneecap)." both of which I've rigidly adhered to.

The day I started I went down to my secretary's office to find out if there were any patients left for me to sort out. I started with only one patient on my waiting list, my predecessor had cleared everything else. I then went down to the outpatient manager's office to sort out how I wanted my clinics to run. She looked a little concerned, took me into her office and opened a large drawer in a filing cabinet.

"These are the outstanding referrals." For the previous twelve months the hospital had just been putting all the referrals made to the previous consultant into the drawer – there were hundreds of them. It took me days to sort through them and put them into some sort of prioritised list. I then started seeing them at twenty every week.

The one patient left for me to sort out surgically was an odd character who'd been involved in a nasty road traffic accident which had left him with multiple fractures. When I took over his care, he had been on our "convalescent" ward at the orthopaedic hospital for four months. I think my predecessor had left him there because he couldn't stand him. He was one of those odd, abrasive characters who, despite verging on being educationally subnormal, thought he knew the answers to everything, and had a knack for rubbing people up the wrong way.

His time hadn't been completely wasted as one of the nurses had taken him under her wing and taught him to tell the time, and to read and write. When I took over his care, he still had two fractures, of his arm and shin, that hadn't joined up. I managed to sort out the arm, but the shin fracture defied all attempts to get it to heal.

I asked one of my senior colleagues to have a look at him and he said he would be happy to take over his management. I'd warned him that the patient was an odd character, but he told me he didn't find anything unusual about him. He changed his mind shortly afterwards though, when a week after he had operated on his leg, the patient went for a swim in a duck pond and the whole thing became badly infected with a really unusual organism.

The department, as previously mentioned, was a slightly odd one. When I arrived, two of the consultants hadn't spoken to each other for over ten years, they both hated the third, and the fourth was just very odd. Our monthly departmental meetings used to leave me feeling I'd wandered into a mad house. Management loved it as they knew the department would, on principle, never all agree about anything, and we were controlled along "divide and conquer" lines.

When I started, my operating lists would have everything on them from bunions to spinal and shoulder surgery, but after I told my colleagues I would be happy to take all the knee and ankle injuries, I very quickly became overwhelmed with the sheer volume of this work and, by default, became a "sub-specialist". I was very happy with this, as I'd always believed the concept of "sub-specialisation" would be of benefit to the patient, something which has subsequently happened all across the health service and in almost every speciality.

Initially I developed my arthroscopic (keyhole surgery) skills down multiple avenues, introducing techniques such as ankle, shoulder and elbow arthroscopy to Yorkshire. For a sports surgeon at that time, the ankle was the most useful addition to my armamentarium, as problems with this joint were common in both footballers and rugby players and dealt with in a similar fashion to many problems in the knee. For shoulders, the development of instrumentation, to do much in the way of surgical repair, would come much later.

Not long after starting at Bradford, I received an invitation to attend a meeting from a firm of developers. They were planning to build a seventy thousand all seater stadium, with a retractable roof, on the site of the Bradford Bulls ground at the top of the M606 at Odsal. The main reason for this location was that they had worked out that there were twenty-two million people living within a two-hour drive of this site.

I had been invited because they planned to have a specialist sports injury centre of excellence in one of the four corner towers and were hoping to attract professional sportsmen and women from around the country. The project continued for a couple of years before finally petering out. Several other doctors and myself spent many hours working on the logistics and planning of the service, all of which was unpaid. The management consultants had very cynically used our enthusiasm for effectively free consultancy. Over the years It was just one of several projects that I was invited to be involved in that never went anywhere.

About twelve months into my job, I went away on a short holiday to return and find that management (despite all the promises I had been made prior to my appointment) had announced our specialist orthopaedic hospital was going to be closed. This was terrible disappointment, as my vision had been to develop it as a top-class NHS sports injury unit.

The orthopaedic department, together with many patients who had been treated there, fought a bitter campaign against the closure. We put together a professional business plan and hand delivered it to the non-executive members of the hospital board the night before the meeting to ratify the closure.

From the local press coverage, management had given the impression that the whole department were fully behind their plans, which was a long way from the truth. I'd love to have been a fly on the wall at that meeting. The plans were put on hold for further consultation, and the closure was delayed by eighteen months. Our fight was doomed to failure because of the then political will, but the chief executive never forgave us. We were moved into inadequate "temporary facilities", which we were still in ten years later, and our department was starved of funds for years to come.

At that point, I was approached by the Leeds General Infirmary to see if I might be willing to jump ship and set up a sports injury unit on the north Leeds, Chapel Allerton hospital site as the "White Rose" centre. Once again, I was involved in multiple planning meetings with their management over the next eighteen months, including writing the job description for the post. I made very sure I would have been the only person in the country to be able meet the exacting job specifications.

The night before the job advert was going to appear in the British Medical Journal, some political manoeuvring went on in the main hospital and the sports injury surgeon post suddenly turned into a joint replacement post and all the previous plans were ditched. My hopes, dreams and ambitions were once again dashed.

While this was all happening, I had been quietly getting on with developing my practice and my reputation as a sports injury surgeon was slowly taking off. The first club to approach me was the Keighley Cougars rugby league club, whose physio had heard about me and arranged to have a chat about how we could look after their injury problems.

He was actually one of the nicest people I've ever met, and we have remained firm friends ever since. He was an extremely good physiotherapist and we learned a lot from each other. Physiotherapy was often a "black hole" to many orthopaedic surgeons, who sent patients for the dark arts of "physio" without having any real understanding of what went on, something you just cannot do if you treat professional players.

Not long after the Cougars, my first football club, Bradford City, came to me as they had been very unhappy about the previous surgeon who had looked after them. I was slowly finding my way through the minefield of looking after professional players, where you not only have to deal with the ego of the patient, but also club physios and doctors, managers, club chairmen and, worst of all, agents who had the reputation of being the "spawn of the devil".

The very first player Bradford City brought to me had a nasty sprain of his ankle. Research at the time had shown that the best way of treating these was to tape up the ankle for support, and get them going as early as possible, within the limits of pain and swelling. Ten days later he was back with an ankle like a balloon. I was surprised and somewhat worried, as it should have been substantially better by that time. I asked him what had been going on.

It turned out things had been going well and he was back walking almost normally when he ran into the manager in a corridor at the ground. The "gaffer" had asked him how things were going but then told him what he needed to do was to hop up and down on the injured ankle until the pain went away. I asked the player if it had hurt and he told me it was excruciating at first, but after a couple of minutes the pain did indeed improve. The following morning, however, it was massively swollen again and much, much more painful, hence his return visit.

I explained that whatever the manager said, this wasn't a brilliant way to treat ankle sprains and we were now back at square one. We restarted his rehab programme, but I was staggered when he turned up another ten days later, having bumped into the manager again, who had repeated the previous performance. In the end he was out for nearly three months instead of six to eight weeks.

This was not an uncommon situation. The manager of another Yorkshire football club had the approach that if you could walk, you could join in full training, with nothing in between. The club physio spent much of his time making sure the manager never set eyes on the players he was caring for.

This type of problem was widespread, with many managers feeling they knew what was best for their players, because they had been players themselves, and not because they had any coaching or medical qualifications. Several years later, I was giving a lecture at the annual Football Association medical meeting at Lilleshall, and asked the assembled audience of club physios and doctors, "Who has seen a player adversely affected or injured by something the manager has insisted on doing?" About seventy percent of the audience put their hands up. One can only wonder what the costs of delayed return to playing, for highly paid professionals for the various clubs would have been, for something that was entirely avoidable.

Perhaps surprisingly, one of the better managers I came across at handling players injuries was Peter Reid. Despite his robust reputation and colourful use of the English language, his approach was to write injured players completely out of his plans until the medical team said they were definitely ready to return. There was never any pressure applied to rush a player back, or complaints if a player was perceived to be taking a long time to recover. The medical team felt it was because when Peter had been a player, he had suffered from being made to play too early after injury and didn't want to do the same to those within his care.

Training in Rugby League at that time was much more scientific. Several of the coaches had come over from Australia, and they in turn had absorbed their training programmes from American Football. Certainly, lower league football was way, way behind, with many of the managers appointed because of their successful careers in playing the game, but actually having no formal coaching qualifications. They tended to coach the players in the same way they had done their own training, with little regard to the consequences of bad practice.

Dealing with managers was a hard-won art. To be fair, they have a difficult job with, every Saturday, a stadium full of fans thinking they all know how to do the job better. Over the years, the tenure of each job seems to be getting shorter and shorter, and not surprisingly many seem to feel very paranoid about their position.

I was effectively one of the back-room team at Bradford City and came to know one or two of the managers quite well. In the days before fitness trainers and sports scientists I was happy to give advice if requested. I'd actually published a book on training, and while not about football, many of the principles were transferable.

One season, having just avoided relegation, I popped down to see Chris Kamara with a copy of the Bradford Telegraph and Argus containing the season's stats. I pointed out that the previous season we had conceded ninety percent of goals against us in the last five minutes of the first half and the last ten minutes of the second and asked him what he thought this implied.

"...They're not fit enough?" I agreed this was what it seemed to show, and we started to talk about the pre-season programme. I explained that to get properly fit takes a minimum of six weeks, and that the then standard preseason programme of a month with a few friendlies, didn't really fit the bill. I presented him with a five-page document "Thoughts on training and injury prevention" which I had put together at home.

"Right Steve. If that's what you think, that's what we will do." I wasn't very popular with the squad, as they were all called back from their holidays a couple of weeks early and really put through their paces. Wayne Jacobs (a great Bradford City player) told me it was the hardest pre-season he'd ever experienced.

It paid off though. Bradford City had a flying start and were top of the division for the first six weeks. Chris recently told me that because of that fantastic run, he was invited to appear as a pundit by Sky television, the start of his long association with the channel, where he now is a regular presenter on a variety of different shows, as well as his unforgettable pop-up appearances, giving snippets of live commentary, on a Saturday afternoon. I hope you'll forgive me Chris, but your brilliance on TV eclipses your record as a football manager!

Chris took the club on a great run winning the last game of the season to sneak into the play-offs. In the play-offs Bradford lost 0-2 at home against Blackpool but then, against all the odds, beat them 3-0 in the away leg. Bradford City then ended up in the play-off final against Notts County at the old Wembley stadium. It was another unforgettable day. One of the most outstanding features of that day was the organisation in getting thirty thousand Bradford fans down to the big city.

The relatively unknown (at that time), managing director of the club, Shaun Harvey, commandeered almost every available coach in Yorkshire. From the early hours of the morning, thousands of fans arriving at Valley parade were marshalled on to the available transport, and as each bus was full, off they went. There was an almost solid line of coaches stretching the entire length of the M1. It was an unbelievable logistical achievement. It had always seemed to me that Shaun had the right stuff. He rose through the ranks to later become the chief executive of the English football league.

The day of the play off final was a lovely sunny day and standing on the terrace between the old twin towers and gazing down Wembley way, there was just a restless sea of claret and amber, as hordes of Bradford fans made their way to the game. The noise inside was deafening, completely drowning out the eleven thousand Notts County fans, and spurring the team on to victory. After the presentation ceremony, "Simply The Best", raucously belted out by over thirty thousand fans was a spine tingling moment I'll never forget.

As is the fate of many managers, a few bad results, and the chairman reflexly reaches for the exit button. Chris was replaced by Paul Jewell, who I knew quite well as I'd treated him as a player. After one home game, before he was appointed, the chairman had asked me for my opinion as to whether I thought Paul could do the job. I told him I thought he was very capable and was sure he would make a good fist of it. Fortunately, this turned out to be the correct prediction, as Paul took the club up into the Premiership – heady days.

The first week Paul was in post, I went down to see him taking him a couple of books I thought he might find useful. One was a tome on team building and the other was called "Dealing With Difficult People". Paul went on to a very successful career in football management at Bradford City and other football league clubs. When I met him several years later, he told me that "Dealing With Difficult People" was one of the most useful texts he'd ever read!

Football is a funny old world and judging by the serial corruption scandals affecting various levels the game, it definitely has its murky side. As a team surgeon or doctor, one of the jobs you get asked to do is to perform a pre-signing medical on potential signings, to advise the club buying the player of any potential risk. I was pretty naive to start with. One manager of a Yorkshire club bought a lot of players who would duly turn up at the clinic for their pre-signing medical. I would examine them, look at their scans and x-rays and then ring the physio to say they were a very high risk and my advice would be don't touch them with a barge pole. I would then be driving home and hear on the radio "** have signed ** for £2.8 million".

After this had happened two or three times, I rang up the physio.

"*, what is going on? I keep telling you the players are crocked and you keep signing them!"

"Aah… but what you don't realise Steve, is the transfer fee includes three hundred thousand pounds in agent's fees and a hundred thousand of that will go straight into the manager's bank account in the Cayman Islands." I have no idea whether that was true, but it might have provided an explanation.

Slowly and steadily, more and more clubs turned up, asking me to look after their squads. It was purely word of mouth among the club physios, doctors and players that brought them to my door. I have never approached any club asking for their work, they have always come to me. I must have been doing something right as they started to come from further and further afield, from Plymouth up to Aberdeen and Liverpool to Hull. Sounds like a lot of travelling for the players, but I was certainly closer for the clubs than Colorado, although my quiet corner of Bradford may perhaps have been seen as a less glamorous location.

In my junior career I'd always had to hide my interest in sports injuries, as they were looked on with disdain by many of my bosses, with the predominant attitude that it was all self-inflicted. I was listening to a conversation between one boss and a patient who liked to run reasonably long distances. I could tell just from the story he had something called "iliotibial band friction syndrome", a pain that generally develops on the outside of the knee after running a few miles. The consultant wasn't very sympathetic. He summed things up to the patient…

"So… this pain only comes on after you have run three or four miles?" The patient confirmed that was indeed correct.

"Well, good god man, if you have a headache you don't bang your head against the wall!" And the patient was dismissed, not even sent for physiotherapy which would frequently have sorted the problem out.

The tide though was slowly turning, and at a meeting of the British Association for Surgery of the Knee in 1993, it was proposed we needed a specialist organisation for sporting injuries. This was the founding of the British Orthopaedic Sports Trauma Association (BOSTA later changed to BOSTAA when we found out BOSTA meant "dung" in Portuguese!). I had spoken briefly at the meeting in support of this.

A couple of weeks later I was on a ward round at the Woodlands Orthopaedic hospital, when I received a message that David Dandy (the surgeon who'd operated on my knee when I was a registrar, and who would later go on to become president of the Royal College) wanted to speak to me on the phone. Somewhat puzzled as to what it could be about, I took the call in the office.

"Steve, Frank (Horan the then editor of the Journal of Bone and Joint Surgery) and I have been chatting. We wonder if you would like to take the post of academic secretary of BOSTA.". I was surprised and extremely flattered and told him I'd love to take the post. My feelings of elation were somewhat flattened when he followed up with, "Yes... We don't want any of those district general types involved." Clearly, he was under the impression I was working in the teaching hospitals in Leeds, rather than a district general hospital in one of the most socially deprived areas in the country. I didn't have the heart to disillusion him and became determined to show them I could do a good job.

I worked hard and think I made a great success of it. I found I had a talent for obtaining sponsorship for academic meetings from orthopaedic product companies and our bank account moved steadily into the black as, at the same time, we developed our reputation for being a serious organisation. I went on to be academic secretary for four years and then later, President for four years from 2004-2008.

On the NHS front, in my early years as a consultant, I developed a bit of a jaundiced view of my colleagues from around the region (and beyond), as I used to spend at least thirty percent of my time re-doing surgery that had been done badly elsewhere. Knee ligament surgery is not difficult to do but is very unforgiving in that an error of only a few millimetres in placing the new ligament and it won't work from day one. Most of the cases I saw had failed because of technical error, some of it fairly gross. As a famous American knee surgeon once said, "Nothing is so bad you cannot make it worse by surgery". My personal philosophy was fairly simple. Put the new ligament where God put the original. Who was I to argue with eight million years of evolution?

I famously (in orthopaedic circles!) screwed up my chances of ever getting on to the lecture circuit in America when I was speaking at a meeting in the Midlands. The faculty included several world-famous surgeons from the States, and I had been asked to speak on "ACL Reconstruction in Elite Sport". I had looked at the list of names and wondered how I, working in a district general hospital in one of the poorest areas of the country, could possibly make an impression on such a stellar faculty from a string of elite units. I started my lecture with.

"Hi, thanks for inviting me to speak. I think I'm here to represent the third world... Yorkshire. ACL reconstruction is not a difficult operation to do... but is a really easy operation to fuck up." I hadn't anticipated the look of horror on my Stateside colleagues faces that I should use such a profanity. It almost stopped me in my tracks. The Brits in the audience all laughed but I hadn't realised just quite how prissy the Americans could be!

A typical example of how awful the treatment that some people were receiving at that time was a twenty-two-year-old girl who came up from Birmingham to see me in my NHS clinic. Eighteen months before she had ruptured her anterior cruciate ligament in her knee playing at a fairly high level of netball. Her injury had actually been picked up at quite an early stage and a surgeon had reconstructed her ligament but, despite extensive rehabilitation and physiotherapy, fourteen months later she had never regained her normal range of movement. She was about twenty degrees short of fully straightening her knee, could only bend it to about sixty degrees, and this had devastated her life. The knee was certainly stable, but so is a joint if you put a large steel pin across it. One of my favourite lines when lecturing was, "Any damn fool can stabilise a knee by restricting the range of movement."

The surgeon treating her had dismissed her concerns with the comment "You wanted a stable knee and you've got one." and discharged her from his care. His level of arrogance staggered me. In desperation, she had somehow found me (I think through the physio word of mouth network), as a sorter out of other people's cock ups.

A plain X-ray of her knee provided the answer as to what was causing her problem. In an operation where the acceptable margin of error in placing the new ligament is about two millimetres, her ligament was about one and a half centimetres from where it should have been.

You're never quite sure how easy it is going to be to get out the old screws and staples, and I wanted her to get back her normal range of movement before redoing her operation. I explained I would have to do the operation in two stages, and that I couldn't guarantee a perfect result, but she was absolutely desperate to have her knee back to something like normal.

The first stage of her surgery was uncomplicated, with the screws, staples and badly placed ligament coming out without any real difficulties. She went back to Birmingham for her post-op rehabilitation and was readmitted about four months later (after follow-up by phone with her physio), for her ligament reconstruction to be done again.

I went down to the ward to have a chat to her before the operation. She burst into tears and it took a minute or two for her to calm down enough for her to speak (I don't normally have that effect on my patients!). In the period between her first operation and readmission she had regained her full range of movement and muscle strength, and now was absolutely terrified that she would go back to the state she had been when I first saw her.

I reassured her that while I couldn't guarantee anything, I didn't think it was likely to happen again. Her surgery was straightforward, and she had a great result, with a both a functionally stable knee and a full range of movement. For a long time afterwards, she sent me a Christmas card every year thanking me and telling me that everything was still OK.

One of the paradoxes of redoing ligament reconstructions is that the more badly done the original operation, the easier it is to redo, as the correct sites of where you have to place the new ligament are often untouched. If you know what you're doing, this makes the surgery pretty straightforward and the result similar to that as if the operation was being done for the first time. All I did was to do the operation as it should have been done in the first place.

Patients, however, think you're some sort of miracle worker, as they have had a badly functioning knee and disability for a long time. They had usually been referred for repeated courses of pointless physiotherapy and sometimes even had repeated arthroscopies, before the surgeon finally acknowledged that something wasn't right and admitted defeat. Another of the peculiarities of ligament reconstruction is that if it is done wrong, it generally doesn't work from day one. When we looked at a large series of patients referred following unsuccessful ACL surgery, over seventy percent of them had realised it wasn't right from the moment they first got out of bed after the operation.

It's a difficult thing for a surgeon when things don't go as planned. There are all sorts of conflicting thoughts running through your mind. There is the worry you have let the patient down and the difficulties of sitting in front of one of your patients and explaining their operation hasn't been successful. This sometimes goes well, but sometimes can result in a torrent of abuse and recrimination. In addition, there is always the spectre of litigation.

No operation works one hundred percent of the time, and no operation is without complications. Every surgeon has a portfolio of failures, don't believe anyone who says they haven't. Sadly, it is what people tend to remember you by. As I once said to Ben Foster when I was redoing his failed ACL reconstruction (done elsewhere), "Goalkeepers and surgeons have one thing in common. All anybody ever remembers you for is the things that go wrong!"

Personally, I have always found the best policy is to front up as soon as you realise something isn't right, and then offer solutions to try and sort the problem out. People generally appreciate honesty. The thing that really upsets patients is when they later find out a surgeon (or physician) has known something isn't right for a long time but has been desperately hiding the truth.

Knee injuries were very badly dealt within the health service, despite having been shown to be the commonest injury causing long term disability from work. It often takes a long time for the problem to be diagnosed. Why that should be is a mystery to me, as a few well-chosen questions usually provide the diagnosis without even having to examine the patient.

In the early part of my consultant practice I was helped enormously by Paul Gascoigne very publicly rupturing his anterior cruciate ligament, live on TV, in a lunging tackle on Garry Charles in the 1991 FA Cup final. There was a blaze of publicity about his injury and treatment, with a TV special and countless articles in the newspapers, including a big piece in the Sunday Times magazine. To tell a patient "You've done a Gazza" immediately brought home the consequences of their injury.

I had some sympathy for the surgeon involved in his care, as the post-operative X-ray of his work was on the front cover of the Sunday Times magazine. Since then I have been at numerous lectures on anterior cruciate ligament reconstruction when, almost inevitably, the picture from the Sunday Times comes up on the screen as an example of a somewhat less than technically perfect reconstruction operation.

A story of a twisting injury of the knee, hearing or feeling a pop or snap, an inability to carry on playing, and swelling within six hours, has a ninety percent predictive value for having ruptured your anterior cruciate ligament. Despite about ninety percent of victims having this story of injury, the diagnosis often seemed to be missed.

I was one of the two authors of a scientific paper published in 1996, "Rupture of the Anterior Cruciate Ligament – A Quiet Epidemic". This showed that in the patients I saw who I thought had an obvious rupture of their ACL, the diagnosis was made by the original treating doctor in less than ten percent of cases, eighty-five percent of them had been to casualty and been discharged (usually after a "normal" X-ray), and the mean time before the diagnosis was eventually made was twenty-two months. I'm not sure this has improved a lot, even with our current, almost universal, access to MRI scanning (MRI scans are not infallible – for most knee problems they are about eighty-five percent sensitive and specific, meaning one in six scans is misleading).

I was still very unsure of where I stood in the world of ligament surgery, at a time when a steady stream of our elite footballers limped off to the States for their surgery, as this was perceived as "the best in the world". I went off to an American Academy of Orthopaedic Surgeons meeting in New Orleans, really to try and get a handle on the level I was operating at, and whether there was anything I should be doing that I wasn't.

It was an astonishing meeting, with an attendance of close to twenty-five thousand orthopaedic surgeons from around the globe. Interestingly, I was told one of the logistical problems was that they ran out of room to park people's private jets at the airport – not something that is generally a problem at the annual meeting of the British Orthopaedic Association!

It was also a great place for a meeting if you are into live music, and I spent many a happy hour late into the night, in small bars with tiny stages, blown away by the quality of the bands and some sensational guitar playing. I developed a biphasic lifestyle, getting up at six thirty, going to the meeting, coming back late afternoon and sleeping for three or four hours, going down to Bourbon Street, drifting from bar to bar, getting back at three in the morning, sleeping for three hours and repeat! This went on for over a week. When I returned to the UK I was completely (if happily) shattered.

While I was at the meeting, I went to almost every session on ligament reconstruction and was reassured to find that the techniques I was using were state of the art. I was surprised that, even in the USA in their big specialist units, they had a significant number of complications and failures. I returned to the UK in the knowledge that the group of us who had trained abroad and returned to the NHS, were every bit as good as the fabled names in the States. All we needed to do now was to prove it.

To help this process I set up a small internet group so we could exchange information and ideas, as well as ask for input if unsure what to do with unusual problems. To be part of this group you had to have a major interest in knee surgery and, most importantly, a decent sense of humour. At the time, this meant a thorough knowledge of all the catchphrases from the then very popular "Fast Show". Those of us who were originally part of this group have all risen to the top of the tree in our field, with several having international reputations.

Rehabilitation was also fairly rudimentary and a bit of a "dark art". The rehab programme after surgery for ligament reconstruction varied enormously across our region, from being on crutches and in plaster for six weeks, to immediate full weight bearing, and everything in-between. As I was treating patients from across Yorkshire, I felt there was a real need to standardise things. I invited physiotherapists from across the region to a meeting to try and work out an acceptable rehabilitation programme following anterior cruciate reconstruction.

It was one of the most terrifying afternoons of my life. Just me, a white board, and twenty-eight physios from all across the Ridings. Physios can be scary people (I know, I was married to one), and their practice was a bit of a mystery to most orthopaedic surgeons. It took a few hours of discussion, but we eventually reached agreement on the "West Yorkshire ACL Rehab Programme", which is still in widespread use today.

In 1997 I was invited back to give a lecture at the annual Football Association meeting at Lilleshall, entitled "Why don't some knee operations work?", based on my experience of sorting out other people's failures. The audience largely consisted of club doctors and physios from around the country, and I don't think it did me any harm.

Niall Quin was a centre forward for Sunderland at the time and had previously had an anterior cruciate reconstruction of his knee at another hospital in the North East (before you say anything this isn't breaching confidentiality – any of these facts are out there in the media!), but sadly was having nothing but trouble.

Niall was a tall, rangy forward who was a brilliant hold up player and was great at winning headers to pass on to his fellow forward. To do this, he had to be able to prop off that leg and following his operation he was unable to fully straighten the knee, so lacked the power and speed he needed. He had already undergone a further arthroscopy (a keyhole operation to look inside the knee) which had apparently not found anything amiss.

One of the Sunderland physios had been at my lecture at the FA meeting, and in desperation they brought Niall down to see me. At that stage he was preparing to retire and had lined up a job with an Irish newspaper. I felt all the problems were due to him being unable to fully straighten his knee out, and suggested he let me look in his knee again. He wasn't desperately enthusiastic about the prospect, but felt he had nothing to lose.

There were no major problems with the reconstruction, but the front of the new ligament had a build-up of scar tissue and bone which were blocking the knee as it was straightening. It was a relatively straightforward thing to sort this out by shaving out the excess tissue. A couple of months later he was back playing, back to his normal high standard and, at a game at QPR, hit the bar three times, had two goals disallowed and scored the winner. He went on to enjoy a great finish to his career, becoming a Sunderland legend with an astonishing goal scoring partnership with Kevin Phillips. He still owes me a promised curry for getting him back playing!

It couldn't have happened to a nicer bloke. They used to say there were only two nice people in football, Niall Quinn and David O'Leary, both of whom I am lucky enough to have worked with. The following year, Niall scored a goal a game for the first ten or eleven games of the season and was interviewed by Garry Lineker on Football Focus. He related the tale of his injury problems, mentioning that it had been me (by name) that had managed to restore him to playing at his best.

The following week, my private secretary's phone almost melted, with dozens of calls coming in from all over the country. It was a bit of a sad time, as patients with complicated problems and bad results from their previous surgery, who kept telling me I was their last hope, came to see me. Unfortunately, many of them were beyond the scope of my meagre skills to make better, and I had to tell a lot of them that there wasn't an operation that I could do to return their knees to normal.

Garry McCallister injured his knee playing for Coventry City in December 1997, some eight months before the World Cup, when he would have been representing Scotland as their captain, leading the team out in the opening game against Brazil in front of eighty thousand spectators. As was often the case at that time, the first surgeon treating him decided that they would try and return him to playing without surgery. However, the first time he tried the knee out and turned on it, it gave way and the reality that it wasn't going to be right hit home.

I reconstructed his cruciate in the February of 1998, and he went on to an uncomplicated recovery, the story of which appeared in the papers as "Banishing the Nightmare of Injury". He then went from strength to strength and a few years later won the "Man Of The Match" in the UEFA cup final, playing for Liverpool. It always gives me a sense of quiet satisfaction when a player I've fixed returns to playing on the pitch, and my office walls were covered with signed pictures from grateful patients.

As a lad growing up in Manchester, there were a whole group of us from my school who used to go to every home game at Old Trafford and stand in the Stretford End, which in those days only had a roof over the back third. We stood there in rain or shine, backs to the crush barriers, when the United team had such legends as Bobby Charlton, George Best and Dennis Law playing for them. There wasn't a prawn sandwich in sight! Like most people, the club you grew up with is the one you hold in your heart forever.

In 1999, Wes Brown injured his knee. Manchester United had an orthopaedic surgeon who had looked after them for many years but was very old school, and Wes really didn't take to him. The club doctor rang me and asked if I could take over his care, which I was only too happy to do. I saw him, reconstructed his knee and when he returned to playing, sat there thinking, "I've successfully treated a Manchester United player, I've really made it!"

Eighteen months later he bust the ACL in his other knee and came back to me to have that fixed as well. Wes went on to a long and successful career, making many appearances for both his club and country. He would have played in three successive World Cups if he hadn't fractured a bone in his foot. He had several more injuries, but was always a fantastic patient, taking each setback as it came, getting his head down and just concentrating on his path back to full recovery.

More and more clubs were coming to ask me to look after their players, at a time when transfer fees and soccer player's wages were increasing almost exponentially After a couple of glasses of wine at one of the FA meetings, I was chatting to Gordon Taylor, the long-standing chairman of the Professional Footballers Association. As footballer's wages were slowly going off the scale, it meant my fees for fixing them probably amounted to no more than a few hours of their income. I mused that what I would really like to do was adopt a "Robin Hood" approach and to charge everyone half a week's wages, so if you were on a low income, your surgery might cost a hundred pounds, and if a premiership footballer, maybe fifty thousand pounds. I felt most people would be prepared to afford this level of expenditure for something they really needed. He looked at me with disdain, and in his characteristic drawl opined.

"I don't think that would be a good idea."

As well as football, many of the Rugby League clubs from across the North turned up at my door, and even The Northern Ballet asked me to care for their troupe.

Dance is a rigorous discipline, and to familiarise myself with what was involved I went to a couple of their training sessions. The intensity and effort they put in would have put many footballers to shame.

During the first year of looking after them, I had seen several of their ballerinas with "stress fractures". This is where a bone develops a crack in it as a result of overuse – a sort of repetitive strain injury. For ballerinas it is very important to maintain a low body weight to facilitate being lifted by their male partners. Most of them smoked, ate little and trained a lot. This meant their body fat percentage became very, very low. When I made enquiries, not one of the patients who had a stress fracture, had a period in the previous four years, and they had essentially switched off their menstrual cycle, developing early osteoporosis and making them susceptible to their bones fracturing.

After success with the Keighley Cougars (I have a team photo signed by the whole team, where I had operated on every single person in the picture, including the coach and the physio!), the Bradford Bulls asked me to look after them, shortly followed by the Leeds Rhinos, and one by one, most of the Superleague clubs from West Yorkshire joined my list.

When I first started, Rugby League was still semi-professional (Brian Noble famously being a full-time policeman, playing for the Bulls on his weekends off), with many of the players on "pay as you play" contracts. This meant if they sustained an injury, they not only lost their income from playing, but frequently were unable to do their daytime jobs either. Not only that, but if their injury was going to prevent them playing for a long time, the club would often decline to pay for their medical treatment privately, leaving them to the vagaries of the National Health Service.

Then the "SuperLeague" was formed, which revolutionised the care of players. Not only did they have a guaranteed income, but the clubs were obliged to make sure the players had appropriate and timely treatment for any injury they picked up while playing.

The only downside for me was that the season was switched to the Summer. Before this, the football, rugby league and skiing seasons overlapped, meaning I was frantically busy over the Winter. Come April/May, the work died away, leaving me to take a summer holiday in relative peace. After the change in the Rugby League season, there was no time during the year when I could get away without three or four texts, phone calls or emails every day requesting advice about managing players injuries.

Rugby League is a brutal and physical game, with a fifteen stone player being considered a lightweight. As the players have become bigger and bigger and faster and faster, the injuries have tended to become more common and more severe. They are also the fittest of any group of players I have treated from any sport. We often had to reset the alarms on monitors in the operating theatre as their resting pulse rates were so slow they kept triggering them.

Rugby league players were undoubtedly the toughest bunch of athletes I have treated over the years and certainly in the early days of the SuperLeague there were some real characters. Brian McDermott who played for the Bradford Bulls (and later in his career went on to an incredibly successful spell managing the Leeds Rhinos) was a truly hard man. He had been a Royal Marine Commando before becoming a professional boxer, and then a rugby league player.

I don't think anyone will forget a needle match in the televised semi-final of the challenge cup against the Leeds Rhinos. He took exception to receiving a vicious knee in a tackle, stood up and with a crisp right hook laid the perpetrator clean out. Two other Leeds Rhinos, rushing in to help their team-mate were also put on the deck with a left, right combination. With three opposition players laid out on the grass around him, the commentator exclaimed, "He thinks he's still in the ring!"

To be fair to Brian, once the red mist had settled, he was mortified and vowed never to let it happen again, describing it as "My mad moment of absolute shame". To add to the grief, his wife Joanne, who was at the game, apparently gave him a "right rollicking"!

Another famous example of their toughness was when the Rhinos were playing Warrington in the Grand Final. Paul Wood received an accidental knee in the groin early in the second half, rupturing one of his testicles. He played on for a further twenty minutes before being taken off. Immediately after the match he was rushed to hospital and had the damaged testicle surgically removed. Can't see anything similar happening in premier league football!!

Knee injuries in the sport of Rugby League are so common I have watched a match between two SuperLeague sides, and suddenly realised there were nine players on the pitch (out of twenty-six) whose knee ligaments I had reconstructed. When the Leeds Rhinos won the triple (Challenge Cup, League Leaders Shield and Grand Final) a couple of years ago, only three players in the squad for the Grand Final had escaped some sort of knee surgery.

They were always a fantastic bunch of people to treat. They followed instructions almost to the letter (one player turned up ten days after surgery looking shattered. He'd been instructed to do his exercises for five minutes every hour and straighten his knee out for ten minutes every hour. He'd taken this quite literally and been setting an alarm every hour round the clock. His knee was in fantastic condition though. I then changed the instructions to "every waking hour".) and just got their heads down and got on with it. Two things always seemed to happen during their rehab. They ended up four inches wider at the shoulder from doing upper body workouts at the gym to get their endorphin fix, and they always seem to sport a new and very large tattoo.

When I started, most of the physios in Rugby League were men, in what was perceived as a man's world, until one club took the brave step to appoint their first female. The players gave her a really tough time over the first few weeks but never managed to break her, and eventually she was accepted as "one of the lads".

In her second week she was in the treatment room, examining a player who had received a mighty whack on the thigh. As was usual after a training session, the players were wandering around the changing room stark naked. One of them strolled in and asked what was happening. The physio explained she was treating a haematoma (large bruise) in the thigh. He asked her if she was going to use a bit of massage and some ultrasound. When she said yes, he told her that wasn't what was needed.

He then stepped up to the player on the couch and whacked him repeatedly on the thigh with his penis, finishing with, "Now that's what he needs." before meandering back out. I'm not sure I would get away with treating patients like this, I'm sure the GMC would have something to say about it!

I was getting busier and busier at work, leaving home before seven a.m., and frequently not getting home until seven p.m., as well as being regularly on call during the week and weekends. Once at home, I often worked late into the evenings preparing lectures I had been invited to give and writing scientific papers. My main operating list at the Infirmary was on a Friday, following which I felt obliged to go in to the hospital on a Saturday morning to make sure the patients were recovering satisfactorily, explain what I'd done during their surgery and discuss their recovery and prognosis (something I did for years, despite this being unpaid).

In my personal life, my wife and I had been blessed with two lovely sons. I don't think you ever really understand the meaning of love until you have kids. The surge from deep within when you look into your newborn's eyes is incomparable. I did wonder at first how I would ever feel the same when we had our second child, but nature has obviously thought this through, and sure enough the love, pure and unconditional, just kicks in.

We decided we would look for a bigger house. I was working hard and earning good money, something that is difficult to adjust to when you have come from a poor background and have experienced what losing everything means. I couldn't help but feel a little guilty and used to tithe my income, dividing the money between Children in Need, Greenpeace and Amnesty International. My accountant used to disapprove, saying as I was paying forty percent tax anyway, why did I feel I needed to give away even more, but I felt it was the right thing to do. This continued until I ended up as the only working adult supporting four adults and four children (more later).

The house my wife and myself were living in had been bought at the peak of the housing market but when we moved out the market had slumped. It took over a year to sell it, despite regularly dropping the price. I must be one of very few people in the country who have sold a house, seven years after buying it, for fifteen percent less than I'd paid for it. Not being able to sell the house left me strapped over a huge bridging loan, in addition to the paying off the large new mortgage.

Having been evicted from our home when I was growing up, left me with a deep fear of the same thing happening again, and I was determined to pay off my debts as soon as possible so, in the eventuality of things going tits up, I would still have somewhere to live. Income from private practice is nice, but certainly not guaranteed. Illness, or a bit of adverse publicity in the local press, and it all disappears. I have seen a few colleagues overextend themselves and run into real trouble when their private income stream dried up.

With two small children, it was a difficult time, as both our mothers were dead and our families lived a long way away, meaning we had no intrinsic support. Weekdays, I would get up at six, make my breakfast, iron a shirt and head off for work before anyone else was up and about. When I got back home after a long day's work, tired and stressed out, the children were often tucked up in bed, fast asleep. Cracks in our relationship started to appear.

One Summer, the night before we were due to drive down to a cottage in Cornwall for a holiday the following day, my wife woke me from sleep at about one a.m. She was complaining she had terrible abdominal pain. At first, like most doctors, I was inclined to dismiss her symptoms, but it quickly became apparent this was serious. We lived out in the country and had no neighbours, so I carried the children down to the car, helped my wife climb in and set off for the Infirmary in Leeds.

On the way, I rang the on-call surgical registrar from my mobile and explained the situation and he met us as we arrived at the hospital. He felt the problem was probably gynaecological and my wife was admitted under the Obs and Gynae team. I took the children home, tucked them into bed and slept fitfully for a few hours.

The following morning, I was going frantic, trying to find out what was happening. The ward just kept telling me that she was comfortable as she'd just had yet another injection of morphine. I pointed out that anyone who has enough morphine is "comfortable", even the terminally ill, but nobody was able to tell me what the plan was.

In the end I managed to track down the consultant under whose name she had been admitted (being in the system has occasional advantages). When I found him, he was actually just about to start an operating list at the private hospital and hadn't seen the patients who had been admitted under his care the night before, or even spoken to his junior staff about them. I left a curt message asking if he was aware he had had a consultant's wife admitted onto his ward, and that

I would be very grateful if he could give me a ring and let me know what was happening.

Shortly afterwards I received a call. He was absolutely furious. Not at me, but at his juniors who hadn't informed him a colleague's wife was lying in one of his beds. He didn't have a trace of embarrassment about the situation and told me he had arranged a laparoscopy (a keyhole operation to look inside the abdomen) a couple of hours later. It was a good job I had pushed for this, as when they looked in, my wife had a twisted ovarian tube that was going gangrenous. A few hours later and this would have ruptured and produced peritonitis. Thankfully it was swiftly sorted out, and she was discharged home that evening.

I was left wondering what would have happened if she had been an ordinary member of the public, and astonished that a consultant should not even bother to talk to his team about patients admitted with potentially life-threatening problems before going to the private hospital. Thankfully, this type of approach to consultant practice is largely gone.

The situation at home slowly and steadily deteriorated to the point my wife and I were essentially living separate lives under the same roof. It was a horrible time. Eventually we grasped the inevitable and agreed we needed to separate. This was psychologically devastating for me as I had always vowed I would never do the same thing to my children as my father had done to me. Once the decision had been made however, there was an overwhelming sense of relief, and our split was fairly amicable. My only advice for anyone else going through the same sad situation is put the children first (everything else will then fall into place) and try to avoid solicitors (who seem to have a talent for taking a perfectly amicable settlement and turning it into an acrimonious war).

I was keen for my wife to keep the house, but she insisted she wanted to move away. Having myself moved to a different house so often as a child, I wanted the children to have some continuity and the stability of having a constant home. At that time there was no money in the bank at all, as I had used it all to pay off the mortgage, so I had to re-mortgage the house to pay a large lump sum to my ex-wife.

My ex-wife moved out and set up home with the boys in a village about fifteen miles away. My way of coping was to throw myself into my job, working even longer hours. I was also determined to remain part of my children's lives, and through some chopping and changing at work, managed to organise things so they stayed with me one night a week and every weekend.

The next phase of my life was about to begin.

9

MAY YOU NEVER

I f you are squeamish or easily upset, it's probably best to avoid this chapter.

Post-traumatic stress disorder didn't exist when I started medical school or moved through the early part of my junior doctor career. Since the condition was described in the early 1980s, one hears of fireman, policeman and victims of accidents or disasters being offered counselling, but personally I have never even been approached, despite having seen and experienced some of the most horrific situations you could possibly imagine.

Certain specific moments and individual patients burn themselves into your memory. Just closing your eyes can bring them into sharp focus, with the associated sights, sounds, smells and emotions instantly brought back, rather like rerunning a movie clip. Sometimes these incidents can be so traumatic they influence both your whole approach to looking after and caring for patients and also the way you think about and approach your own life.

On my very first day on my attachment to a surgical ward as a medical student, the houseman was taking the six of us round, filling us in on the details the patients and their problems. We came to a side room with a closed door, where he explained there was a poor lady who was terminally ill with inoperable ovarian cancer. She had been admitted as an emergency with intestinal obstruction, but when she was opened up on the operating table, the whole of the inside of her abdomen was matted together with tumour, which had also spread to her liver. She was not expected to live for more than a few days.

As we shuffled past, I peered in through the small, round observation window in the door. As I did so, she suddenly sat up, opened her mouth and vomited faeces. Cruelly, the tumour had fused together the back of her stomach and her colon. Our eyes met, and her anguished and terrible look of distress and horror burned itself straight into my brain, and is something that I can instantly, and vividly, recall to this day.

Whatever your beliefs, your god (or fate) has some terrible ways in which your life can be brought to an end. I have witnessed many of them. It is probably why medics develop such a black sense of humour, just in order to cope with the horrors they have to deal with. I have never understood the general public's fascination with horror movies and crime dramas on the TV. I guess when you've experienced the reality of having to try and save someone screaming in pain, trying to hold their guts in their abdomen and getting covered in their blood, it's not quite so titillating any more.

I recall sitting with a group of non-medical friends when I was about thirty. None of them had even seen someone die or had to deliver desperately bad news to anyone. Medics and the emergency services are set apart in that they deal with these things on an almost daily basis. It can be difficult to cope with.

Certainly, when I was a student and junior doctor, it was regarded as part of normal practice to help patients die. This wasn't "murder" or "killing" but helping an individual through the last phase of their lives, and something doctors had been doing for centuries. One thing

I have learned from my career through medicine is that there are worse things than dying.

Back then a patient would be brought into the hospital during the terminal phase of their illness, and if there was no prospect of improving them, a discussion would take place with their relatives (and the patient themselves if they were compos mentis enough, although this was rarely the case). The offer to "keep them as comfortable as possible" was usually accepted with relief and gratitude. A suitable prescription for diamorphine would be made, and over twenty-four to forty-eight hours, the patient would drift off with dignity, pain and stress free. I never met a set of relatives who were not grateful for this kindness for their loved one.

Then came Harold Shipman, who abused his privilege as a physician, and was clearly mentally ill. Because of this single deranged individual, doctors are now reluctant to prescribe patients morphine at all, in case they suddenly face a murder charge.

I had first-hand experience of this, when a close relative was admitted to a hospice with inoperable cancer. They slipped into a coma and were placed on the "Liverpool Pathway". The Liverpool Pathway was introduced to try and rationalise terminal care, but in my experience was a horrific way for people to die. Fluid and food were withdrawn, so essentially the patients died from thirst and hunger. Somehow, the government were persuaded it was a great idea, and hospitals were incentivised to use it by receiving a financial reward if they hit their target for the number of patients put on it. Inevitably, downward pressure came from management, but most of my colleagues got around this by giving appropriate analgesia, and then enrolling the patient on the pathway when they only had a few hours to live.

In my case, after a couple of days watching their relative desperately sucking on the damp swabs used to moisten the lips, the family asked me if I, as a medic, could have a word with the team involved in their care, to see if the inevitable process could be made more comfortable.

I went to have a word with the palliative care registrar, to see if he thought some morphine might be a kindness. He was absolutely horrified and told me that giving morphine would amount to "euthanasia". I pointed out that withdrawing fluids was a certain way to kill someone, but it was likely to be unpleasant and drawn out, but he explained that this was "passive", so was acceptable, whereas giving morphine was "active" and therefore not. I guess you have to try and justify things so you can sleep at night. If you treated a dying animal like that, I'm pretty sure the RSPCA would bring a prosecution for cruelty, but in humans it seems to be OK? Vets are not accused of being "murderers" or "killers". I just pray that when my time comes, for the sake of both myself and my family, the physician looking after me will have the moral courage and compassion to help me through my final hours and allow me to die pain free and with dignity. This is obviously a personal view, but I think we need a wider, more sensible and less emotive debate about the issue.

In our relative's case, it took a further six days to die, and we watched as they became a withered husk of the person they had been. Immediately afterwards I wrote a letter to the BMJ, outlining my experience, entitled "Shipman's Curse", but they declined to print it. I think they thought it would have been too controversial. Nobody is saying it should be compulsory to be eased out, there wouldn't be any draconian directives or targets for the terminally ill. I think we need a debate, for individuals to have a choice, and for doctors to be able to provide appropriate care for their patients in the most difficult of times.

I digress… back to the patients.

When I was a houseman at Coventry, one of first patients I will never forget was a Chinese student in his early twenties, who arrived in the admissions unit vomiting copious amounts of blood. I've never seen anything like it before or since, he seemed to be exsanguinating onto the floor, walls and ceiling, as we were desperately pouring blood transfusions into him through multiple IV lines. I was literally soaked to the skin in his blood.

We eventually managed to gain control and stabilise him, but it turned out he had "Australia Antigen positive hepatitis", and early liver cirrhosis, despite being so young (we were all subsequently tested for what would have been a career ending and life shortening infection but fortunately none of us had contracted the virus). Over the next week, he had two further episodes of vomiting large amounts of blood, to the point where the blood bank at Coventry ran out of supplies of his blood type.

After discussions and consultations, it was decided he needed to be transferred to the specialist liver unit at Kings Hospital in London. I was delegated to be the accompanying doctor (they didn't ask for volunteers!), and was put in the back of the ambulance with him (lightly sedated), twenty eight units of blood and other blood products and a "Sengstaken Tube", a type of catheter you shove down the gullet and then inflate, to compress the bleeding veins at the lower end. I was allowed a plastic apron and some gloves and goggles but wasn't confidant of the outcome if he had another catastrophic bleed during the journey. The back of the ambulance would quite literally have become a "bloodbath".

The ambulance set off at breakneck speed. As we hit end of the M1 we were met by two police cars who shepherded us through the centre of London. With sirens going and blue lights flashing, one would race ahead and block the next road junction to allow us through, and then they would leapfrog each other and repeat. I couldn't help but admire the utter professionalism with which they did their job.

I've never been across London in a faster time. We even went around the Marble Arch roundabout at fifty miles an hour. We arrived at Kings still in one piece and grateful that nothing untoward had happened. I gave his hand (he'd held my hand the whole way down) a squeeze and told him we'd arrived. He squeezed my hand back and thanked me for helping him.

Despite everything, he sadly passed away a few weeks later, a long, lonely way from home.

Certain experiences are so horrific you never forget them. When I was a casualty officer in Stoke, I was grabbing a swift cup of tea in the office one evening, when a phone in the corner I'd never noticed before, started ringing insistently.

"That's a funny ring tone." I queried.

"It's the 'bat phone.'" the charge nurse tersely replied. What it meant was the police were ringing to say they were on their way and needed a doctor to go out to the scene of an accident.

I was hurriedly squeezed into a high viz jacket with the words "DOCTOR" on the back and told to pick up the emergency bag.

"What's in here then?" I asked.

"Everything we might need." replied the charge nurse with a grin. I unzipped the top and peeked inside. I gulped as the first thing I recognised was an amputation saw.

Seconds later, a police car screeched to a halt outside, we piled in the back and it took off at speed, blue lights flashing and siren blaring. It was cold, dark and raining and a scary ten-minute drive took us to the scene of the accident.

Two lads in a hot hatch had obviously been driving at high speed when they hit a small humpback bridge. The car must have taken off, flipped over and landed on its roof. The passenger had been thrown out and was lying in a crumpled heap on the wet tarmac, blood pooling around him. He was clearly dead.

The one the police were worried about, and thought might still be alive, was still in the car and although the car was upside down, he was held in his seat by his seat belt. The car was a mass of smoking, twisted metal and was clearly leaking petrol.

I was asked to crawl underneath, half expecting to be cremated at any second, until I could reach up to the guy trapped in the driver's seat. He actually didn't look too bad from where I was looking at him. I reached towards him.

"Can you hear me?" Are you OK?" As I gently shook his shoulder, something dropped onto the "floor" from the other side. I squirmed further in and looked round. The thing that had dropped out, was in fact a piece of his brain, as half his skull was missing. I wriggled back out of the wreckage.

"Sorry, there's nothing we can do. He's dead." Somewhat crestfallen at our inability to help, we were taken back to the hospital, while the police set up their forensic investigation.

I've witnessed and dealt with some horrendous bits of trauma over the years, but not once have I been offered any counselling or advice on how to deal with it. It seems to be assumed that as a doctor you have a natural ability to cope with the horrors you have to manage.

Working in Sheffield with Mr. E. we would be referred some extraordinary cases from around the region. One patient, transferred from another city, had one of the most appalling stories I have ever heard, before or since.

She was a young teenage girl who had been out shopping with her mother on Christmas Eve. At the top of a nearby hill, a bus driver nipped out of his empty bus, leaving the door open, to get a packet of cigarettes from the paper shop and two, fifteen year old lads thought it would be a great laugh to jump onto the bus and drive off. They soon lost control and it careered down the hill, running right over the top of the girl.

She sustained horrific multiple injuries, including a ruptured bladder and ovaries, a ruptured kidney and spleen, a ruptured bowel, injuries to her chest and a completely smashed up pelvis.

She very nearly died and spent six weeks on intensive care having multiple operations. It was only as she started to recover, they realised that every time she turned her leg out, her hip would dislocate out of its socket. Her pelvis was essentially in bits.

She was an unbelievably courageous young girl with a lovely, caring mother. Neither of them could understand what they had done to deserve such an appalling fate. They were such a nice family. I couldn't understand it either, but it is something you see a lot of as an orthopaedic surgeon, where one second someone's life is great, the next it's been turned upside down, through no fault of their own.

We took multiple X-rays (no CT scanning in those days) and put them up on X-ray boxes around the room. We looked at them for ages, trying to convert the two-dimensional images on the screens into a three-dimensional model in our heads. It's a bit like a three-dimensional jig saw where some of the pieces might be missing and some are no longer the original shape. A provisional plan was made of how it might all be put together again.

We were in theatre for fourteen hours to reconstruct the first side and then six weeks later, another eleven hours to do the second. Mr. E was a genius at what he did, and I will never forget the two procedures. I moved on from that job before her discharge, but I often still think of her, wondering how things turned out.

One of the attractions of the discipline for orthopaedic surgeons, is that primary bone cancer is very rare. The downside is that when it does occur, it often affects young teenagers and frequently has a very poor prognosis. These tumours are often picked up accidentally when the patient sustains an injury (or thinks they have had an injury), and an X-ray throws up something suspicious.

A colleague in Bradford, in the week running up to Christmas, asked me if I could arthroscope the knee of a fourteen-year-old lad who had apparently been injured playing football the previous week (no MRI scanning at that time). His plain X-rays were normal, so he was added to the list, but I was puzzled when I didn't find anything much.

The first week in the New Year his parents brought him back for review and listening to the ongoing story something just didn't sound right. I sent him for a further X-ray and just on the edge of the film was a very small "Codman's Triangle", one of the first X-ray findings of an osteosarcoma, a particularly aggressive form of bone cancer.

I then had the very difficult task of sitting down with the patient and his parents and explaining that this was very serious, and it looked like a form of bone cancer. There are only two centres in the UK dealing with this condition, and I had already spoken to the National Bone Tumour Centre in Birmingham and arranged his admission the following week. Despite surgery, he died eighteen months later.

In this special type of situation, I find giving bad news particularly difficult. The parents are crying, the patient is crying, and you are sat there trying to be professional and hold it all together. Having children myself gives an insight into how it must feel, and it truly rips you apart. You can never banish the anguish you see in a loving parent's eyes; it lives with you forever.

Hanging on the wall of my office is a print of Leonardo's "L'Uomo Vitruviano". On the back is a message of thanks from a young man and his family for the care I had given him.

At the age of thirteen, he had been admitted to hospital following an accident where he had sustained a nasty fracture of the thigh bone just above his knee. The consultant whose care he was under had taken him to theatre and pinned the fracture in place. Unfortunately, the operation became badly infected, which proved difficult to control, and it took several weeks of intravenous antibiotics before it seemed to have cleared up. It was as he was recovering, and they were trying to get him going again, that they realised he had hardly any movement in the knee joint. He was referred to me to see if anything could be done.

I took him to theatre to see if I could work out what was going on. There was only about five degrees of movement in the knee, and I had great difficulty getting an arthroscope into the joint. To my horror it became apparent the kneecap was actually fused to the end of the thigh bone and the normal shiny white surface of the joint had been completely eaten away by the bacteria, leaving him with just bare bone rubbing on bare bone. This was an impossible situation. Much, much too young for a joint replacement and in constant pain from the damaged joint, I felt the only thing I could do would be to fuse the knee joint solid. This is an operation that is a last resort, as it leaves you with a permanently, completely stiff knee joint and a short, straight leg.

I had a long think and rang a colleague in London to ask if he would be willing to give a second opinion. Professor Fred Heatley was a great orthopaedic surgeon. A brilliant lecturer and thinker, with an encyclopaedic knowledge of orthopaedic history, he could always be relied on to give a sensible opinion.

The family went down to London for the consultation and were impressed by the attention they received. Fortunately for me, the professor agreed that fusion was really the only option.

The other problem with this particular patient, was that the growth plates (responsible for the bones growing in length) on either side of the knee were still open, indicating he still had some growing to do.

Fusion necessarily shortens the limb, and I didn't want to make the situation worse. A standard operation would have closed the growth plates in this leg, while the other leg would have kept on growing, resulting in a huge difference in length from one leg to the other.

I gave it some more thought and made up a technique using pins above and below the growth plates, held together with some external scaffolding (if only we'd had "Ilizarov" frames at the time). The knee joint was successfully fused by twelve weeks later, getting rid of his pain, the frame was removed, and the growth plates remained open with the bones continuing to grow in length, so he didn't end up with devastating shortening of the leg. In addition to the print, some years later he sent me a letter saying he remained well and had been accepted into medical school.

You don't become a doctor to reap the praise, but it is nice when patients take time to write or send a card. I have folders full of "thank you" letters, which I occasionally pour through during periods of self-doubt.

When you are a sub-specialist you often get referrals, from other consultants, of patients who have had devastating injuries or compli-cations and have reached the end of the line in what can be offered in their local hospital. Many were told, "Well I can't help you but there is a guy in Bradford who might be able to do something." and they would arrive full of hope and expectation.

Many times, I was able to help, but sometimes I had the difficult and emotionally draining task of explaining that there really wasn't anything that I could do to improve the situation. It is particularly hard when patients have been told that you are their last hope but there is really no point in giving people unrealistic expectations.

When you first start, there is always the temptation to try and surgically sort out anything that comes your way, but this is slowly tempered by experience, until you hopefully develop a realistic idea of your own limitations. No matter how good you are, sometimes things do not go as planned or hoped for and, if you are a caring clinician, those patients stay with you forever. You analyse these cases over and over in your mind, trying to work out if there was something that could have been done differently to have changed the outcome.

Over the years, attitudes have undoubtedly changed, and some patients have become more demanding and aggressive. In Bradford, in the NHS, I have had the "I pay your wages", approach on numerous occasions, when patiently trying to explain that we couldn't do their operation or investigation this week as there were more pressing problems that needed dealing with.

In Bradford, with its offensively high unemployment rate, this was often a bit ironic, as I would look down at the patients records to see "unemployed" next to "occupation". I never did resort to countering with, "Actually, it's the other way round", no matter how tempting it might have been.

One of the joys of being a clinician is seeing and dealing with the vast cross section of humanity that come through the door. You never know, day to day, what will turn up. Everybody can become ill or be injured, whatever your beliefs, sexuality, star sign or background, whether you're rich or poor, aggressive or shy, unpleasant or just really nice.

Sadly, attacks on health service staff have become a regular occurrence, despite the fact we are only doing our best to try and help. I have been threatened and physically assaulted on several occasions, something that became a real worry after two plastic surgeons in Wakefield were stabbed to death for declining to remove a tattoo (the NHS won't fund this procedure).

Sometimes, the patients are just very odd. I was asked to see a gentleman for a fifth opinion about his troublesome knees. His problems went back over several years, but he had every fact relating to his various meetings with a multitude of doctors at his fingertips and was keen to relay them to me. If I'd let him ramble on, he would have taken the whole clinic up, so after a few relevant questions and an examination, I cut to the chase and offered to have a look inside his knees, as this was the only intervention he hadn't been through. I did warn him that I may not find anything but that if I didn't, it wouldn't mean he didn't have problems, just that I couldn't cure them with minor surgery. On this basis he was happy to proceed.

I wrote to his doctor outlining the conversation we had and physical findings and mentioning I found him an odd character. He somehow obtained a copy of this and took great exception to its' content. I arrived at lunchtime the next day to find my secretary physically shaking, having just come off a phone call from him. It took a lot to rattle my secretary, so it must have been bad.

The gist was that he was demanding an apology, demanding I returned his call straight away and threatening that if I didn't, he would report me to the GMC. I felt a little aggrieved, having been the only clinician he had seen in several years who had offered to try and help him. I have never taken kindly to anyone threatening my secretary, and tried to phone him straight back but there was no reply, so I sent a letter explaining that he had now skewed our clinical relationship to the point I would be unable to treat him with the required degree of clinical detachment and so was discharging him.

The next day I went into the office to find my secretary, white and shaking, in an even more frightened state. The patient had received the letter and phoned her, telling her to tell me that "The end of the world is nigh and only the righteous will survive." and that I was just a "snake in the grass and that I would receive my just desserts." and several other biblical type threats. I contacted management and explained the situation, but they didn't seem particularly interested.

The following morning a large, padded brown envelope arrived, addressed in red ink. It seemed to contain something about the size of a video cassette. This was a time when stories about letter bombs regularly appeared on the news, so I wasn't desperately keen to open it.

Once again, we contacted management who took the parcel off and X-rayed it. It did indeed contain a video cassette which, when played, contained scenes of the patient throwing Death Stars into dummies, and several other "Ninja" type activities. It also contained what appeared to be a piece of parchment (like the sort of thing you mock-up in school) with many biblical quotations from the book of Revelations, all in red ink, presumably intended to look like blood.

I was getting seriously worried, and ended up speaking to the Trust's solicitors, suggesting we take out an injunction to prevent the patient coming anywhere near me or the hospital. They were spectacularly unhelpful, as they thought it unlikely be a problem, but suggested perhaps I should check the corridor before coming out of a clinic and look under my car before driving home! In the end, after contacting an ex-patient of mine high up in the police force, an officer went round to have a quiet word and the situation faded away. It was months before I relaxed into my normal routine though. No one from management came to see me and I never received any kind of help or support.

Management were similarly unhelpful when I was physically attacked on the ward. Another rather odd patient (I seemed to attract them!), who was waiting to go to theatre for a minor operation, was kicking off about something he was unhappy with, and shouting and swearing at the nurses, just as I arrived to do a pre-theatre ward round. One thing I would never tolerate is abuse of the nursing staff. Their job is difficult enough as it is.

I walked into the bay where his bed was allocated to explain we had a zero-tolerance policy towards abuse of the staff, and I was therefore cancelling his operation so he could pack his bag and go home. The next moment he had me up against the wall, holding me at the throat (this is definitely a major disadvantage of wearing a standard tie!) with one hand, with the other hand raised and ready to punch me.

Two thoughts went through my mind. "Am I allowed to hit him first?" And, "Please don't break my glasses, I have an operating list to go and do." I managed to talk him down and back into a chair, without having to use any force. Five minutes later, an overweight, wheezing, sixty-year-old hospital security man (summoned by sister when things kicked off) arrived to provide back up! The police later arrived and escorted the patient out of the hospital. To give you an idea of his insight, as he was being frogmarched off the ward, he turned and called to sister, "When will Mr. B be contacting me to rearrange my surgery?"

Over the next three weeks the hospital "stress counsellor" came to see sister four times, to make sure she hadn't suffered any adverse effects from the incident, but I didn't receive a single piece of support.

There are definitely some odd patients, but then medicine is an odd profession. You are exposed to tremendous suffering and sadness as well as unbelievable bravery and strength of will. Over the timespan of my career, my memory has been filled with a vast collage of faces, emotions, triumphs and tragedies, and it has been a massive privilege to have been a part of it all. It might not be the best paid or the most respected, but I'm pretty sure not many of my generation would have swapped it for anything else.

10

SMOOTH OPERATOR

And so I moved into the second phase of my career. Getting slowly wiser and very slightly more mellow, learning to pick my battles rather than trying to fight everything, and one failed marriage behind me. Reputation established, but still wracked with self-doubt and the feeling that sooner or later, someone would tap me on the shoulder and tell me I shouldn't be there and get back outside. This feeling never left me until the day I retired. I think this affects many who have had success but come from way outside the establishment. I recently discovered this feeling actually has a name – "The Imposter Syndrome".

In many ways it's probably not been a bad thing. A colleague of mine in London told me he had always been afflicted in the same way, but felt that the feelings of self-doubt gave you fire in the belly and just drove you to constantly questioning your practice, striving to be a better surgeon, and continually trying to improve. It always seemed that just as you thought you had an operation down to a "T", something would happen to let you know you weren't quite as good as you thought you were!

While you never stop learning to the day you retire, the first ten years of a consultant's practice are a massive learning curve. Before becoming a consultant there was always the option to "let the boss have a look at it" and then suddenly, you are the boss and the buck stops with you. For my generation this wasn't too bad, but for the current generation of trainees, who do very little unsupervised, this must be a massive jump. In my time as a senior registrar you could list patients for surgery in the knowledge that you would probably have moved on before their admission date arrived. After becoming a consultant, you know that you will be responsible for the outcome for the rest of your career.

You slowly learn to deal with patients who you may be seeing for years to come, the subtle arts of "bedside manner", and coping with the constantly shifting quicksand of the NHS. You would think that everything should be in place to allow you to operate with the minimum of stress and the maximum efficiency, but this is rarely the case, and almost every day a new set of difficulties would appear.

After my marriage failed, I threw myself into my work. I was doing a phenomenal amount of surgery, nearly two hundred and fifty ligament reconstructions and roughly a thousand knee arthroscopies a year, putting me in a very small, select group operating at this level. I think I was getting slicker and quicker, although speed was never my primary aim. Being slightly slower and getting the operation perfect is better than a fast but shoddy job – like many things in life!

Dealing with the stress of it all was difficult. Patients expect a cheery greeting and a ready smile no matter how crap you are feeling inside. The culture in the Health Service is you just suck it up and crack on. Even taking time off for physical sickness was regarded as "poor show" and showing a lack of commitment to the cause. One of my senior registrar colleagues was asked if he took his job seriously when he asked for time off to attend the birth of his first child.

Taking time off as a junior meant another colleague had to cover for you and work flat out, and generally if you missed a night on call things were swapped round so you just did it when you returned. You didn't go off sick unless you were physically incapable of walking on to the ward. When I was a casualty officer in Stoke, a vomiting bug swept through the ranks of the junior doctors. I was last to succumb and was told that as I was the last one standing, I would just have to hold the fort. I remember being in the plaster room manipulating a lady's wrist fracture when waves of nausea overcame me. I just turned around, threw up into the sink, rinsed my mouth out and carried on. I'll never forget her perturbed expression.

Things have certainly changed among the junior ranks. A colleague of mine in a different hospital was ploughing through an overbooked hand surgery clinic when the phone on his desk rang. He answered it to find the senior house officer, who was meant to be helping him, on the other end of the line. The junior doctor explained he was taking the afternoon off sick as he was suffering from "Hayfever".

"Hayfever eh… You poor thing. What was the name again?" The doctor spelled out his name which the consultant carefully wrote down on the pad in front of him. He then replaced the receiver and then proceeded to put a big red cross through the name – career over!

Being a consultant surgeon is perhaps unlike many other jobs, in that if you do take time off sick, no-one sees your patients in the clinic or operates on the patients on your waiting list, they just stack them up for your return, so a couple of days off just means you can look forward to a compensatory frantic period of a week or two on your return.

I was once suffering from the flu (real, proper flu!), with a raging fever, aches and pains all over, sweating for Britain and with an associated viral conjunctivitis that made my eyes bright red, like those of "Darth Maul" from "Star Wars". The phone at home went off and I reluctantly answered it to find a colleague ringing me to say a thirteen-year-old lad with a rare knee injury had been admitted to the hospital. It was a type of injury that needs sorting out urgently and there was no-one else in the hospital who could deal with it.

I climbed wearily out of my bed, shaved, showered, dressed and drove in to the hospital. The path from the front door to the theatres had been cleared and my theatre scrubs had been laid out for me. I changed on my own, put on my hat and mask, went into the clean air theatre, scrubbed up, carried out the operation and left the registrar to sow-up the skin. I carefully put my theatre scrubs, gloves, hat and mask into a large plastic bag and sealed it, redressed, drove home and collapsed into my bed.

Back then patients came first, before any family commitments, personal problems or illness. I can't imagine this happening today; the ethos is now totally different. I can, however, understand the present generation of consultants not going "above and beyond", given the way they are treated and the lack of respect they are afforded.

Coping mechanisms for the stress of it all varied from one colleague to another and it's no wonder alcohol is abused by many. My personal relief valves were running and rock climbing. Evenings off (depending on the weather) would see me soloing around the rock faces of the local crags or jogging through the fields.

People often look at me quizzically when I tell them I find rock climbing relaxing. Certainly, soloing (climbing without ropes or protection) requires absolute concentration. One mistake can result in serious injury or even death. Having to put everything else into the back of your mind and focus on the rock in front of you, moving as smoothly and efficiently as possible, was a way of banishing the cares and concerns of the day. I suppose in current parlance it was a form of mindfulness. Rock climbing and surgery do have some similarities. Problem solving while under real stress, with the consequences of failure being quite substantial, are common to both. Being able to calmly work out your next move, while being stressed out and at the very limit of your abilities, is a transferable skill to many walks of life.

Jogging through the fields was almost another form of meditation, as you sink into the rhythm of one stride after another and get closer to the nature around you. Not infrequently the answer to something you had been puzzling about would just pop into your head. For me, it was a great way to recharge the batteries after a long day in the operating theatre.

In total, I have performed roughly sixteen thousand knee operations over the course of my career. People sometimes ask me "don't you get bored?". This has never been the case. There is the satisfaction of completing an operation beautifully, the reward of any craftsman in any field ("Zen and the Art of Motorcycle Maintenance", with its concept of the pursuit of "quality", had a big and ongoing influence on me after I read it as a student). Also, every case is different. You have to do an awful lot of cases to start recognising when something unusual is actually there. I would see things I'd never seen before right up until my retirement, but it was only through having done thousands of cases that I was able to actually realise that what I was looking at was different and significant.

Having done so many operations it gets difficult to go anywhere without running into an old customer. They usually bound up to you with a cheery "hello" and "thank you", to which I generally reply, "How is the knee?", knowing I'm on pretty safe ground.

On one short snowboarding trip to Grindlewald in Switzerland, three ex-patients came up to talk me in the departure lounge in Manchester airport. When we arrived in the resort, I quickly readied my stuff, bought a lift pass and headed up to the top of the mountain. At the summit, as I stepped out of the third bubble lift, the first person I met addressed me, "Oh, hello Mr. B. Good to see you." It was a lady whose knee ligaments I had fixed a couple of years previously.

For about the first fifteen hundred patients or so, I could pretty much remember all the details of each case and then things started to blur as my "hard drive" became full and every new fact going in meant something being archived to free up space. You tend to remember the complicated and difficult cases, or the famous ones, but the rest is a bit of a blur. My intrusion in people's lives is more significant than theirs in mine. This isn't being condescending, but most people will hopefully have just one ligament reconstruction in their lifetime, whereas I was doing ten to twelve ligament reconstructions a week.

I was never one to jump on bandwagons. If I had an operation that worked well in my hands, I would only change if something seemed to offer a radical improvement. I stuck with the surgery I was happy with, even when the "trend" was to move onto something else and colleagues rushed off to try something new.

I'm very glad I did, as I have saved myself a lot of grief. As the years have rolled by, techniques have arrived in a blaze of publicity and then shuffled off in disappointment, leaving an unhappy group of patients, and their surgeons dealing with the aftermath. As long-term studies in large numbers of patients have been produced, the type of ACL reconstruction I started with and stuck with, has thankfully been shown to produce the best outcomes.

In many ways, a group of us who started at roughly the same time in the early nineties, were pioneers in the field of knee surgery in the UK. Although techniques for anterior cruciate ligament reconstruction had been around and been tested for a while, they were still evolving, and the techniques for more complex and unusual injuries were being developed as we went along.

Not infrequently, an injury or problem would turn up that you hadn't come across before and there was no guidance as to what to do in the published literature. You would think hard about it, sometimes discuss the case with a colleague in another part of the country and, if the patient's symptoms warranted it, make up an operation.

The most challenging cases were the knee dislocations, where someone's knee has literally been ripped apart, disrupting three, or all four, of the ligaments holding it together. Scanning sometimes helped, but the deciding factor was always the assessment of what was functional and what was not, tested with your hands, when the patient was anaesthetised and their muscles fully relaxed, immediately before starting.

Frequently, what you thought was intact would turn out not to be and some of the structures would be damaged beyond repair, requiring some novel ways of reconstructing them using other structures from around the injured joint or the opposite knee. These operations would take upwards of three to four hours and are both mentally and physically punishing for the surgeon. The ability to work out what was going on and devise solutions on the spot was hard won, through hours and hours of less dramatic surgery and endless combing of scientific papers.

Whereas, when I'd been training, the standard treatment for a knee dislocation was plaster for twelve weeks and then a block-leather gaiter and walking stick for life, the aim was to try and return the patient to some sort of normality. One of my greatest achievements was to operate on a SuperLeague rugby player who had his knee disorganised by an opposing eighteen stone forward, reconstruct and repair three of the four ligaments in the joint and return him to playing for a further five seasons.

One day I turned up in theatre and was nervously approached by the then theatre manager. Would I mind if a trainee ODP (Operating Department Practitioner – a member of the team who can help either the anaesthetists or scrub team) scrubbed up and assisted for the morning's operations? I reluctantly acquiesced and resigned myself to doing my job despite the "assistant", which is never easy if they haven't a clue what they are doing.

I examined the patient in the anaesthetic room and then went to scrub up as the patient was set up on the table. After putting on my gown and gloves, I stood up at the table and looked across at my "assistant". A pair of twinkling green eyes, between a surgical hat and face mask, stared back at me. For me, it has always been the eyes. I agree with William Blake that the eyes are the windows of the soul. Some women's eyes sparkle for me and most don't. These eyes connected to something deep inside me and feelings that had been dormant for a long while started to stir.

I have had the odd disappointment when the removal of a surgical face mask exposes a face you'd rather have left covered, but this time a pretty face with a ready smile revealed itself. In the coffee room, after the list finished, we started chatting and something just clicked. I had failed in my marriage she was very unhappy in hers. It's an old, old, cliched hospital romance story but one thing led to another and we are still happily married twenty years later. Our family was initially expanded by her bringing her son from her first marriage, who fortuitously, was the same age as my two sons. They all got on extremely well together and have grown up as true brothers. We were later blessed by the arrival of our fourth son to complete our modern family unit.

A couple of years after that initial meeting, we had moved in together and for the first time in a long time, I actually felt cheerful. I remember walking down a corridor in the hospital, smiling and softly humming to myself and suddenly thinking "I'm happy!", puzzling as to how long it had been since this strange feeling had been part of my life.

The operating theatre was not all fun and games or a hotbed of passion and was frequently a source of enormous stress. At one stage, I turned up in theatre to do a complex knee reconstruction, likely to take three to four hours, to find a scrub nurse who I'd never seen previously, who greeted me with a smile and, "I've never scrubbed for a ligament operation before."

My heart sank. This was going to be difficult enough as it was. I went into the anaesthetic room to find a locum SHO (the most junior grade) anaesthetist and an ODP who had come from an agency and likewise, had never seen one of these operations before or had any idea of how I liked things set up.

To further add to my rising stress levels, the only person we could find to assist me was a second-year student nurse from the ward, who'd never been in theatre before. Nobody had thought to warn me of the circumstances I would have to deal with. I couldn't really cancel things, as we had acquired a donor ligament (same as for any type of transplant) for use in the operation, which somebody had taken out of the freezer a couple of hours before to thaw out (the only thing done as it should have been!), which couldn't be re-frozen and which had cost several thousand pounds.

So, with mild trepidation we got underway. Things were going fairly smoothly, if a little bit slower than usual, when we reached the point in the operation when, to minimise the chances of causing a major injury to blood vessels in the back of the knee, I needed x-ray control (in the form of an image intensifier), while I carefully ran a ten millimetre drill through the joint.

The radiographer arrived with the X-ray machine and proceeded to tell me, and try and demonstrate, it couldn't be used in such a way to get the imaging I wanted. The clock was ticking and every second was precious, as there was a tourniquet on the leg to control the bleeding. I exploded.

"For fucks sake... turn the fucking thing the other way round!" She didn't even know that could be done. I took a step back and it suddenly dawned on me that I was the only person in theatre who actually knew what they were doing or had any idea of what we were trying to achieve. It was a very lonely feeling. (I apologised to the radiographer afterwards, which she accepted graciously, saying she understood how stressful theatre can sometimes be).

This sort of scenario happened all the time in the NHS. You gradually learned to cope with missing or faulty equipment, inexperienced staff and non-availability of assistants. In fact, almost any situation that could be thrown at you. As I once said in a meeting with the DOH "Surgeons do their job despite the system, not because of it." Almost every day brought a new problem that had to be worked around. It constantly felt like you were sliding down a razors edge between triumph and disaster. It's no wonder so many of us die young. In fact, I remember reading a report from the Royal College stating that the average life expectancy for a surgeon retiring at sixty-five was... nine months. The increasing demands of patients, managers and politicians, all mixed in with poor working conditions, made trying to do the best for your patients a constant, stressful challenge.

At one time we were desperately short of nurses both in the operating theatres and on the wards (sound familiar?). The hospital looked afar, and at one stage two thirds of the nurses in our department had been drafted in from the Philippines. Some of them were very good, some not so good, and many saw a post in the UK as merely a steppingstone to a job in the US. It was not a situation that was sustainable, but lessons never seem to be learned.

During my early years as a consultant it was very different in the private hospital. They understood the importance of you working consistently with the same team so everyone gets to know what is expected of them, what equipment will be needed, and a bond of trust is formed between the staff, keeping the surgeon calm and happy. "A calm and happy surgeon is a productive one." as one of the managers in the private hospital once said to me.

I had the same team of nurses for every list and a pair of fantastic and skilful anaesthetic colleagues (Dr. S and Dr. E – thanks for everything guys) who shared my desire to start promptly on time and crack on with things. We shared the same sense of humour, but Dr. E wasn't so keen on my musical tastes! The time used to fly by, and it was always fun.

I always had music playing in theatre. Usually a mix of my eclectic tastes in rock. I generally am aware of it at the beginning of a case, but as you get to the technically critical bits it becomes white noise in the background, then comes back into focus as the operation winds down towards sewing the skin. There is actually a study from Australia which demonstrated that surgeons operate more efficiently when they have music of their own choosing playing in the background.

In the NHS it was very different. The theatre manager decided she wanted all her staff "multi-skilled", which meant the nursing staff were frequently precipitated into a theatre with a surgeon they hadn't previously worked with and scrubbing for a procedure they had never seen before. It was no wonder the atmosphere was often fractious.

As my reputation grew, I was flattered to receive an invitation to become a member of the Football Association and the Rugby League Medical committees at roughly the same time. These posts were unpaid, but interesting to be a part of, and I think we did some decent work in improving the standards of care across the board, for both players and spectators, at all levels of the game.

We were instrumental in introducing standards for crowd care, and immediate resuscitative care, with the development of a number of required courses for the medical staff involved. The introduction of defibrillators at pitch side, and for the crowd doctor, was one of our interventions (the same via the Rugby League medical committee), spurred on by the appalling scenes when Marc-Vivien Foe had a cardiac arrest when playing for Cameroon in the Confederations Cup semi-final in Lyon in 2003.

We introduced cardiac screening for football trainees, supervised by a consultant cardiologist from Papworth hospital. This could produce some difficult moments, when an asymptomatic trainee, who always seemed to be "the next Wayne Rooney", would be found to have Hypertrophic Obstructive Cardiomyopathy (HOCM), a condition that can cause fatal cardiac arrest during exercise. Our chairman, Myles Gibson (a wise old neurosurgeon from the Leeds General Infirmary), was absolutely brilliant at delivering, with kindness and compassion, to a devastated young lad and his parents, the bad news that their career was over before it had begun.

I thought my time as a junior doctor had been sexually prolific, but my murky past was put in the shade by some of the goings on of young (and not so young) footballers. I had become concerned as I had seen two elite level professional footballers with swelling of the knee and ankle which turned out to be swelling of the lining of the joint as a secondary effect of a sexually transmitted infection.

We co-opted a doctor from a league club who, in addition to their standard type duties, did a few sessions in the local hospital Genito Urinary Medicine clinic ("clap clinic" to you and I). They had expressed an interest, as out of curiosity they had tested the squad of the club they were looking after and found thirty percent of them were chlamydia positive. The doctor told us that the culture of the club at that time was to film your sexual exploits onto video, which would then be shown on the team coach on the way to the next away match. With the number of lurid tales being published in the tabloids at the time, I could well believe it. Despite the reluctance of the higher ups at the Football Association (I got the impression that they felt the whole thing was rather unsavoury), we managed to disseminate a "sexual health" information programme down to the clubs and trainees.

During my time as president of BOSTA, the problem of sports injuries was receiving an increasingly higher profile. The government was encouraging the population to take more exercise to "improve the health of the nation", but there was no safety net for those who then sustained an injury in the process, putting them back into an overstretched NHS, which tended to regard these injuries as low priority. It was also recognised that most of the injured were in the adult working population, therefore costing the public purse a large amount of money in benefits.

The Faculty of Sports and Exercise Medicine was established with two main aims. The first was to look after the health of the sporting population and the second, to recognise and treat injuries in a timely fashion, minimising the cost to society. As the President of the British Orthopaedic Sports Trauma Association I was involved in the discussions around the setting up of the syllabus. Sadly, I am not much of a political animal or empire builder, and the importance of the surgical side of the programme was swiftly sidelined by the physicians.

Early on in this process, I wrote to Richard Caborn (the minister for sport at the time and the main government representative in setting up the Faculty), expressing my concerns. I received an invitation to go down to his offices in London and discuss what I saw as the problems. I took a day's leave and carefully prepared my arguments. I arrived fifteen minutes ahead of my scheduled appointment but sat for over an hour waiting to meet the main man. I was ushered into his presence to be asked.

"So, what is it you've come to see me about?" Despite the fact it was he who had requested me to come down and see him, he had absolutely no idea why I was there, and the meeting, for which I'd had such high hopes, was a complete and utter waste of time.

Very quickly, the surgical management of acute (or chronic) injuries, received less and less emphasis, to the point where the "principles of surgical management of musculoskeletal injury" appears as one line on page thirty-four of the current syllabus. After seeing a semi-pro rugby player completely mismanaged by a doctor with the diploma from the college, and trying to pick up the pieces twelve weeks after he should have been referred, I felt I had no option but to resign my honorary fellowship of the college as, to my mind, it was no longer fulfilling the original criteria for which it had been created.

A good example of a sport that puts considerable burden on the NHS is skiing. I had become concerned that a bigger and bigger proportion of my ligament injury practice seemed to be skiing injuries. When we looked at the problem in 2006, the number of skiing injuries had tripled over the previous twelve years. The problem for the NHS is that while their holiday insurance covers them for any treatment needed abroad, as soon as they cross the UK border, they are put back into the health service (even some UK private health insurance policies exclude skiing injuries). We estimated that this cost the NHS about eight million pounds a year. We also calculated that your chance of sustaining a significant injury while on a week's skiing holiday is... about one in seventy, pretty high by most sports standards.

Part of your job as an orthopaedic surgeon, is to deal with "Trauma" i.e. anyone arriving in a broken state through the doors of A&E. In addition to the genuine accidents and "slips and trips", anyone who has watched "You've Been Framed" or read an edition of "The Darwin Awards" will appreciate there is no end to the stupid things that people do that really, really don't end well. Unlike Humpty Dumpty, the NHS can, and does, put them back together (most of the time!).

It also exposes you to a substratum of society that most of the population rarely come into contact with. The NHS fixes everyone, a burglar falling off a roof at two in the morning, a joyrider writing off the car he's stolen, and people shot, stabbed or beaten up. Many are very unpleasant people, who live their lives not caring about the norms of civilised behaviour.

In Bradford, there was periodically a turf war between the local criminal gangs controlling the drugs trade, and we would get a series of admissions of individuals shot in the knee or elbow, or sometimes with major life-threatening injuries. For a week or two there would be armed police officers looking bored, standing outside the ward as the injured recovered to the point they could be arrested and accompanied down to the police station.

Many of the younger patients of this type came from appalling social backgrounds. Missing fathers, absent or drug dependent mothers making their living by prostitution, the children largely left to fend for themselves. When you treat them, you can't help but feel that this is a terrible waste of a life, and that they are doomed to spend most of their lives living at her majesty's pleasure.

One of our customers was a sixteen-year-old joyrider who'd crashed the car he had stolen and ended up having both legs amputated. He was full of bravado and a pretty obnoxious young man. When he had finally healed and was discharged, being pushed out of the ward in a wheelchair, his final shouted message to all around him was, "This isn't going to stop me stealing cars!" The wicked thought that occurred to me was "What, those little, blue ones?".

Another of my patients was a career burglar, who had lost one leg at the thigh in some previous injury and now had a problem with his other knee. I saw him in outpatients and listed him for an arthroscopy, but every time we sent for him, he was back in Armley prison. I couldn't help but think that having a false leg made him not too difficult to identify or improved his ability to run for it if disturbed.

We would then arrange another appointment in outpatients, to make sure nothing had changed, put him on the waiting list again, but when we sent for him, surprise, surprise he was back in prison. It was like a revolving door. This went on for a couple of years before we managed to get him in for his surgery. I chatted with him on the ward before his operation. He actually seemed a fairly pleasant guy and was always polite and thankful to everyone for his care.

"**..., every time we send for you, you're back in Armley. You're not very good at this burgling lark. Why don't you try something honest?". He sighed.

"Well Mr. B, it's all I know how to do." He did then extend the offer that if I ever got burgled and let him know, he would help get my stuff back.

I've had a few similar offers from the dark side of society over the years. One patient, grateful for the outcome of his treatment, told me that if I ever needed "a shooter", to just give him the nod. Another who I put back together, offered to supply his services if anyone crossed me and needed "sorting out".

Not all criminals have a soft centre. One of the things that really upsets me is when people steal from hospitals. The NHS treats anyone, no matter which side of the tracks they have come from, as well as their families and friends. If you steal something from a hospital and then get injured or ill, it might be you that ends up suffering. Unfortunately, this logic clearly doesn't appeal to some, who really are the lowest of the low.

At the BRI we had a five-day ward on the top floor. This is a ward where patients only requiring a few days in hospital can be admitted, with the ward closing Friday evening and then opening again Monday morning. After one weekend, the staff arrived and walked onto a completely empty ward. Everything had been taken. Mattresses, sheets, duvets, pillows, all the kitchen equipment, TV and even the bedpan washer. Hospitals are trusting environments and in the days before CCTV and ID badges, someone looking official in a brown coat and with a clipboard, could just walk in and walk out again with anything movable. The result was a lot of cancelled patients and scarce resource taken up replacing the stolen goods.

The oddest group of trauma patients are those who feign accident and injury in order to either obtain opioid painkillers, or because they have a warped love of being in hospital or having surgery. Over the years you develop sixth sense of when something is not quite right, which can stop you from making a terrible mistake.

One afternoon when I was in clinic, A&E asked if I would see a patient with a "locked knee" (when one of the cartilages tears and the torn bit gets trapped in the joint, stopping it from bending or straightening), who seemed to be in a lot of pain. He was brought round for me to have a look at and sure enough, any attempt to move the joint made him scream with pain. I noticed two small and fairly fresh, scars on the front of his knee and asked him if he'd had recent keyhole surgery. He went on to tell me he had a similar episode of locking three weeks before and had been admitted to a London hospital and undergone an arthroscopy but that they had been unable to sort out the problem.

Things just weren't ringing true. He told me he was a semi-professional soccer player but then made the fatal error of telling me he was a goalkeeper – he was about five foot seven! I asked who had done his surgery, and he mentioned a professor at a London teaching hospital who, unbeknown to him, was actually a personal friend. As the patient was still screaming every time we tried to move him, I sent him up to the ward with the instructions not to give him anything stronger than paracetamol.

I rang my friend and told him the story.

"Oh, you've got our "Munchie". (Munchausen's syndrome is a mental illness when somebody feigns illness or injury to obtain treatment they really don't need). I went up to the ward to be told by the nurses he had been desperately asking for morphine for the "agonising pain" he was in. I spoke to him.

"Hi… I've spoken to the professor and I'm afraid I don't believe a word you've said. The police are on their way to interview you with regard to trying to obtain controlled drugs by deception." A miracle occurred. His knee suddenly straightened and the next moment he was sprinting off the ward, never to be seen again!

One similar type of patient came to see me privately, having had multiple operations on his knee following a complex ligament injury some years before. He'd just returned from the States where he had just had his Posterior Cruciate Ligament redone, for the second time, at the Hospital for Special Surgery in New York.

The surgery and an overnight stay in the hospital had cost him ninety-six thousand dollars! When he left, they told him he still had some laxity (looseness) of his previously reconstructed anterior cruciate ligament and that this would need redoing for the third time. It was this he'd come to see me about. He clearly loved surgery and seemed to have unlimited funds. In the previous four years he had spent a total of eighteen months on crutches after his various operations. I examined him and as far as I was concerned, his knee felt completely stable.

I told him I didn't think he needed anything further doing and that I didn't think further surgery would make any great difference to his knee stability (and it is to restore stability that this type of surgery is done). He was adamant however that something needed doing and went away very unhappy. I think he found someone in Europe who took his shilling, but last thing I had heard, he'd had to have a knee replacement.

I found myself head of our orthopaedic department by default. All the other consultants in the department had done their stint and when the then clinical lead became ill, it was my turn. It's not a position many people choose to do and the average tenure of this type of post around the country was in the region of eighteen months.

You are suddenly "a manager", responsible for budget setting and business planning without any training at all, running a department with an annual budget of roughly twenty-three million pounds a year. Trying to juggle not only management demands but also colleague and patient's aspirations is a difficult task at best. Trying to organise a group of independent minded orthopaedic surgeons is like trying to herd cats. I held the post for eleven years, becoming one of the longest serving clinical heads of department in the country, at a time when our department expanded from five to fifteen consultants, and during several reorganisations of the health service and hospital.

I never regarded myself as some sort of dictator trying to impose my personal vision on everyone else. I preferred to move forward by consensus. Sure, I had my own ideas of where I wanted the department to go and might try and persuade others to my point of view, but I didn't get the hump if the majority disagreed. I didn't regard the department as a personal fiefdom or try and gain any personal advantage from my position.

My proudest achievement was having a department where we all spoke to each other, so very different from when I had first arrived at the BRI. This made us a very powerful unit, as the standard management tactic of "divide and conquer" just didn't work. We achieved a lot but were constantly asked to do more. I always tried to lead from the front and always stood up for the staff against some awful management initiatives. I think you can make things work by two ways, either through fear or respect. If people are afraid of you, they will try to not displease you, but if people respect you, and know you are looking out for them, you can achieve so much more.

The wage structure as a consultant was a weird set up. The pay increased year on year for the first five years and then remained static, with any pay increase dependent on "Merit Awards". These were highly prized, as once obtained, they were never taken away (this has now changed, and they are reassessed every five years) and counted towards your pension. They were supposed to be awarded for "activities above and beyond" turning up every day and keeping your nose clean.

Around the year 2004 I was doing OK. My private practice just kept on growing but I was also contributing what I could in the National Health Service. I was not only a major income generator for the Trust and head of the orthopaedic department, I had become the non-designated, regional referral centre for complex knee injuries. I enjoyed teaching and represented the hospital on the regional postgraduate education committee as well as organising a yearly mock exam for the trainees. At a national level, because of my perceived expertise I had been invited to be president of BOSTA, I was chairman of the National Allograft (donor ligament) Users committee, was an examiner for the Royal College FRCSOrth exam, and was on a team of five producing national guidelines for "Best Practice Anterior Cruciate Ligament Reconstruction". I had published (on average) two scientific papers a year and was being invited to lecture around the country and abroad. I was on both the Football Association and Rugby League medical committees and was the British representative on the "Union Internationale des Associations d"Alpinisme.

Out of the blue, I received a letter saying the Royal College had nominated me for a national "B" merit award (merit awards at that time started with a "C", usually awarded at local level, then progressed to a "B", an "A" and then top of the range "AA"). I was extremely flattered, but not optimistic of winning out against national competition, and wondered what would happen if I applied locally.

One of the peculiarities of the system, was that the decision as to who received merit awards was made by the consultants in our Trust who had already obtained one. As an example of a self-fulfilling prophecy, the biggest department in the hospital (anaesthetics), had the biggest proportion of merit awards and therefore the most people taking part in the vote!

A colleague told me that when my application was discussed, it was felt that I was earning enough money already (in my self generated private practice), and the two awards went to an A&E consultant and a radiologist who was close to retirement, who's only achievement seemed to have been turning up at nine and leaving at five, Monday to Friday, for thirty years and not upsetting management. Apparently, it was felt it would "boost his pension". Nothing to do with achieving anything which might deserve the term merit. Not that I'm bitter in any way! I never did receive any NHS recognition.

There were three surgeons in our hospital who suffered from a considerable amount of jealousy, purely based on our ability to generate income in the private sector. Given that at the time, any form of advertising was frowned upon by the GMC, we had all become successful through our own endeavours and being good at what we did. There was a general surgeon, a plastic surgeon and myself. We actually got on well together, having a mutual respect for each other's achievements.

One of the very few things I like about the USA is that if you are a success there, people look at you and say to themselves "I want to be like him. What do I have to do to achieve what he has?" In the UK, it seems to be more "Who the hell does he think he is?", as they run a key down the side of your car, or slag you off behind your back or on social media. It doesn't seem to matter that you started with absolutely nothing, nobody has given you a helping hand up, and you've never progressed by damaging or defaming anybody else, if you've done well, you're fair game. There is no celebration of success.

I think I suffered more than most as my practice was so high profile. At the private hospital, a steady stream of top-class sportsmen and women were coming to see me, purely based on my "word of mouth" reputation. About that time, I looked at Sven Goran Eriksson's England squad and had operated on over a quarter of them. I lived out my sporting ambitions vicariously and, to this day, can't watch a game of football or rugby league, at any level, without there being at least one player I have treated running around on the pitch.

In the local area, I was looking after Leeds United, Bradford City and Huddersfield Town football clubs and the Bradford Bulls, Wakefield Wildcats, Castleford Tigers, Leeds Rhinos and Huddersfield Giants Rugby League teams (makes me sound more like a large animal vet!). Further afield, I was treating many soccer players from the premiership down to non-league, as well as top class participants from many diverse sports, from all over the country.

It is sometimes assumed that because you are treating these high earning players you must be earning a fortune. This is not the case! In fact you are paid little more than a standard BUPA fee, despite clubs asking for almost immediate access and treatment, and you needing a massively higher indemnity insurance (some insurance companies won't insure you at all for treating professional players – one club doctor was recently sued for thirteen million pounds). I have even had accountants from a top premiership club querying why my fees were above the standard BUPA fee, for treating a player earning well over a hundred thousand pounds a week!

Most of the players were great, with just the occasional prima donna. Some stand out in your memory. One day the physio from Middlesborough brought an injured player down to see me. It was immediately apparent he was in a different league (as it were) to most – intelligent, articulate and insightful. We had some interesting conversations about the club and particularly the role of managers. Gareth Southgate was his name – I wonder what became of him?!

Treating sportsmen and women from the elite level is potentially somewhat stressful, but "you either have the big match temperament or you don't". When operating on a premiership player, the club physio and sometimes the club doctor, will come to watch the surgery. This is useful in terms of being able to discuss what you are doing and why, as well as the post-op rehabilitation, but when you pick up a knife and they are standing behind you, it doesn't make for a more relaxed atmosphere. You have to be able to put all thoughts about how much this individual is worth, what they are earning or what would happen if anything went wrong to one side, put yourself in "the zone" and concentrate on doing what you do best.

There is then always a long rehabilitation period and the inevitable nerves of the "first game back". In 2010 two of the Leeds Rhinos greatest players were injured within a few weeks of each other. Jamie Peacock is a true "Man of Steel", and as tough a customer as you are ever likely to meet. Danny McGuire was a mercurial and creative player, and one of their top try scorers. Not only were they both injured at roughly the same time but they both had the same unusual, complex ligament injury of the knee.

Ligament reconstruction of these injuries is tricky in a normal individual but the outcome in the highest of demand sports is unpredictable. It is a tough conversation with a player, when you have to tell them their injury is potentially career ending, and very difficult for the player to get their head around. (There was an interesting TV interview with Danny, about his career, when he went into detail about this.)

Fortunately, everything went well and they both came on as subs in the same first game back. I'd never seen Jamie Peacock look nervous, before or since. It was nerve wracking for me just watching, so what it must have been like for him I can't imagine. He was hopping from foot to foot and bouncing up and down on the spot. The moment came when he took the ball for his first carry. He made a few yards then disappeared under a pile of opposition players and my heart went into my mouth, but he emerged unscathed and, a few minutes before full time, carried the ball ten yards, popped the ball up in the air for Danny McGuire to run onto, burst through the opposition line and score. Jamie Peacock went on to finish his career on a high, and Danny McGuire was playing until recently. He is currently still the SuperLeague all-time leading try scorer.

My association with Bradford City continued to be close. After a superb season in the championship, the club had climbed into the Premiership by winning the last game of the season away at

Wolverhampton Wanderers, and then stayed up by the skin of their teeth by beating Liverpool 1-0 in the last game of the following season. That game was a magical afternoon. Arriving an hour before kick-off, as I climbed out of the car outside the ground, the atmosphere was like nothing else I've ever experienced. It was like thick, static electricity in the air.

Sky TV football pundit Rodney Marsh had foolishly stated that Bradford were the worst team ever to have reached the premier league and that if they stayed up, he would shave his head on the pitch at Valley Parade. The following season started with Bradford City's chairman applying a razor to Marsh's flowing locks as he sat in the centre circle, to loud cheers from the crowd.

Unfortunately, the seasons after that weren't so brilliant, and year by year, the club steadily slid down the leagues. We then had a period in the doldrums, followed by an exceptional season or two when the club ended up in the League Cup final at Wembley (the first ever club from the second division to achieve this – unfortunately getting absolutely slaughtered by Swansea), after beating several premiership clubs on the way. The next season they had a great FA cup run, unexpectedly coming from two-nil down to beat Chelsea at Stamford bridge when Chelsea were well clear at the top of the premiership. (Jose Mourinho's face was a picture, although he was unexpectedly very gracious in defeat).

One of the darkest moments in Bradford City's past was the fire disaster in 1985, when fifty-six people died and over two hundred and fifty were injured. It was a desperate day I remember well. I was working as a registrar in Sheffield, seeing a patient in A&E when I looked up at the TV in the waiting room. The final game of the season (when Bradford had gained promotion to the next division) was being televised and events unfolded live. I will never forget the image of one of the spectators staggering out of the stand being consumed in fire and being knocked to the ground by a policeman desperately trying to put out the flames. It was a terrible time, still fresh in the memories of staff at would become my base hospital.

In 2015, it was the thirtieth anniversary of the event and there was a big push to raise money for the Burns Unit, remembering those who had passed. That year the crowd were fond of singing "Everywhere We Go", with the Kop belting this out in grounds all over the country. I approached the chairman and asked if he would be happy for me to produce a charity single based around the chant, with the proceeds all going to charity.

At that time, I had not long formed a band – Never2Late – and so saw this as a chance of combining two of my favourite things in life. We had a great time putting it together, helped enormously by "Peak Recording", a sound studio in Bradford who provided their services free of charge. My vision was to record the crowd singing the chorus, get the players to sing the verses and intersperse the verses with sound clips of some of the highlights of the previous couple of seasons that the local radio stations provided us with.

It was a logistical nightmare! I had thought orthopaedic surgeons difficult to organise but trying to get footballers together in the same place, at the same time, was an interesting exercise. The captain (Steven Darby – now tragically diagnosed with motor neurone disease) and vice-captain (Andrew Davies) helped a lot, and I will always be grateful to them. It would have been even better if they could have sung in tune, but it's amazing what autotuning can do! It was also very difficult to get the crowd to sing in time but again, it is mind blowing what can be tweaked in a modern recording studio.

The single was released as a digital download and sold thousands of copies. We reached number three in the "Official Independent Singles Breakers Chart" in May 2015. Eight places below us, at number eleven, was a single, "Know Me From", by some guy called Stormzy. I often wonder what became of him. We raised a decent sum for the Burns Unit and for several years after there was still a trickle of sales.

Looking after a professional team is a fragile business. You are not employed by the club and neither do you receive any sort of retainer. You are only ever as good as your last case. I looked after one team from the northeast for fifteen years and never had a problem, then one case didn't work out and I never saw a player from that club again. You are also vulnerable to a change of manager, which often goes hand in hand with a complete change in the backroom staff, or even the whim of an agent or chairman. One premiership team flies all their first team players to Barcelona (by private jet!), to see a surgeon who operates on several different joints, rather than send them to an appropriate super-specialist in the UK.

You will be looking after a team and having no problems, then the manager changes, brings his own backroom staff with him and the referrals dry up. What then often happens, is that you suddenly start getting referrals from a brand-new club and find the physio from the previous club is now working there. It's all about building relationships, where there is a mutual sense of trust, in them knowing you are not going to operate on everybody who comes in through the door, that when you do operate the outcome is likely to be good and, probably most importantly, you can accurately and realistically predict time frames for returning to playing.

There was sometimes a feeling expressed by colleagues that operating on these top sportsmen and women was elitist, and that it was better to concentrate on the ordinary man on the street. I always countered this by pointing out the example of Formula One racing. Car manufacturers spend a fortune developing systems that function at the very limit of performance, which then filter down into the bog-standard cars that you and I drive around. If you can do an operation that functions at the cutting edge of sport, then that can only be of benefit to the less demanding weekend warriors. Certainly, if an operation can stand up to the rigours of rugby league it will probably be more than adequate for mere mortals.

There is a common misconception that patients receive something different in the private sector, but in terms of the treatment this isn't the case. A better menu, a choice of appointment times and a guarantee the consultant will be doing the surgery, but I don't know of anyone who does a different or lower standard of surgery in the NHS. You don't get a "better" operation because you go privately.

In fact, if I had something major wrong with me, the private hospital would be the last place I'd want to be. There is generally a skeleton staff at a private hospital once the operating lists for the day have finished, with usually the most senior doctor on site being an SHO of variable standard. I had an argument with the chief medical officer of the health care company running our local private hospital, who suddenly announced that all consultants working in the hospital should have their "Intermediate Life Support" (a fairly high standard of resuscitation) qualification, as this would "make the hospital safer". I pointed out that a hospital is as safe as its weakest point, which for twelve hours a day, was when there were no consultants in the building at all, and if he didn't feel that this was safe, he should close the place down.

I also mentioned that when I was in my private clinic, there was an anaesthetist next door and a cardiologist not twenty yards away in another clinic. The last thing a patient would want was me getting in the way of their resuscitation! The only time we ever had unanimous agreement in the Clinical Management Group (a collection of senior managers and heads of departments) at the Royal Infirmary, was when a similar proposal was put forward and I asked if there was anyone around the table who would want their cardiac arrest managed by an orthopaedic consultant, which received a resounding "No!".

This type of pointless posturing became increasingly prevalent with the introduction of annual appraisal, introduced to try and stop the appearance of another Harold Shipman. Initially, it was a purely paper exercise with an "appraiser" from our department who would sign us all off in a day of meaningless questions and answers. It was simply not fit for purpose.

One of the interesting things you reviewed together were the complaints with your name on them. In fact, any complaint by a patient under your care was attributed to you, even if it was about the toilets not being clean or the food arriving cold. One memorable complaint with my name on it, that I didn't even know about until I attended my appraisal, was by a cage fighter whose knee ligaments I had reconstructed one afternoon. During the night after his surgery, the hospital "bed managers" thought it appropriate to put a homeless person with pneumonia into the bed next to him and he caught fleas.

The appraisal process was beefed up again with the introduction of "mandatory training". This included such esoteric items as knowing which colour fire extinguisher to use in which type of fire, "customer care" and "lifting and handling" modules (something as an orthopaedic surgeon, I clearly knew nothing about).

In my usual fashion, I point blank refused to take part (in the mandatory training), as I couldn't see what relevance it had to my ability to practice medicine safely (an opinion I had in common with the head of the General Medical Council). Indeed, mandatory training isn't required by the General Medical Council in order to be seen to be fit to practice. Most of the modules were set at health care assistant level and were completely irrelevant to my daily job of work.

Eventually, the private hospital threatened me with withdrawing my practicing privileges if I didn't complete the various modules, with no right of appeal. The burden was somewhat eased when a member of the theatre staff told me to just keep hitting the return button on the computer keyboard. I couldn't believe it could be that easy, but sure enough, I didn't read any of the text and just kept hitting the button until a message appeared, "Congratulations. You have completed the **** module. Please print out your certificate". I did six and a half hours of mandatory training in roughly thirty-five minutes.

Their appraisal process was so "robust and fit for purpose", they brought in an orthopaedic surgeon who had passed his appraisal, to do "choose and book" NHS work, who had a string of complications (despite repeated warnings from the staff) before he was stopped from operating. When he left, his waiting list was reviewed and, certainly in the cases I looked at, two-thirds of them did not have the indications for the surgery he had listed them for. My colleagues specialising in joint replacement told me they had a similar experience, cancelling about half the patients he had listed for joint replacement. The implications were that he had possibly performed inappropriate surgery on hundreds of patients. He was able to tell you which colour fire extinguisher to use though.

At my last appraisal, my appraiser sent back my form saying that in the section "What do you want to achieve in the next year?" I wasn't allowed to put, "To have remained sane in the face of the relentless tide of bureaucratic bullshit that threatens to overwhelm me on a daily basis." Most doctors just want to get on with treating as many patients as possible, to the best of their abilities but clearly, managers and politicians have other ideas. Most of the process isn't fit for purpose, and it seems to be box ticking for our leaders. Annual appraisal certainly doesn't seem to have stopped the regular appearance of rogue doctors in the media.

As a consultant you are also subject to the seemingly arbitrary policies dished out by the DOH, in order that politicians can reassure the voters that they are doing everything they can to improve the health service. A classic was the "bare below the elbow" policy, introduced in 2008 in response to public concern about hospital acquired infection. Because some bacteriologist had cultured bacteria from shirt cuffs and ties, we were instructed to wear short sleeve shirts and abandon our ties and jackets.

At our hospital, a meeting of all the heads of departments was called to discuss the introduction of the policy, and we were told we would be responsible for disciplining staff who failed to comply. I asked for the evidence that this policy had been trialed and had been shown to be effective. There wasn't any. I asked that if I could name a hospital where everyone wore their jackets and ties, nobody rolled up their sleeves and they had no MSRA, would they be prepared to accept that the policy had no basis in science?

The medical director told me he thought that would be difficult to do, so I pointed out the window at the private hospital across the road, where they had a zero MRSA infection rate. In reality, this was because they had a bed occupancy of less than eighty-five percent and screened all the patients before admission, two approaches which *had* been scientifically shown to reduce infection. We were then told, whatever the science, we would be doing it anyway and would be disciplined if we didn't, "because we say so". I do sometimes wonder if was yet another government ploy to demean the status of consultants.

Patients often have a touching faith in the powers of medicine to overcome death. Almost all of them seem to believe that if they have a cardiac arrest they will be revived. As clinical lead I had to sit for over an hour listening to a couple's complaint that on admission the SHO on the ward had suggested in the event of a cardiac arrest, resuscitation might not be appropriate for their ninety-two year old, blind, deaf and doubly incontinent mother with Alzheimers and a fractured hip, and they therefore felt we weren't taking her care seriously.

Yet another recent initiative in the NHS (following in the wake of the private sector), was to get all consultants to obtain their "Advanced Life Support" qualification in resuscitating patients with a cardiac arrest. This sounds great but is both time consuming and costly to the health service (like all mandatory training). When an anaesthetist at the BRI did a study on resuscitation rates, if you weren't in ITU, CCU (Coronary Care Unit), A&E or the operating theatres, the successful resuscitation rate could be stated in round figures i.e. zero. I was recently speaking to a consultant anaesthetist from the Mid-Yorkshire Trust, who told me that they had done a similar study with very similar findings.

The last few years have seen attacks on consultants by the Competition and Marketing Authority, the Private Health Information Network, Data Protection and insurance companies (the "relentless tide of bureaucratic bullshit"!). After halving their fees, insurance companies started ringing me up to tell me I am "overcharging" and advising patients they shouldn't come and see me for the same reason. This last I was particularly aggrieved by. I hadn't put my fees up for twelve years, but the medical insurance companies tied in new consultants to contracts stating that they would abide by the private health insurance company's fee structure (otherwise they wouldn't be allowed to treat their customers), and then a few years later halved the fees, effectively fixing the fees at an artificially low level.

Our last chief executive at the BRI told me he felt sorry for me as "When you worked through medical school and then worked your butt off to become a consultant, this is not what you signed up for." He was right. The last thirty years have seen massive changes in consultant status from virtual God (something I'd really rather not be), to being treated as just another one of the team, although your name is on the end of the bed, the buck stops with you, you are responsible for decision making and accountable for anything that goes wrong. I don't think anyone nowadays wants the "God" status, but surely respect, accountability and responsibility should go pretty closely together.

11

MONEY'S TOO TIGHT TO MENTION OR WHAT'S WRONG WITH THE NHS? - POLITICIANS AND MANAGERS.

This is going to be a long chapter! There won't be much humour and what I say will probably ruffle a few feathers. The facts are quoted from and easily checked via Google, and this chapter documents the personal experience I have had, over the years, of many mishaps in managing the health service.

Politicians seem to hate doctors, particularly hospital consultants. I often wonder if this is because in surveys of trustworthiness, doctors and vicars always come out at the top and politicians somewhere near the bottom, usually between used-car salesmen and estate agents. A YouGov poll in January 2019 found that eighty-five percent of people have "little or no trust in their MP." It doesn't seem to matter which political persuasion they may be, the poor old NHS is used as a political football by successive governments, with patients and the front-line staff being kicked from pillar to post.

Politicians seem to love changing things, even when they seem to be working well. During my career I have seen several reorganisations of the health service, each one costing billions of pounds to implement. My experience is that not one of them has been responsible for substantial improvements for patients and staff.

In my own consultant career, this started with Margaret Thatcher's reforms, with the setting up of hospital "Trusts", and the introduction of the "purchaser-provider split" with GP fundholding. The premise of the latter was that General Practitioners know what their patients need and would be best placed to decide where funding should go. At the same time, it would introduce an element of competition into the process. This was seen as a way to "break the power of the consultants".

Before this, any GP was free to refer any patient, to any consultant, in any hospital – true patient choice and a logical system given that the taxation for funding the health service is collected centrally. Afterwards, patient referrals were largely restricted to where their GP's practice had made contracts for hospital care. It also led to a massive explosion in bureaucracy.

In our hospital, which had become a "Trust", we now needed managers to make and monitor contracts, managers to bill the practices, managers to make sure the bills were paid etc., etc. When I was a registrar at the Bradford Royal Infirmary (BRI), the hospital ran with a general manager, a matron and an accountant with a few support staff. By the time I left some thirty years later, managers outnumbered consultants by approximately three to one.

Whereas before Thatcher's reforms I was left to organise my operating lists based on clinical priority, I now received a list every week of patients that needed to be seen and operated on in line with the various contracts, irrespective of whether their condition was urgent or not. My department actually had twenty-seven different contracts made for us (without the involvement of any of the consultant staff), all with different time frames in which patients had to be seen or operated on, making the system impossibly complicated. Like most of my colleagues, the list of manager's requests was filed in the bin, and I continued to treat patients based on their individual clinical needs.

One of the interesting things about the contracts was that they were made by a hospital manager who had no understanding of what our department did, and general practitioners who generally had a similar level of knowledge. The sophistication of the process was such that the GPs were buying "Finished Consultant Episodes". This meant an outpatient visit, plus or minus surgery, for each individual patient until discharge. Bizarrely, they were all paid at exactly the same rate, whether it was a minor procedure on a toenail or a complex revision joint replacement.

A good example of this level of understanding was when one year we were asked, by the then Area Health Authority, to reduce the amount of "trauma" we did by ten percent. When our manager approached me to ask if this was reasonable, I had to explain to him that "trauma" involved people who had injured themselves or been involved in accidents and was therefore something over which we had no particular control!

Understanding why these reforms were perceived as a good idea was difficult to understand, although I suppose it did massively increase the number of non-clinical people employed by the health service. Years later we learned that one of Margaret Thatcher's trusted GP medical advisers at the heart of the health reforms (Clive Froggatt) was found guilty of writing himself prescriptions for heroin and had a heavy dependence on the drug at the time. Enough said!

Thatcher's brilliant achievement, however, was diverting attention from the fact that not enough money was being put in at the top of the system and shift blame to those on the ground for "not using what they had efficiently enough". The NHS slowly and surely became chronically malnourished.

Before these reforms, we treated and operated on as many patients as we possibly could throughout the year, maximising the use of our facilities. Afterwards, hospitals all around Yorkshire would stop operating on elective (non-emergency) patients around December or January as their "funding" had run out (in Bradford it was felt this approach was "politically unacceptable" so we had fifteen percent of our operating lists cancelled on a rolling basis, so for two or three years I had a paid day off every sixth week!). Staff weren't laid off and wards and operating theatres stood largely idle, but were kept running to deal with emergencies, so the "saving" to the NHS must have been minimal, at the cost of patients waiting long after they could have been treated.

We were being constantly urged to try and run our service as a "business". There is however one fundamental difference between nationalised healthcare, and a business trying to make a profit. The more work we did, the better and more efficient our service and the better our reputation, the more money it cost the government and taxpayer.

As my own reputation grew, I received more and more referrals from GPs, for patients from all over the UK who wanted me to try and sort out their knee problems. This became a real headache, particularly after waiting time targets were introduced, and I became seen by management as a liability, rather than an asset.

Government changed but the attitudes didn't. In 1999 one of Tony Blair's trusted allies, Alan Milburn, was appointed health secretary. I was driving into work at seven in the morning, when Radio 4 played his opening remarks on air. I nearly choked as I heard, "All we need to do to sort the health service out is to get the consultants in off the golf course." Alan Milburn seemed to have a particular dislike of hospital consultants, rumoured at the time to be something to do with his parentage.

So, the Labour government's big scheme at the time was to introduce a new consultant contract with the thinking being, that if they only paid consultants for what they did, and consultants spend most of their time on the golf course or in the local private hospital, then they would save at least thirty percent on the consultant wage bill. Up to this point consultants were paid a fixed salary and, in my experience, most of my colleagues worked well above and well beyond what they were paid for.

After some serious negotiations the government put the new contract to the consultant body, and it was rejected by a sizeable majority. The government then turned around and told us we were having it anyway, and then proceeded to roll out the new salary structure, making it compulsory for newly appointed consultants.

Contrary to Alan Milburn's and the Labour party's seemingly deeply held beliefs, it turned out the vast majority of consultants were working far in excess of the predictions (for those of us working at the front line this was blindingly obvious). In my hospital, several consultants were told they had to do less work as they were working in excess of the permitted hours. Instead of saving thirty percent on the wage bill, it ended up costing the government thirty percent more. You may recall Gordon Brown being asked where the "missing NHS billions" had gone, and hear him explaining the money had gone on the "expensive new consultant contracts", neglecting to mention the fact it was his administration that had insisted on implementing them, against the wishes of the majority of consultants.

(It seems that lessons are never learned. In 2018 the current Conservative government unilaterally changed pension regulations affecting a large number of consultants. Colleagues were receiving tax demands, out of the blue, for sums in the order of fifty thousand pounds, and given three weeks to pay. A 2019 survey of surgical consultants found nearly seventy percent of consultants were considering early retirement and had already reduced the amount of time they were spending working in the NHS, as to work longer hours meant such punitive taxation they were effectively working for nothing.)

The Labour government made a similar fiasco of the new General Practioner contract. This included the option for dropping out of "on-call" for the loss of a few thousand pounds in income. I have been told the DOH believed less than ten percent of GPs would take up this option, but it turned out to be something nearer ninety percent. Again, anyone who has worked on the ground could have predicted this, but sadly not our leaders, and is yet another example of how the people at the top are disconnected from the reality of the front line.

This led to the situation where suddenly there were no on-call GPs at night, with the urgent setting up of "NHS Direct" and all the problems and costs that this produced. Amazingly, and apparently completely unpredictably, this put huge pressure on the ambulance service and A&E departments across the county. Who'd have thought it?!

Alan Milburn was also responsible for driving forward the "Private Finance Initiative" where health authorities were strong-armed into seeking private financing for new hospital buildings and infrastructure. Deals were sanctioned which financed eleven-point-eight billion pounds in building hospitals in England but will cost seventy-nine billion of taxpayer's money to pay back over thirty years, at which time the buildings will no longer belong to the health service. Who exactly has benefitted from that?

There are numerous reports in the press about Alan Milburn's track record. Shortly after his tenure as Health Minister, a contract was awarded to a company called Alliance Medical to carry out MRI scans on NHS patients in order "to reduce waiting lists". This it singularly failed to do even when, as reported by Labour MP Kevin Jones, purchasing authorities were instructed to send their patients to Alliance facilities, often many miles away from the patient, and sometimes when the local hospital MRI scanner was under-utilised.

According to the Guardian, the contract cost the NHS sixteen million pounds but only sixty-two thousand of the one hundred and thirty thousand paid for scans were used – i.e. the taxpayer paid full price for less than half the work. Weirdly, not too long after his resignation as health minister, Alan Milburn took up a directorship of the company that owns Alliance Medical. Apparently the two were completely unrelated.

He has continued to be true to his socialist principles, and in an article in the Financial Times, hectored his previous parliamentary colleagues to continue to utilise private healthcare as part of the delivery of NHS services. In 2018 his company, AM Strategy, which generates income from "private healthcare consulting", reported cash in the bank of four-point-six-three million pounds.

During this time of change I became head of the orthopaedic department at the Bradford Royal Infirmary (mainly because I was next in line and nobody else wanted to do it!) and, because of this role, I was asked to give a lecture on "Choice and Capacity" at the Royal College of Surgeons in London. The Labour Party had introduced the "Eighteen Week Target" from referral to treatment and only two disciplines were likely to struggle to hit this – Orthopaedics and Plastic Surgery.

A meeting was therefore arranged between heads of orthopaedic departments from around the country and the Department of Health, as they wanted to try and understand what the problems and potential solutions might be. This turned out to be the inaugural meeting of The British Orthopaedic Directors Society, set up in response to the perception that the then leaders at the college were unrepresentative of opinion on the ground. Interestingly, I gave my lecture, went off to another meeting in the college and when I returned, was surprised to find I had been proposed, seconded and voted in as vice-president of the society, without ever seeking office!

I was continuously fascinated by the apparent lack of understanding of the representatives of the DOH, who seemed to struggle to grasp the situation at hospitals around the country. One of their major problems was that they couldn't understand why the number of consultants in our speciality of orthopaedic surgery had doubled, but waiting times had gone up, their feeling being that this was a situation being deliberately manufactured to boost consultant's private practice.

To try and explain, I showed them that when I arrived at Bradford, the hospital was doing less than ten knee ligament operations a year. By the time of the meeting I was doing one-hundred and fifty reconstructions a year and we'd just employed another knee surgeon to cope with the demand – something that hadn't existed ten years before. The rapid introduction of new technologies, the increasing demands of the elderly population, the need for redoing a large number of the original tranche of joint replacements (much more complex and time consuming second time around), and directions from above that junior doctors were no longer to do operating lists of their own (as a registrar and senior registrar I had, on average, three unsupervised operating lists of my own a week), all conspired to mean that demand constantly outstripped capacity.

In several meetings between The British Orthopaedic Directors Society and the DOH, I was consistently impressed by their lack of insight into the way the organisation they were nominally running, actually worked. We even had Lord Warner (Minister of State at the Department of Health at the time) come to talk with us. I won't forget our meeting! I had been detailed to meet him at the front door of the Royal College of Surgeons in Lincolns Inn Fields. He arrived three quarters of an hour late, stepping out of his taxi and striding up the steps to the front desk. He was a tall, imposing figure and addressed the receptionist with a superior air.

"I've come to talk to some surgeon chappies." I stepped forward, introduced myself and asked him to follow me to the lecture theatre where the assembled group of thirty to forty heads of orthopaedic departments from around the country had been waiting, for what we anticipated might be a constructive dialogue. He stood up to speak and weighed in with, "Of course, all you surgeons love long waiting lists." He had clearly arrived with preconceived ideas not based in reality at all, and over the next thirty minutes, nothing he said changed our initial impressions.

We never really achieved much, despite our willingness to be involved in positive change. It seems that politicians make up their minds first, without ever considering the evidence, then look for advisers and any poor piece of research to support their ideas, ignoring experts from the field and the often overwhelming weight of evidence that is out there (they never seem to learn – recently Michael Gove stated "we've had enough of experts").

This was coupled with what seemed to be a top down culture of bullying. The DOH usually sent one of their "Hatchet Men" to our meetings. He was a small, very overweight individual with thinning greasy hair, who was clearly used to getting his own way by a mixture of threats and intimidation and was one of the most unpleasant people I've ever met. The others of his team, who he used to drag along from the DOH, seemed scared stiff of him and terrified of saying or contributing anything that might be deemed not to be strictly within government thinking. He seemed completely non-plussed by coming up against a group of consultants who were both not at all intimidated and refused to agree with everything he said!

As long ago as 1990, the British Orthopaedic Association published a "Blue Book" about consultant practice. Within this was the fact that in hospitals which mixed emergency and elective (non-emergency) work within the same site, about seventy-eight percent of them experienced interference with, or even complete cessation of routine surgery. In Bradford, we were lucky to have the Woodlands Orthopaedic Hospital situated in beautiful countryside, several miles from the main Infirmary. This allowed the smooth running of the elective surgery part of our department. Patients would receive their date for surgery without the worry their operation might be cancelled because there were no beds due to emergencies.

Situated in what had been originally an old country house, and surrounded by rhododendrons and woodland, it was a great place to work or be treated. Patients used to love it. Deer would occasionally wander onto the lawns and, in their recovery phase, patients could walk outside into the fresh air and sunshine. Orthopaedic patients are not generally ill, they usually have problems with a particular joint but are otherwise well, so this was an ideal environment for them. There were lovely little hospitals like this all around the country.

Then the Conservative party decided that small independent hospitals could not be financially viable and decided to close them all. We fought a bitter campaign to keep the hospital open, but it was always going to be a losing battle. We were made a lot of promises by management that our service would be better than before, we would only be in "temporary facilities" for two years before moving to a brand new, purpose-built unit, and that our elective beds would be ring-fenced.

After the Woodlands Hospital was closed and we were shoehorned into the main hospital, the ring fencing of our beds lasted all of three weeks before they started to be used for emergency admissions from other departments (resulting in cancellations of our routine surgery), and ten years later we were still in our "temporary facilities".

Following Alan Milburn, we had John Reid as Health Minister. The government had decided that what we needed was a number of small independent, elective hospitals around the country (sound familiar?) – the "Independent Sector Treatment Centres" (ISTC). John Reid stated he was proud to roll out this programme "to break the cartels of consultants who artificially inflate waiting lists to boost their private practice", rhetoric that may have come from his time in the young communist league. When I heard this, I had to wonder what planet he was on. Trying to organise groups of consultants is like platting fog, and in forty years I've never come across anything resembling a cartel!

In Bradford, an ISTC was built at Eccleshill, about two miles from where the previous Woodlands Hospital had been! Brand spanking new, with three operating theatres and an MRI/CT scanner, facilities that the Infirmary was crying out for. To incentivise private healthcare providers to take up the running of these centres, they were promised they would be paid for a fixed amount of work at ten percent above the rate the hospital Trusts were being paid. Rather like the Alliance Medical contract, they were paid the full amount irrespective of whether they completed all the work. In addition, they were allowed to cherry-pick their cases, so anything difficult or complicated, or patients who had other significant health problems, were referred back to the Infirmary.

A good example of how little the DOH understand how things work was when hospital Trusts around the country complained that the ISTC's and private sector were getting all the straightforward knee replacements, and they were left to do the complicated ones, even though they were paid at roughly the same rate. Instead of increasing the fee for the complicated ones, the DOH decided to reduce the fee for the straightforward cases.

Within twenty-four hours, a private hospital in Leeds was ringing consultants telling them they couldn't do NHS knee replacements anymore, as with the changes in fees they couldn't make a profit on this procedure. This of course meant these "non-profitable" cases went straight back to the main NHS hospitals.

The ISTC in Bradford was a peach! My department purchased some day-case operating sessions there, on a weekly basis, as we just didn't have enough operating theatres or beds in the Infirmary. I turned up on the first day, impressed by the shiny, modern facilities. The first thing that struck me, however, was the level of staffing. The theatre coffee room was full of people dressed in purple scrubs, and my operating list had twice the number of staff as I would normally expect. This included a top pay-grade sister who sat on a stool for the whole list, hitting a button on the computer to note the time of arrival of the patient in theatre, hitting the same button to denote the time they left and doing nothing else. When we had finished, half the staff who had been in the coffee room at the start of my list were still there.

Even more astonishing was to find out that of the three theatres, the second was only used about half the time and the third had never been used at all. It's only function at the time was that the staff used it to do aerobics at lunchtime. This state of affairs carried on for years. I'm not sure if the contract for work was ever fulfilled, yet another great use of taxpayer's money.

At that point the Infirmary was desperate for more operating space, and in a facility where the beds would be protected from being taken by emergency admissions. The contract for running the ISTC was coming up for tender again and the consultant body approached senior management in the hospital with a business plan to take over the ISTC to run as an NHS facility. This got rebuffed as it would be "politically unacceptable" for the ISTC to be seen to have failed!

It must be great being a politician, spending other people's hard-earned cash with no come back, no matter how much is wasted. For reasons I've never quite understood, the orthopaedic department in Bradford was one of three centres around the country to take part in

"The Lorenzo Project" – the development of a flagship data capture system in the NHS Information Technology programme.

Our department were all very enthusiastic about taking part and eagerly awaited our first meeting with the representatives from the company who had won the tender to develop the programme. They arrived full of promises that within eighteen months we would have a working model to trial.

Within five minutes of starting discussions with them, it became glaringly obvious that they had absolutely no idea about the size and complexity of the task they had taken on. Over the next couple of years our department must have spent thousands of hours working with them (unpaid!) to try and get something off the ground.

Two and a half years later there seemed no prospect of anything happening, so as the head of department I made enquiries about what penalty clauses there might be in the contract for late delivery, fairly standard practice across the industry. Surprise, surprise there weren't any, and four years after we started, the project was abandoned. The reported cost to the taxpayer of the failed, national IT project was in the region of four billion pounds, with absolutely nothing to show for it. We never did find out exactly where the money went!

Lessons were obviously not learned and recently the "Care.data" programme was abandoned at a cost of a mere seven-point-five million. Where does all this money go? Someone, somewhere is profiting from all this, but it's definitely not the Health Service!

Costs are always something politicians seem intensely interested in. During Labour's tenure, the "NHS Confederation" was tasked with identifying areas where savings in NHS spending could be made. I attended a meeting with them at the British Orthopaedic Association headquarters at the Royal College (weirdly, chaired by Mark Baker, the first and short-lived chief executive of the BRI – see below). One of our major proposals was that the NHS should use its purchasing power to drive down the cost of commonly used joint replacements. At that time (and it's still the case), each hospital negotiated its own contract with the companies selling them, who for their part seemed to run rings around the individual purchasing departments. As an example, in our locale, this had resulted in the Halifax Royal Infirmary (about three miles as the crow flies from our hospital), paying more for exactly the same joint replacement than we did in Bradford, because they were a "smaller user".

One of the surgeons in our unit originally came from Belgium and a friend of his from back home told us that the knee replacement our department used was thirty percent cheaper in their hospital than it was in ours. That was despite the fact the knee replacement was actually manufactured in the UK. At one point we seriously considered hiring a van, driving over to Belgium and filling it with knee replacements, but were told by the company they would refuse to honour any warranties if we did this.

We pointed out to the NHS Confederation that we were all part of the NHS, so why wasn't there a nationally negotiated price? It would be a bit like a car manufacturing company which had three different factories, having a component supplier charging them a different price for the same component at each factory, based on how many each factory used.

This was thought to be a great idea and off they went, but nothing happened! Indeed, many years later in 2015, Lord Carter came up with exactly the same idea! One wonders who is pulling which strings to prevent such an obvious and simple way of saving the tax-payer millions of pounds from happening.

We did see the forming of the "NHS Supply Chain" which was supposed to drive down the costs of essential items such as dressings or office supplies by bulk purchasing, but it was when I was clinical lead of the orthopaedic department, I discovered a ream of A4 paper was cheaper at "Staples" office supply store than through the NHS Supply Chain. I approached management and offered to drive my car down to Staples and fill the back of it with paper for the department but was told I couldn't do this as it had to be bought through official channels.

The number of examples of poor government thinking go on and on. Waiting lists are a political hot potato and constantly (and rightly) concern politicians. During my time in the NHS, initiatives to reduce these have been many. Unfortunately, the only thing the government seems to care about is getting the numbers through. They don't seem to care about who does the surgery or what the quality of the outcomes are, as long as the operations get done quickly.

A classic example was a lady in her mid-fifties who came to see me with a poor result after knee surgery. Eighteen months previously she had injured her knee, and her GP referred her to myself. At that time the Area Health Authority was screening all letters from GPs in their area referring patients for a hospital appointment. Her referral letter was intercepted, and she was redirected to a private hospital in Leeds where the government had funded a "waiting list initiative" for a shed load of orthopaedic surgery to "shorten waiting lists".

She told me that on her first attendance she met a European orthopaedic surgeon who had been flown in by the hospital to do the work. What she didn't know at that stage, was that the surgeons were being contracted for a months work at a time and then would be replaced by another European surgeon, this continuing until the funding ran out.

The first surgeon told her he wasn't sure what the problem was and organised an MRI scan. At the next follow up, a different European orthopaedic surgeon reviewed her and told her the scan showed she had ruptured her anterior cruciate ligament in her knee and that she needed it reconstructing (this is often not indicated in patients of this age). She was listed for surgery.

When she came to the hospital for her operation, yet another European orthopaedic surgeon she had never met before performed the surgery, told her everything had gone well and discharged her. She was never happy with the result. When she attended for follow up and complained that it didn't feel right, a fourth different surgeon organised a second MRI scan.

When she attended to discuss the results of that scan, a fifth orthopaedic surgeon told her the scan showed the operation hadn't been done correctly and would need redoing, but she would have to go back to her GP now, as the contract had ended and they were all going back to Europe! At this point, eighteen months after her injury, she was referred back to me to try and sort out and redo her badly done operation.

At the same time the radiologists (the experts in interpreting x-rays) in Leeds were raising concerns about the post-operative X-rays of the joint replacements that had been done by the same group of surgeons. The European surgeons had apparently been told they had to use a particular joint replacement they were unfamiliar with. The radiologists reviewing the post-operative check x-rays are on record (and appeared on the TV programme "Inside Out"), as reporting that some sixty percent of the X-rays raised concerns about the technical outcome of the surgery. Poorly done joint replacements lead to early failure and prolonged pain and suffering for patients. Re-doing major surgery like this is more time consuming, is less successful, has higher complication rates and is very, very, much more expensive.

Getting it right first time is the best way! If you ask any surgeon about how they would organise an operation for themselves, top of the list is always "who will be doing it?". Waiting times (unless excessive), and geographical location of the hospital are of secondary importance. Successive governments only seemed to care about the figures they could put in front of the voters and many, many patients have suffered as a consequence.

As you've probably worked out, I have a fairly low opinion of politicians. I work in a profession where my practice has to be demonstrably evidence based and my performance and outcomes are constantly monitored. One slip can result in suspension, being sued or even struck off, something our leaders seem largely immune too.

Even well-intentioned efforts by politicians can turn out not to be quite what they were supposed to be and cost the taxpayer large amounts of money that is desperately needed elsewhere in the health service.

The National Institute for Clinical Excellence (NICE) was set up with the aim of providing evidence based, best practice guidelines for treatments across the health service. Part of the problem is that if

NICE declare a particular treatment the best, then the lawyers cotton on to it immediately, and if a patient hasn't received that particular line of therapy and has an adverse event, it becomes difficult for an individual clinician or hospital to defend a claim. Hospitals therefore scramble to adhere to NICE guidelines, without necessarily critically examining them.

The question is however, are NICE guidelines all they are set out to be? The common perception is that they are unbiased and scientifically based.

In orthopaedics, two of our common complications after major surgery are deep vein thrombosis (DVT) and pulmonary embolus (PE), the latter of which can be fatal. Over the last forty years there have been many approaches to try and minimise this risk.

I attended a lecture not long after NICE produced their guidelines for DVT prophylaxis. NICE's recommendation was to use chemical prophylaxis (drugs that are either injectable or taken by mouth) to thin the blood, for variable periods of time after a joint replacement. The lecturer from the British Orthopaedic Association pointed out that in formulating the recommendations, the committee seemed to not have taken into account evidence about any adverse complications from the therapy and ignored the large amount of data on the use of Aspirin. The products recommended were marketed by two big pharmaceutical companies and it seemed that a significant proportion of the clinical advisers on the committee received sponsorship from those same two companies.

Subsequently, even the American Academy of Orthopaedic Surgeons, in the most litigious country in the world, have recently published a recommendation saying that aspirin is a safer and acceptable form of DVT prophylaxis. In a publication in the British Bone and Joint Journal, it was estimated a switch from NICE recommendations to aspirin would save the health service over twelve million pounds a year.

Similarly, NICE recommendations on bariatric (weight reduction) surgery (for which they were very much in favour, at potentially an enormous cost to the health service), had a committee which included four doctors who made their living from bariatric surgery and of the two patient representatives, one worked for a company selling bariatric surgery and the other was a health blogger who promoted bariatric surgery on YouTube. The assumptions made about the cost benefits, again seemed to be made on the basis of the surgery having a hundred percent success rate and no complications (which is far from the case), and with no requirement for further surgical intervention, monitoring or dietary supplements.

The problem is that NICE committees are voluntary and not well remunerated. They therefore seem to attract those who might have a vested interest in the subject under discussion. A journalist called Zoe Harcombe has blogged extensively about this, but apparently, NICE seem to think that as long as you declare a vested interest, it has no bearings on the validity of the recommendations!

The poor old NHS is subject to bad decision making by politicians who may be of poor quality, but the quality of hospital managers is generally worse! I could write another whole book on "managers I have known" but I'll just give a few prime examples. Margaret Thatcher's reforms were meant to attract high quality managers from industry into the NHS, but this it spectacularly failed to do. All that seemed to happen was the same, poor quality managers were given new job titles, paid a lot more money and carried on as before. Promotion through the management ranks in a hospital generally tended to come from within.

At the BODS meeting when I gave my lecture to the DOH, every middle manager in our hospital was either an ex nurse or ex medical secretary, all of whom had always worked in our hospital. Some were managing annual turnovers of their departments in the region of twenty-five million pounds, with no business qualifications at all (this included the chief executive). In fact, at that time, the only member of staff at the BRI who had actually obtained an MBA was one of the anaesthetists.

Really great ward sisters would feel they had to move into management, as there was no way for the system to pay them more for staying at, and continuing to do brilliantly, the job they were already doing. Frequently, this meant losing a fantastic member of the clinical team and getting a not very good business manager.

At the time of my lecture one of the "managers" in our department had been my secretary when I first arrived at the BRI, so the person who had originally taken my dictation, was now dictating to me which patients I should be operating on! They all seemed to be terrified of making a wrong decision, so made no decisions at all.

Approaching our, hopelessly out of his depth, hospital business manager with an innovative idea for improving the service was always met with kiss of death phrase.

"Well, I think what we need to do is to set up a working party to have a look at this." Members would be recruited, meeting dates arranged, which were then frequently changed at the last minute, meaning you couldn't attend without cancelling an operating list or outpatient clinic, and the weeks would become months and drag on and on until the project died a death. Which basically meant nothing ever changed.

My first example of the management that was to come, was as a senior registrar at the Leeds General Infirmary (LGI). A new, keen as mustard, theatre manager was appointed. Eager to make his mark, he commissioned a time and motion study of the theatre porters in the ground floor, four operating theatre suite. The theatre porter's job was to collect and return patients to their respective wards and to fetch and carry equipment as necessary.

There were two of them working at any one time, and the study showed that each of them only worked fifty percent of the time. "Aha!", thought the new manager, "two theatre porters, each only working fifty percent of the time, we only need one", so to save the wage of the most poorly paid member of the theatre team, the manager removed one of them.

The knock-on effect was entirely predictable to anyone who has worked in an operating theatre suite. Whenever two of the theatres finished a case close to each other, one theatre would then stand idle, waiting for the porter to be free and fetch their next patient. So, to save the wage of one poorly paid porter, whole theatre teams would stand idle for forty-five minutes at a time and inevitably patients would be cancelled off lists.

Shortly after this, the LGI was offered the chance to become a "Trust", something viewed with suspicion by the staff but as potentially a great thing by management. The management made a great play of balloting the staff as to whether they wanted to go down this avenue, but when eighty-seven percent of them voted against it, they took the hospital into Trust status anyway. To add insult to injury, at a time when funding for anything was extremely tight, the management commissioned a decorative mug to celebrate their achievement of obtaining Trust status and issued one to every member of staff. The following day the chief executive turned up to find a mountain of these mugs outside his office, returned in silent protest.

One of the first things the management proceeded to do was to close the "consultant's dining room", as it was "elitist". These facilities existed in almost every hospital and actually served a purpose. It was the only place you met your colleagues and learned about developments and advances in other fields. In addition, a lot of interdepartmental referrals could be sorted out on an informal but confidential basis. So, if a consultant on an orthopaedic ward had a patient who had a problem with their urinary output he would approach the physician with an interest in kidney problems, discuss the case and arrange for one of the appropriate team to visit the patient. With the demise of the consultants dining room this system, which worked pretty efficiently, disappeared and it was replaced with a paper request system with the inevitable delays, lost paperwork etc.

I think the main reason the management closed the consultant's dining room was it was seen as a place where objections and opposition to management policy could be discussed and organised by the consultant body, and the closure at the LGI was replicated in hospitals across the country. Interestingly, three or four years later the dining room was reopened but as an exclusive "management dining room".

Occasionally (not often!), I felt some sympathy towards our managers. In the top down culture of bullying in the health service, they are caught between the politician's unrealistic and dishonest demands, and the harsh realities on the ground.

The Bradford Royal Infirmary, where I was to take up post, was one of the first hospitals in the country to obtain Margaret Thatcher's vaunted "Trust" status, but within seven months the first chief executive , Mark Baker, was crucified in front of a Commons health select committee and resigned, after they deemed his trust application had been "over optimistic".

The first year of our Trust's life was actually monitored by Sir John Harvey-Jones for his BBC television series "Troubleshooter", at a time when the change to the Trust had "exposed such weaknesses in its management and accounting systems", that it was forced to consider returning to district health authority control.

He found "There is nothing but disappointed people, being let down in this place", that the government's promises that "money would follow patients" had been unfulfilled and there had been a failure to deliver promised benefits to staff and patients. Talking to my colleagues who are still working there, little has changed and indeed, this seems to be common across hospitals around the country.

After Mark Baker, a new chief executive was then appointed and through my early years at the BRI, became one of the longest serving chief executives in the NHS. His management style, however, was to set up layer upon layer between himself and the front line. Each manager seemed to tell the manager above what they wanted to hear, so by the time the message reached the top, everything in the rose garden was smelling sweet.

Our Trust was seen to be one of the top performing in the country, apparently hitting our budget year on year. We became one of the first ten "Foundation Trusts" in the country and our chief executive was awarded a CBE for "services to the health service". Within twelve months however, it became apparent that our success and financial stability was a house of cards, we were in fact deep in debt and the chief executive "took early retirement"… CBE to "retirement" in twelve months.

Hospital managers often seem scared of consultants and are reluctant to involve them in decision making in their Trusts. This is difficult to understand. We have an intimate knowledge of our fields, are generally highly qualified, well-motivated and reasonably intelligent. We are also likely to be working in the same hospital for our entire working lifetimes and have a vested interest in making it successful, as opposed to most hospital chief executives, who are a bit like football managers in that their tenure averages about eighteen months before they move on.

As an example, when I was appointed at the BRI as a consultant with a special interest in arthroscopic (keyhole) knee surgery, I was told there was no funding to buy the additional equipment I needed to actually carry out my role. The instruments we had were inadequate and antiquated, so I ended up buying a set of instruments out of my own pocket, which I used for every case for the next ten years. For the first three years I was in post, each time I carried out a ligament reconstruction, we had to borrow almost every item of kit until, because of my growing reputation, one of the companies agreed to supply us with it all, in return for us allowing them to bring surgeons from other hospitals across Europe to see how it all worked in practice.

Almost all the consultants I know care deeply about their patients and the staff who work with them. There may be the odd bad apple in the barrel, but the houses of parliament are hardly immune from this. Unlike politicians though, it seems every time a rogue consultant somewhere in the country oversteps the mark, it is used as a big stick to beat the rest of us.

Because of the top down culture of bullying, hospital managers become obsessed and fixated on hitting the targets they have been set, irrespective of the harm done to patients. One only has to look at the North Staffs scandal, where patients were being sacrificed on the altar of performance, to see the harm that can be done. Image is all. In days gone by, if hospital consultants felt something wasn't right and patients were coming to harm, they wouldn't hesitate to approach the local press or media. At the BRI the policy was that approaching the press without going through the Trust's press officer, resulted in instant dismissal. So much for a culture of openness.

During my time as clinical lead, our department set up a home internet group, after a colleague in another hospital discovered that management were clandestinely accessing intradepartmental communications between consultants. I guess the title Hospital "Trust" is a bit of a misnomer.

Recently we have seen managers at West Sussex hospital asking staff to provide fingerprints and handwriting samples to try and identify the author of an embarrassing whistleblowing letter containing allegations of errors in a patient's management. According to the Guardian, "all the doctors asked for fingerprints and handwriting were told non-compliance suggested guilt". The Trust's tactics were described as "harassing and totally at odds with the Trust's stated commitment to a culture of openness and speaking up"!

Whilst there is apparently protection for "whistleblowers", on the ground this seems far from the case. Management and the NHS will always find a way to get back at you if you raise a concern that is embarrassing to the establishment (who wants an HMRC investigation!). In my experience, most staff just put their heads down and get on with treating their patients, as to raise concerns is seen as potentially career ending.

I have mentioned problems with purchasing across the NHS before, but these problems reach right down to the day to day running of a hospital. Purchasing departments are often responsible for buying equipment they know nothing about and the number of times I have heard "well, it's the same as the other one but much cheaper", doesn't bear thinking about. This usually means it is an inferior product and frequently is not fit for purpose, wasting scarce resource.

Our department once lease hired a camera stack for performing keyhole knee surgery. This seems like a great idea as, just like every other sphere in life, improvements in tech march on apace, and after three years we would be able to upgrade to the latest all singing, all dancing equipment. That is… it seemed like a good idea until it went wrong and nobody in management could work out who we had leased it from. Our own medical physics department refused to mend it, as the hospital didn't own it, and we ended up cancelling all keyhole surgery for six weeks. Eventually it was decided that we would fix it in house and work was resumed. The camera stack was junked a couple of years later, but I often wonder if there is still a sum of money going out every month for a reason no-one can fathom.

Orthopaedic product companies run rings around purchasing departments in hospitals and not infrequently the apparent cost saving from switching from one product to another disappears due to some fine print in the contract that has been overlooked.

One of my favourite examples of the sophistication of purchasing in the NHS, was when our department needed to upgrade the camera stack that you need to be able to see and carry out keyhole surgery. These are expensive bits of kit, in the region of fifty-thousand pounds. In the NHS, if you were buying anything over fifteen thousand pounds, it had to go out to tender, so we proceeded to go through the laborious process of trying out different products, even though there was agreement among the surgeons as to which system was most suited to our needs.

A few days before the decision was due to be made, I was contacted by the rep from one of the companies whose product we didn't like, who offered to put in two camera stacks for nothing, if we changed one of our other contracts to use their companies particular make of disposable shaver blades (small instruments used during keyhole surgery). We had previously tried these shaver blades, and they were vastly inferior to the ones we were already using.

I immediately rang the rep of the company of the system we did like, and was best suited for the surgery we did, and asked if they could match the offer. He rang back a short while later with a deal that would give us *three* camera stacks for nothing, if we kept the contract for *his* company's disposable shaver blades. Not surprisingly we went with this offer.

On the day the contracts were to be signed I received a phone call from the rep.

"Steve, what's going on? I keep telling this guy in purchasing that we're going to give you the camera stacks for nothing, but he's insisting we take fifty-two thousand." I told him I'd get straight back to him and rang the purchasing manager.

"What's going on? They're going to give us the camera stacks for nothing. Why are you insisting they take fifty-two thousand?" He proceeded to tell me that the money had been allocated for a camera stack and therefore *had* to be spent on a camera stack. I could not dissuade him, and even the suggestion we used the money to buy disposable shaver blades instead, fell on deaf ears. I rang the rep back.

"Take the money." I can't believe that this sort of problem is not being replicated across the whole of the NHS on a daily basis. There is massive scope for improvement, but the bottom line is, there is a desperate need to involve the people who actually do the work in buying equipment for their speciality. Cheapest is not always best!

The quality of management is a constant gripe by staff working in the health service. The fact that NHS Trusts feel the need to spend something in the region of four-hundred million pounds a year on management consultants speaks for itself. The sad fact is, that this expenditure rarely produces any positive change. Talking to colleagues from across the country, what generally seems to happen is that management consultants come in to look at a certain problem, charge a lot of money and then tell you what you knew already. Certainly, this was my experience at the BRI.

I first came across this shortly after my appointment as a consultant. The London School of Economics came into the hospital, as a management consultancy company, to plan our future as an organisation. The hospital spent a lot of money on this and the consultant body was called to a presentation of their conclusions.

Apparently, we couldn't survive unless we moved to a new, purpose-built unit which would be so efficient we would be able to reduce our bed base from one-thousand-three-hundred and eighty, to eight-hundred and fifty. When I voiced my disagreement with this, saying that the demographics of the population was changing with increasing numbers of the elderly, with evidence that in orthopaedics the number of hip fractures was projected to double in the next ten years, I was dismissed as just being difficult.

The management spent a lot of time doing presentations across the Trust of the findings and the plans for the future, to various departments and groups of staff. Sadly, as occurs all too often across the NHS, the plans were scrapped two years later (a mere seven-hundred and fifty thousand pounds down the pan). The hospital has since built five new wards and still can't cope with the demand for in-patient care. Money well spent!

Management consultants have been into our hospital a few times, at enormous expense on each occasion. Their interventions never seem to have made a substantial difference. On one occasion, without any discussion, management brought in a management consultant to look at the way our orthopaedic outpatient department was run. If they had asked me, I could have told them what the problems were in ten minutes. He spent six weeks with us before presenting his conclusions. He was a pleasant chap and clearly a very bright cookie and I eagerly anticipated hearing his conclusions. I looked at him across the desk and asked him what he thought?

"Honestly? It's difficult to see how it works at all. It seems the problem is, that when something isn't working, the rest of the system adjusts round the thing that is wrong, to make it work, rather than sorting out the thing that isn't working in the first place. This has been going on for so long and on so many levels I can't see how it can be fixed." Although this sounds a bit negative, he had hit the nail right on the head and our outpatients just continued as it had before.

I thought he was dead right. Since I left the NHS a few years ago, I have thought about this a lot and have come to the conclusion that the only way of fundamentally fixing the NHS would be to scrap the whole thing and start again from the ground up. This is never going to happen though, so the staff struggle on trying to do their very best for their patients, despite whatever the politicians and the system throw at them.

Certainly, in the past and right up to present there has been an antipathy between hospital clinical staff and management, which can be bitter. Management seem to have an inherent distrust of consultants, and consultants certainly don't trust management. Why there should be this conflict is difficult to understand, given that treating as many patients as possible to the highest of standards should be a common goal.

Most surgeons, given the opportunity, will operate until the cows come home, without the need for any prodding. Hospital managers should be there to facilitate clinical work and not be "the enemy". There are far too many of them, building little empires and doing jobs not directly involved in delivering care. Before leaving the BRI I found myself wandering down a corridor in the management sector of the hospital and couldn't understand why there were so many job titles on doors that left me struggling to know what their purpose was.

We need more direct involvement of the front-line staff and a multi-party parliamentary committee overseeing things, rather than the NHS being used as a political plaything. I also think the NHS needs to fundamentally reassess what it is there for.

When the Health Service was first set up, treatments for many conditions were rudimentary. We have since seen an almost exponential rise in what medicine can do, but a linear increase in funding. This of course means the gap between what we can do and what we can afford gets greater every day.

As individuals, we each need to take more responsibility for our own health and not expect the NHS to be a failsafe for any form of aberrant behaviour. The government needs to take more responsibility for the health of the nation, not bow down to pressure from corporations and be prepared to take decisions that might not be immediately popular.

Difficult decisions need to be made as to what the NHS is there for and this needs widespread consultation. Rationing is an inevitability and not everything should be available on the NHS. At the moment rationing is effectively in place but is done by covert means

238

to avoid political fallout. I just wish our leaders would be more open and honest rather than try and convince everyone that everything in the rose garden is smelling sweet when all those on the frontline can smell is bullshit.

12

SHOULD I STAY, OR SHOULD I GO

Management may be pretty poor in the NHS, but in the end, it was they that forced my hand into retiring a few years early from the NHS. Not because I was bad at what I did, as by that time I had a national and small international reputation in my field. Mainly because I am not much of a political animal and have never been afraid to speak the truth as I see it. I have always been an advocate for the patients and staff against injustice and incompetence, something that just didn't sit well with those in the offices.

At the BRI we had the appointment of a dynamic, new chief executive, after our previous one had "taken early retirement". He was clearly highly intelligent and well qualified, arriving with a new broom and completely reorganising the management structure to put clinicians into the decision-making framework.

Whereas we never saw the previous Chief Executive around and about in the hospital, the new one would don scrubs and help out as a health care assistant on the ward, something previously unheard of, and this brought him much credibility with the staff. Each department had a management team appointed, with myself continuing as clinical lead in orthopaedics and with our own line manager. We were promised that if we achieved and exceeded our targets and budgets, part of any profit would be ploughed back into the department.

Our department bought into the new ethos and set to with a vengeance. My own "management style" was always to try and involve everyone in the decision making and give everyone some ownership of the department by delegating roles and responsibilities. We had weekly meetings, discussing problems and solutions, any complaints and what we could learn from them, and everyone was welcome to come and pitch ideas for improvements.

After the first year, the orthopaedic department, previously so often the butt of disparaging jokes by colleagues in other specialities, was held up as a shining example as how it should be done. Despite hitting all our targets ahead of time, keeping to budget and even making a small profit, none of the promised funding came back into the department, and the department and staff started the slide into disillusionment.

On a completely different note, about this time, a colleague invited my wife and I to a masked charity ball. I wasn't very keen, but my wife thought it might be good fun and, after all, it was for a good cause. I think the prospect of shopping for a new ball gown might have had something to do with it! In retrospect I'm glad we went as it was an extraordinary evening, giving me a glimpse into a world so very far removed from my own.

I began to realise we might be out of our depth when we arrived at the hall in our Volvo estate, to find the front lawn covered with a selection of Ferraris, Range Rover Sports and a smattering of Lamborghinis. Listening to the hubbub of cut-glass accents as we were welcomed into the grand entrance hall further put me on edge and my hackles started to rise. Wearing a Venetian mask was actually an advantage as it hid my expressions as the evening unfolded.

As it turned out, my colleague's table was full, and we were precipitated onto a table of complete strangers. The lady on my right started to make small talk asking me what I did a for a living and then,"And where do you work?"

"Bradford" I told her. She thought for a moment, beamed at me and exclaimed, "Oh, Bradford... Daddy bought my brother a mill in Bradford for his twenty-first birthday." She then started quizzing me about my children and where they went to school. I told her my eldest son was at Ermysted's (a top-rated state school in Skipton). She looked puzzled.

"Ermysted's... Ermysted's... I don't think I've heard of that one." I explained it was a state school with a superb record of scholarly achievement. She looked shocked.

"A state school?!" She was clearly struggling to process this bit of information and turned to talk to someone else. The lady on my left had her husband sitting next to her. He seemed a bit odd and very disinhibited. He went off to get more drinks and she turned to me.

"You'll have to forgive *, he's not been the same since an accident when we were hunting in Scotland last year. Yes... he got shot in the head... they weren't sure he was going to survive at first and he was on intensive care for six weeks." And then with peals of laughter, "He's never been the same since!"

And so it went on. I felt completely like a fish out of water and then teleported into the middle of the Sahara. This was a privileged world I'd never been exposed to and was unaware still existed. There were Tamsins, Aubreys, Jemimas and Marmadukes, like some bizarre adult version of Playschool. When the dancing started, a significant portion of the assembled throng disappeared into the kitchen, presumably to smell the freshly baked produce, as they all came back with white powder around their noses.

I guess it was all a bit stranger as, being the designated driver, I was on sparkling water so observing from behind my mask with a clear head. It felt like I was an extra on the set of some weird Fellini movie. It was certainly an eye opener and brought home to me we were still a very, very, very long way from the dreams of a meritocracy I'd grown up with.

From the orthopaedic department's point of view, I think the shit really hit the fan in the Winter of 2009, which was particularly harsh.

At that time our bed occupancy in the department was running at a hundred and five percent, as we often put two or three patients through the same bed on the same day, with the ward cleaning team kept frantically busy. That winter, the hospital was completely unprepared for the influx of emergency medical admissions. Very quickly, our beds became blocked with outliers from other hard-pressed wards, and we had to start cancelling routine surgery on a regular basis.

The hospital business manager of the time insisted we bring in everyone listed for surgery on a particular day, irrespective of how many beds we thought we were likely to have, as he couldn't contemplate the possibility of not utilising a potential operating slot. The poor patients were then sat out in a corridor, on uncomfortable plastic chairs and having had nothing to eat or drink from midnight the night before. If a bed did become available, the patient was assessed by the anaesthetist and then consented for surgery, still in the corridor, before getting changed for theatre.

We had four theatres with eight lists each day, but because of the bed situation we were only able to manage a few cases during what should have been a busy daily schedule. This meant at two o'clock in the afternoon, Sister would go out to those still in the corridor (often fifteen plus of them), to tell a lot of disgruntled and hungry patients, they wouldn't be getting their operation that day and they could go home. The poor woman was then repeatedly subjected to a torrent of verbal abuse, which she handled as tactfully as she could. How she coped with this I still struggle to get my head around and, after a couple of weeks of this, she started to look increasingly frazzled.

I raised my objections the following week at the next clinical management group (CMG) meeting with the chief executive and top-level managers. I told them I felt it was not only an unacceptable way to treat patients and staff but was also clinically unsafe. The chief executive came back with, "Oh, that's just shroud waving", his favourite phrase whenever concerns about clinical safety that might impact on throughput were raised. I was appalled by their attitude, where hitting targets was clearly the only thing that seemed to matter. Clinicians were constantly asked to cut corners, but if anything went wrong, management then turned around and dumped on them from a great height.

The next week the same thing was happening, and I rang the Business Manager.

"Hi…, you know the discussion we had in the CMG meeting last week?" He reluctantly acknowledged he remembered it.

"There are seventeen patients out on the corridor and we actually have no beds at all. I'm going to tell them you are responsible and give them the location of your office. They should be there in ten minutes, so I'd get your excuses ready – they seem pretty upset to me."

"You can't do that!" was his panicked reply.

"I can, and I will. You can't treat patients like this. It's unacceptable." Needless to say, after this incident, the way we organised admissions was changed in very short order, to patients being rung at home at seven-thirty in the morning to be told whether they needed to come into the hospital or not. I don't think management ever forgave me.

The following April the deputy clinical lead, our line manager and myself were summoned to see the chief executive. He wasn't in a great mood and proceeded to lay into us, complaining that we weren't going to hit our financial or waiting list targets for the year. I pushed a spreadsheet across the desk to him.

"As you can see, we have had four hundred and eighty-seven cases cancelled this winter because we have had no beds. If we had been able to do these, we would have achieved our waiting time targets and had a profit in terms of income." He looked disdainfully at me.

"But that's your problem." We then entered into a rather robust discussion, where I agreed I would be prepared to accept responsibility if I was in control of the resource, but we had just been through six months of never knowing day to day how many, if any at all, beds we would have, with constant firefighting to try and maximise our throughput.

"But you have to find strategies that allow you to cope with this." Quite how we were supposed to do this I never found out. Whilst I may be OK as a surgeon, my ability to magic up empty beds out of thin air is somewhat limited. After this period, management seemed to have fallen out of love with me. I think the major problem was that I saw my role as representing patients and the orthopaedic department in management, and they saw my role as representing management in the orthopaedic department. While these two stances sometimes sat comfortably together, very often they did not.

So, after eleven years as the head of the orthopaedic department, during which time the department had undergone radical changes and was both one of the most efficient and one of the biggest income generators in the hospital, I was given the opportunity to resign or told I would be removed from my role. By that time we had a department of fifteen orthopaedic surgeons who actually worked cohesively and talked to each other (this was a very rare situation in hospitals around the country!), something I was very proud of.

Stepping down was actually a relief, as we were constantly being asked to achieve the impossible. The previous three years we had been instructed to reduce our budget by five percent per year each year, at the same time as inflation was annually running at five to six percent. During this period, despite steadily deteriorating finances, we were told we had to increase throughput and improve quality and outcomes. There really is only so much blood you can squeeze out of a stone!

No longer having responsibility for running the department, I got my head down and concentrated on seeing and treating patients to the best of my ability, and as many of them as the system would allow me. I would see about fifteen new patients and thirty to forty follow ups in a clinic session and was operating on upwards of a dozen a week, beds and staffing permitting.

Some twelve months later I was summoned to see the chief executive. I asked his secretary what the meeting was about. "Oh, just a catch up." I was told. This was a common management tactic whenever clinicians might be involved, trying to prevent you from any preparation. It would be impossible to get an agenda and then when you turned up, something would be sprung upon you which you then had to deal with while thinking on the hoof.

On this occasion I had a fair idea what was coming, as the nursing staff had tipped me off. After the initial exchange of pleasantries, the Chief Executive opened with.

"Steve, we've been monitoring your outpatients, and on average you leave the clinic three quarters of an hour before it is due to finish. What have you got to say about that?" As the nursing staff had forewarned me this was occurring, my arguments were well marshalled.

"Well, on average I see ten to fifteen new patients and thirty to forty follow up patients in the time I'm there. Mr. * in the clinic room next to me, sees a total of just six new patients, and his clinic often overruns by up to an hour costing a significant amount of staff overtime. Which makes you more money and which would you rather have?"

"But if you were there for another three quarters of an hour, you could see more patients."

"That is true, but the problem is I can't hit my waiting list targets as they are at the moment. If I saw more patients this problem would get significantly worse. I do not want to see patients, discuss their problems and potential surgical solutions, agree a plan and then have them shipped off to some other hospital and surgeon so they don't breach their waiting time. That doesn't help anyone."

He clearly wasn't convinced and looked unhappy. At that time, I was one of only two consultants in the Trust still on an old style, what was called a "maximum part time contract". There was a set of regulations (The Whitley Council Regulations) that applied to this style of contract and I pulled the relevant photocopied sheet out of my bag and slid it across the table to him.

"As you know, I am still on an old-style contract. These are the regulations that apply to it. As you can see, I am actually entitled to half an hour's travelling time, to and from any clinical commitment. I have in fact been working in excess of what I am paid for and have been doing so for the last twenty years, putting in countless hours of unpaid overtime for the NHS. In addition, I have never been able to take my full allocation of annual leave in any year since I started, which has also been unpaid. To comply with the contract, I'll make sure I take all my annual and study leave, take a patient off every operating list and shorten my clinics further, is that really what you want?"

He looked down at the paper with distaste, scanning through the relevant text. He looked up at me and violently shoved the document back across the desk at me.

"Get out!" was all he said, so I gathered my things and left. As I have previously said, the NHS is an unforgiving beast and if management are out to get you, they will find a way to make your life intolerable. Any unsubstantiated complaint by a patient and you could find yourself on gardening leave, guilty until proven innocent. This was despite the fact I had worked thousands of unpaid hours over my time as a consultant and was a major income generator for the hospital, attracting work in from all over the region and beyond.

It was therefore with great sadness that I decided I had to jump before I was pushed, and shortly afterwards announced I would be leaving after serving my three months notice. I would be able to carry on doing some NHS work in the local private hospital through the "choose and book" system, so my old patients could always find me if they needed me.

In the private hospital in which I most recently worked, there were five orthopaedic consultants, all of whom have a national/international reputation in their respective fields, who have left different hospitals in the NHS for no other reason than hospital management have pissed them off one too many times. None of them have been motivated by money. It is difficult to understand why this should be the case and why NHS managers should think their hospitals are better off without these highly skilled and highly motivated individuals.

The biggest change for me on leaving the health service was that I was suddenly in charge of my own working life. I no longer had managers telling me which patients they wanted me to operate on and when, and in the private sector I was valued as an income generator rather than as a waiting list liability. I no longer had to give six weeks notice if I wanted to change an operating list or clinic. My private secretary just shuffled things round if I was asked at short notice to lecture at a meeting or had an urgent case to do.

I also had more time on my hands! To celebrate, I went to Glastonbury that Summer, one of the many things on my bucket list. Despite the awful weather and a sea of sticky mud, it was a unique, life affirming and joyful experience. There are people from all walks of life, different generations, ethnicities and orientations just getting along and having a good time. It gave you hope for the future. As Hendrix is quoted as saying "When the power of love overcomes the love of power, then the world will know peace". Glastonbury also inspired me to pick up my guitar again and form a band (Never2Late – we're even on Spotify!) – swapping my scalpel for an axe!

Writing and performing our eclectic mix of tunes became one of my passions and something I could carry on into my retirement. We may not be particularly good but enjoy it immensely. Maybe one day I'll be on the stage at Glastonbury instead of in the swaying crowd. One can live in hope!

One the saddest changes I have seen during my long time in the Health Service is the attitude of consultants to impending retirement. As a medical student and junior doctor, I came across quite a few consultants who were coming up to the end of their working lifetimes, and without exception they were not looking forward to leaving their work behind. They all told me they would miss the work, the patients and colleagues, and had all thoroughly enjoyed what they felt had been a very worthwhile career.

Now, it is completely different. Politicians have managed to demotivate a group of people who are generally not motivated by financial gain but by an altruistic desire to help people and do good. The consultants who are coming up to retirement that I meet now, seem fed up and miserable and just can't wait to get out. It is a very sad state of affairs.

I feel blessed that I have at least enjoyed some good years, when I felt the standards in the hospital were very high and staff genuinely cared (and had the time to do this) about the patients who had put their trust in them. I have been lucky to have been able to work my entire life without thinking whether I am going to gain from recommending a particular type of treatment. This is the beauty of the health service. You can decide on a treatment plan for a particular patient without it having any bearing on your income, so decisions can be based on purely clinical grounds.

Although I have been very fortunate to have been fairly successful, money has never been my motivation. Indeed, to the day I retired, I have had no idea what my fees were for consultations and surgery in the private hospital (they've always been managed by my accountant and secretary), a fact patients often found astonishing. I have been driven by the desire to do the very best for the person in front of me and to make every operation I do as technically perfect as I can make it.

I feel genuinely sorry for the few in my profession who seem to be motivated by the pursuit of mammon. I know of one consultant in Yorkshire who, together with his anaesthetist, works out the maximum they can screw out of the insurance company for each and every case. It's not what it should be about. Now, there are even some who actually employ "media consultants" to manage their various social media accounts, constantly posting on Facebook, Twitter and Instagram, in order to try and increase their private practice. At least I have been spared that. I did have a website, but it mainly contained my CV and a few basic details of my career.

I'm not going to pretend the money isn't nice, but if you are good enough and care enough about your patients, word goes out and the financial rewards roll in. The real rewards, however, are in the form of knowing you have genuinely helped people and the satisfaction that you've done a good job. In my long career, I have performed something over twenty thousand operations, most of which have gone OK, and I've returned many top-class sportsmen and women back to the playing field.

Sadly, a very few procedures have not turned out how both the patient and myself would have wished, despite the fact I have always tried to give my very best. If you are a caring clinician, it is those few patients who stick with you and haunt your dreams through the night, rather than the many successes.

I look back over my time as a doctor and am thankful for some great colleagues and the enjoyment and fulfilment the journey through the Health Service and beyond has given me. I feel deeply sad for the current generation of clinicians who are never likely to experience this. Sure, there have been some very dark moments but put on the scales, they don't even begin to tip the balance. As the song says, "Regrets, I've had a few…"

Working in a profession where your knowledge and skills can be literally live saving and certainly life enhancing, has been a true privilege. During my time the poor old health service has been kicked from pillar to post by successive governments of different political persuasions. I fear for my young colleagues, where politicians and managers seem to want to reduce them to merely technicians doing their bidding and no longer being advocates for the poor old patients who are slowly being reduced to units on a production line.

The old NHS may have had its faults but at least the staff genuinely cared about those needing their skills. It will be a sad day indeed if Westminster finally manages to stamp this out.

The journey of putting down this story has been a long and winding road. I couldn't have done it without a little help from my friends and the constant encouragement and support of my family, who kept telling me I had to document my story. During the process I have learned a lot about myself as well as about the strange and wonderful entities that are medicine and the health service. At times, my career felt like I was just blowing in the wind as I drifted from post to post never knowing where I'd end up, or even whether I'd ever make it. I got out when I was still at the top and avoided the inevitable, long, slow decline into incompetence and irrelevance that a few surgeons opt for. Some of it seems so long ago and there have been mixed emotions of both pain and pleasure in dredging it up. I have left out as much as I put in, so I'm not quite running on empty yet and life is a long song with more verses to be written…

EPILOGUE: LAST MAN ON EARTH

To my patients, I wish you well and thanks for letting me share a small part of your lives. To those few where things haven't turned out as either of us would have wanted, I can only apologise, but can assure you I was always trying to give my best. As a caring clinician the hurt stays with me forever.

My thanks go to those club doctors, physios, colleagues and all who have put their faith in me over the years – much appreciated.

You may have noticed all the chapter titles relate to songs. Music has always been a massive part of my life. I was lucky to be at university during the seventies, a fantastic time of musical change and some of the best lyricists there have ever been. The songs have been chosen from some of my favourite artists and put together make a reasonable playlist, but if you're interested, I would urge exploring the artist's catalogues further.

After Midnight – J.J.Cale. A laid-back song maker with short, tasteful guitar solos.

Follow Your Heart – John McLaughlin. One of the greatest modern guitarists, for me, eclipsing both Clapton and Hendrix.

No More Heroes – The Stranglers. One of the best of the punk generation, their music has stood the test of time.

I'm Not Like Everybody Else – The Kinks. Light years ahead of their time. Best version of this is the live one. My band always finish with this!

Raised on Robbery – Joni Mitchell. One of the great singer songwriters. Try her album "Hissing of Summer Lawns".

Bring It On Home – Led Zepplin. Great band. Saw them on their first tour, and was totally blown away, for the princely sum of six shillings and eight pence, supported by "Blodwyn Pig"

Do They Know It's Christmas – Bob Geldorf may not have produced much great music but anyone who watched it will never forget the "Live Aid" concert – "Give us your fucking money". Someone who got off his arse and helped the world.

The Pretender – Jackson Brown. Played with the Eagles for a while before branching out on his own. Truly great lyricist and songsmith.

May You Never – John Martyn. Unique talent and brilliant guitarist with an unusual technique. Sadly, no longer with us. Saw him live in Birmingham when Danny Thompson, his bass player, had the trots and had to keep running off the stage during the set.

Smooth Operator – Sade. An extraordinary talent who exploded on the music scene.

Money's Too Tight to Mention – Simply Red. A superb band, whose live set is every bit as good as their recordings.

Should I Stay, or Should I Go – The Clash. Another of the punk era whose talent made them one of the survivors when so many were like mayflies.

Last Man on Earth – Loudon Wainright III. A great and quirky wordsmith, and this song contains one of my favourite ever verses

"Kids used to say their prayers at night
Before they went to bed
St John told us that God is love
Nietzsche said he was dead
This thing we call existence,
Who knows what it all means,
Time and Life and People...
Are just glossy magazines."...

COVID-19 POSTSCRIPT

This book was written and completed during the twelve months before the coronavirus pandemic suddenly hit the world, just as we were about to publish. I felt something needed to be added.

When I was a trainee an old consultant said to me, "If you're around long enough, you'll see the same things coming around again." The appalling lack of foresight and lack of provision of personal protective equipment in the current crisis stirred a few memories.

I was a senior registrar in Leeds when the AIDS epidemic started in the late eighties. The hospital was a centre for major trauma cases with people unconscious and with multiple injuries being rushed in by ambulance to be put back together by multidisciplinary teams. There was little chance to take a history or delve into their personal or medical histories and they were often bleeding profusely from many different wounds as they arrived through the front door. Studies coming from the States were suggesting that it was even possible to be infected by the virus by inhaling the vapour produced by drilling and reaming bones when fixing their fractures.

We had meetings with the hospital management to explain the problem and request that we were supplied with the new (at that time) exclusion hoods which had their own independent and filtered air supply and might afford some protection from a disease that at that time was incurable. I sat in stunned amazement as management gave their view.

"We don't think it's likely to be a problem and anyway, it's too expensive." I guess it wasn't their lives or those of their families being put at risk.

As we enter our second spell of "lockdown" the British Medical Association report just twelve percent of hospital doctors said they were fully protected from the virus at work. At my old base hospital, the doctors are manufacturing their own protective gear and improvising to get around the lack of promised ventilators. Teachers at my son's school are 3D printing desperately needed face masks.

I have previously expressed my low opinion of politicians and nothing of their management of the current crisis has changed that. It's not just the leaders in our country, it's been right around the world. In 2015 Bill Gates gave a TED talk entitled "The next outbreak? We're not ready." which pretty much predicted what would happen and how the world desperately needed to prepare for what seemed inevitable. Absolutely nothing happened. Governments around the world have now scrambled to try and mount a response to a problem that has been predicted for a while.

In the UK, the health minister Matt Hancock stated to parliament on the twenty-third of January 2020: – "The public can be assured that the whole of the UK is always well prepared for these type of outbreaks", that "The NHS is well prepared and well equipped to deal with cases arising in the country" and "The UK is one of the first countries to have developed a world-leading test for the new coronavirus." It now seems he might have been a little optimistic in his reassurances.

A Sunday Times investigation reports that there was "a complacency at the heart of government" and our stockpiles of PPE had been "run down and were out of date". Boris Johnson apparently did not attend any of the five virus meetings held by COBRA and indeed spent twelve days on a holiday at a "grace and favour" mansion in Kent. The Sunday Times describes it as "The thirty-eight days when Britain sleepwalked into disaster". Bizarrely it is reported that the UK sent over two hundred and sixty thousand pieces of PPE to China, and seeing Michael Gove repeatedly refusing to give a straight answer to the question "did we send PPE to China – yes or no?" did little to suggest the report was wrong.

According to the Independent, the panicked DOH spent sixteen million pounds on coronavirus testing kits, described by Boris Johnson as "as simple as a pregnancy test" and which in his learned opinion had "the potential to be a total game-changer." Unfortunately, when tested at Oxford University, they were found to be insufficiently accurate and so now half a million of the tests are gathering dust in storage.

In Britain, we have seen our prime minister at the front door of number 10 applauding the NHS staff (quite rightly) who are putting their lives on the line on a daily basis. This is the same Boris Johnson who in 2017 voted against a Labour amendment seeking to award nurses above the annual salary increase of a below inflation one percent and the Conservatives "cheered and applauded" when the Labour amendment was defeated. He now freely admits it was the care provided for him by two nurses from abroad (one from New Zealand and one from the European Union country of Portugal), who are part of the NHS family, who saved his life and that NHS workers kept putting themselves in harm's way risking "this deadly virus".

In 2008, the greed of the financial sector brought the world to its knees but within a couple of years, the City was back awarding staff big, fat bonuses at the end of the year. For those of us working in the public sector, it was a different story. What followed for the staff were wage freezes and then an annual pay increase of one percent or less for the next ten years of a Conservative government. Spending on the health service was cut and when I was clinical lead of the orthopaedic department, we were asked to reduce our spending by five percent per year for several consecutive years, at a time when inflation was running at five to six percent.

The effect of this, according to the Health Foundation, is that earnings for NHS staff have fallen by twelve percent over the last decade, resulting in severe difficulties in recruiting and retaining staff. For doctors, the British Medical Association estimates that in real terms medical staff are earning thirty percent less than ten years ago. The current rounds of applause and campaigns for medals are all very nice, but if the politicians truly value the NHS and its staff, what they really need to do is to actually pay them a decent wage and to reverse the many years of underinvestment in the health service that the current crisis has brought into sharp focus.

If there is anything positive to come out of this, it is that the pandemic has demonstrated we all live on the same planet and it doesn't matter what political persuasion you are, which country you live in or what religion you may be, we all share the same fragile hold on life. We can't fight a pandemic based on geographical or party-political lines. In the UK we now have a leader who has experienced first-hand how important our health service and its staff are. Let's hope he doesn't have a short memory.